The
IRREDUCIBLE
NEEDS *of*
CHILDREN

The
IRREDUCIBLE
NEEDS *of*
CHILDREN

*What Every Child Must Have
to Grow, Learn, and Flourish*

T. Berry Brazelton, M.D.
Stanley I. Greenspan, M.D.

A Merloyd Lawrence Book

PERSEUS PUBLISHING

Cambridge, Massachusetts

Many of the designations used by manufacturers and sellers to distinguish their products are claimed as trademarks. Where those designations appear in this book and Perseus Books was aware of a trademark claim, the designations have been printed in initial capital letters.

A CIP record for this book is available from the Library of Congress.
ISBN 0-7382-0325-4

Perseus Publishing is a member of the Perseus Books Group.

Project Editor: Marco Pavia
Text design by Jeff Williams
Set in-10.5 point Galliard

1 2 3 4 5 6 7 8 9 10—03 02 01 00 99
First printing, September 2000

Perseus Books are available at special discounts for bulk purchases in the U.S. by corporations, institutions, and other organizations. For more information, please contact the Special Markets Department at HarperCollins Publishers, 10 East 53rd Street, New York, NY 10022, or call 1-212-207-7528.

Find us on the World Wide Web at http://www.perseusbooks.com

For Christine Lowell Brazelton
and
Nancy Thorndike Greenspan

The authors wish to thank
Merloyd Lawrence, whose insight and dedication
made it all come true

Contents

Introduction

As a pediatrician and a child psychiatrist caring for the families in our practices and engaging in studies of child development on a broader scale, we have become deeply concerned about the unmet needs of children in this country and abroad. Although there have been admirable initiatives in public health, education, pediatrics, and the law to improve the lot of children, few have tried to identify the fundamental requirements of a healthy childhood. In this book, we have set out to identify the very most basic needs, the kinds of care without which children cannot grow, learn, and thrive. Once these are recognized, plans to ensure that these requirements will be met can be more easily designed and evaluated.

We have also become aware of certain stresses on young families that have increased significantly in our lifetime. Under these stresses, mothers and fathers find it hard to meet the needs of their children. Few families can face these stresses and the tensions they create without outside support. We have allowed these tensions and conditions to multiply without the cultural supports that could be mustered. In investigations (1989–1991) by the National Commission for Children[1], it became apparent that our country lags behind a number of other cultures in supporting strong families. We risk paying a terrible price in our children's later behavior—drugs and antisocial and violent acts. As one CEO asked, "Will it cost our country much to create the necessary supports to meet the irreducible needs of infants and children?" Compared to what? We can no longer afford to ignore what our neglect of these needs means to our children's ultimate development. Our grandchildren will live together in a society with the offspring of neglected families. So will yours.

In our work as physicians and advocates for children, both of us have seen signs of great hope; new awareness and new programs that make the best interests of the child a top priority are developing nationwide. We hope our effort to clarify the basic needs can help point to further remedies, remedies that will demand the response of national and state governments, of communities, of business, and of individuals. No one layer of our society can face them alone.

Early childhood is both the most critical and the most vulnerable time in any child's development. Our research, and that of others, demonstrates that in the first few years, the ingredients for intellectual, emotional, and moral growth are laid down. If they are not, it is true that a developing child can still acquire them, but the price rises and the chances of success decrease with each subsequent year. We cannot fail children in these early years.

The "irreducible needs" we will lay out are experiences and types of nurturing to which every child has a *right*. In a society as affluent as ours, no one of us has a *right* to ignore them. Yet once we define these needs, it becomes clear that our society is failing many of its families and small children at present.

As physicians deeply committed to the well-being of children, we can no longer stand by with the complacency that silence implies.

At the White House Conference on Infant and Child Development a few years ago, there was a consensus that appropriate early experiences were vital for intellectual and emotional growth. When this consensus emerged, the president asked an essential question: What specific types of experiences are most important and how much each of them is necessary? No one attempted an answer. Child development professionals have never clearly articulated an answer. Fathers and mothers are asking the same question. They want to know the specifics of how to raise happy, confident, creative, intelligent, emotionally healthy children. They want their children to grow into adults who can nurture their own children and be reflective enough to lead a diverse, complex world into the future.

In the chapters that follow we will try to answer the question asked by the president and so many parents. Avoiding vague generalities, we will identify seven irreducible needs of infants and children.

Addressing these seven irreducible needs will take us all on a journey into our attitudes and policies towards children and families. It will lead us to re-evaluate our convictions and our daily practices in child care and family functioning, education, health care, social services, and our legal system. In order to illustrate just how thorny these questions are, we have included a sample of our own dialogue as we tried to identify each need. This dialogue is drawn from actual transcripts of discussion we had over a period of time. They give the flavor of our collaboration as well as suggest how we developed the recommendations.

As will be seen, the dialogues and recommendations are based on a synthesis of our clinical and research experience rather than a review, other than very selective, of the studies on the topics discussed. Due to the limited number of studies in some areas many of the most important questions (such as how much nurturing care a baby requires each day) must be addressed by integrating clinical experience with the available research. This at least creates a frame of reference for setting current standards as well as for future studies and discussion. The chapter-by-chapter notes at the end of the book offer some reviews of the literature and also some of our related research.

The most dramatic recent example of the results of neglecting a small child's needs are the orphanages in Romania and other countries that were doing little more than warehousing infants and young children. In these settings, without warm nurturing or appropriate social and intellectual interaction, children developed severe physical, intellectual, and social deficits. Four- or five-year-olds were able to communicate only with a few simple gestures, such as reaching for food. When upset, these children would often frantically bang or sometimes bite their own arms. They had no language or ability to use pictures to communicate basic needs or wants, let alone more rapid communications, and only fleeting capacities to receive comfort or warmth when hurt or upset. With intensive help, these children have made gradual but consistent progress. They have been able to learn to reach out, be warm with others, communicate with gestures, and develop beginning capacities for language and thinking. But these remedies are a long and slow process, however, requiring many years, and the results of the early deprivation are often never fully remediated.

While this is an extreme example, warning us all about the impact of institutional care, there are other inadequate forms of care occurring in the United States and other industrialized countries right beneath our noses to which we pay too little attention. These include the situation of children who get into our foster care system and go from foster home to foster home because they are difficult to care for. There are also the children who are neglected or abused even when living with a biological parent or parents. Abuse and neglect is increasing, not decreasing.

When children are put in foster care programs because they've been neglected or abused at home or because their parents are unable to take care of them or have given them up, they often have problems controlling their impulses and relating trustingly to others. They have deficits in language, cognitive, and social skills, often due to early patterns of abuse or neglect, such as prenatal biological insults (e.g., a mother ingesting toxic substances). As children are shifted from foster home to foster home, their problems usually become more severe. We see patterns not unlike what we've observed in Romanian orphanages—aggression and impulsive biting and hitting, unable to play with other children or feel compassion or caring for others.

The children who are living with their biological parent or parents and are deprived of the ordinary experiences that would enable them to be warm, loving, and caring are often in families with multiple problems, such as mental illness or severe antisocial patterns in one or both parents. The children aren't provided opportunities for nurturance, interaction, or learning. Here, too, we see chaotic, impulsive, self-absorbed, aimless children with severe language, social, and emotional difficulties.

In reading this, one may sigh with a sense of relief thinking that in your community such patterns of multiple foster care placements or neglect and abuse are very rare. But there is another trend occurring, both in the United States and around the world—a new type of institutional care. This type of care is part of every community. Approximately 50 percent of young children are now reared for significant parts of the day by persons other than their biological parents.[2] Here, we're not talking about after-school programs for school-aged children. We're talking about infants and toddlers in the first three years of life. From the 1970s through the 1990s, there has been a transformation of the attitudes of families towards raising their own children. During this time, there has been a huge increase in the number of families giving up the care of babies, toddlers, and preschoolers to others for 35 or more hours a week. In other words, large numbers of infants, toddlers, and preschoolers are spending the lion's share of their days in nonparental care.

More important than mere numbers are reports regarding the quality of this care. These are not encouraging. The most comprehensive study of the quality of day care reported that the vast majority of center-based care was not of high quality (over 85 percent was not of high quality for preschool children and over 90 percent was not of high quality for infants and toddlers).[3] Similar reports have emerged around other non-parental child care arrangements, such as family day care.[4] In addition, most states in the United States have very weak regulations governing care.[5] New findings regarding daycare options for mothers on welfare are especially alarming. These "Wave 1 Findings" are from the Growing Up in Poverty Project 2000.[6] These findings suggest that day care for such families is of very poor quality (eg. instances of toddlers wandering aimlessly about). The findings about overall lack of care suggest that quality of care is an important contributor to a child's development.[7]

The day care debate gets confused however by focusing only on research reports that maintain it's the quality of care that counts, not whether children are in institutional day care or family day care or cared for by parents. The reports stress that the quality of nurturance, interaction, and sensitivity to the child's cues are what's associated with their development status. It is true, and makes common sense, that quality would be an important variable and certainly, as indicated above, there's no guarantee that biological parents will always provide good quality care. But, what tends to get obscured in these academic discussions is the fact that at present most non-parental care (as revealed in a number of studies, including the study that documented that quality counts) is not of high quality.

We do know that quality child care is essential to the optimal development of small children. In our present setup, as indicated above, only 10% or less of infants and toddlers have access to high quality day care. The rest wind up with care that anyone with real options would not trust. Nor do the parents of these children. When a parent must leave a small child in less than optimal child care, that parent is bound to grieve. The grieving can take many forms: denial, detachment from the child, and anger and/or depression at the workplace that demands the separation. If we want motivated workers we need to offer them optimal child care or flexible hours that permit parental sharing of care.

With over half the nation's children receiving one form or another of nonparental care, the question is whether we want to allow a type of care that is not providing children the needed nurturance and social and intellectual interaction. We have to ask whether this nurturance is possible in settings where caregivers are caring for four or more babies (and later six or more toddlers), are paid minimal wage, and given little training and little incentive to avoid staff turnover (among those who can get better jobs). In Chapters 1, 3, and 4 we describe in detail the kind of nurturance that is needed by children in any setting.

Even when children are cared for at home for the first few years, there still are worrisome trends. There has been a shift towards more impersonal, rather than emotionally nurturing types of care-giving for infants, toddlers, preschoolers, and children. A recent report from the Kaiser Foundation revealed that on average, children are spending five to six hours a day in front of the TV or computer screen.[8] During this time, children are not receiving nurturing warmth or age-appropriate social or intellectual interactions.

But this is just one sign of the movement towards impersonal care. Many families are overly scheduled. Both parents are working to make ends meet or to improve the family's economics, leaving little relaxed family time. Education is becoming more impersonal as it is, more technologically oriented, losing the personal touch. Families in their own relationships with one another are also moving towards more impersonal modes of communication. E-mails are replacing lunches together and time in front of the screen is replacing many other forms of personal interaction. Recreation as well as work is taking place in a more impersonal atmosphere, with less interaction among and within families.

One of us (S.I.G.) was recently struck by how pervasive this shift is towards impersonal modes of care. A visit within the same week to two very different settings attempting to provide nurturing care revealed some striking similarities in what might be called "institutional love."

In the first setting, a woman sat in the corner of the room looking at the floor. Around her crawled four babies who seemed to relate only to their own bodies and the objects they can see or touch. One of them got her hand caught in a toy. The woman went to her, pulled her hand free, said, "O.K." and then moved silently back to her chair. Another baby banged on his half-filled bottle of milk. The woman picked him up, put him stiffly on her lap and faced him towards the wall while the baby sucked down the rest of his milk. When the baby was finished, she put him back on the floor without a word. The room was quiet. There were no signs of the familiar gestures, sounds, and expressions that tie people together.

Was this an overwhelmed, economically disadvantaged mother in a worrisome family situation? Or an over-stressed home day care facility in a poor neighborhood? No, in fact this was a scene in an upper-middle class day care center for infants and toddlers. The woman was an aide earning the minimum wage. The director of the private, well-run, fully accredited center said, "She is the norm."

In another room in the same center, a smiling woman animatedly exchanged words, grunts, smiles, laughs, and gestures with five toddlers as they rolled trucks back and forth and giggled at one another. The children pointed at, crawled over, and made sounds at each other and the woman caring for them. Using subtle movements of hand, face, and voice she engaged all five toddlers at once.

"Who is she?" S.I.G. asked.

"Oh, she is the assistant director, substituting for one of the aides who is sick," replied the director.

"Is it possible to have more of the staff that cares directly for the babies show her warmth and interactive skills?" S.I.G. asked.

"Occasionally we have caregivers similar to her, but in general we don't and people with her skills quickly get to higher levels. We can't afford to pay someone like her to spend time with the infants," the director responded.

A few days later, in the second setting, S.I.G. saw similarly unresponsive aides sitting in their chairs. One was telling an elderly woman, "Sit down and stop babbling or you won't get your ice cream." In another room, six other elderly women were sitting and staring silently into space while two more aides sat behind their table looking bored and indifferent. A woman pleaded unsuccessfully for a back rub and later confessed, "I just need some human touch." Another woman brightened up when an aide talked to her and was unnecessarily thankful for the little conversation.

This setting is one of the city's best institutions for the elderly. Here, too, the food, cleanliness and medical care are excellent.

This is "institutional love." It is provided at either end of the lifespan for both the poor and the well-to-do, for those who, because of their age and helplessness, need to depend on others for their care. We all know what this kind of care is like. What we don't want to think about is that this care is what we are providing for those we love.

Surely, one may rationalize, with enough money we can have good services. In fact, in some workplaces parental involvement in on-site day care creates a sense of an extended family. "Cooperative" nursery schools benefit from parent participation. A compassionate head nurse in a home for the elderly may instill a personal touch. But, sadly, these are the exceptions. The irony is that if we as a society keep this up, in 80 years the current infants will be back in these impersonal surroundings and it will feel strangely familiar.

One of us (S.I.G.) has questioned whether we are creating a new view of human nature reflected in our impersonal child care policies and interaction patterns, a concrete, materialistic one.[9] In this view, we are more concerned with the brain than the mind and with biology and genetics than experience.

Such views are reflected in mental health treatments. Children are being put on three and four medications to deal with complicated family patterns and stress. A recent study in *The Journal of the American Medical Association*[10] revealed that alarming numbers of preschoolers were put on medications not approved for very young children, with three-quarters of them not having concurrent psychological or family therapy to teach new coping capacities. More and more children are not being helped enough to deal psychologically with the stresses in their lives. There is little exploration of feelings and attempts to work with families to alter maladaptive patterns.

When children are in stressful relationships and family circumstances, even attempts at using appropriate medications rarely work because the stress is ongoing. While the medication may work temporarily, it rarely works for a long period of time. This leads to a second and third medication or higher doses of the original medication. Recently, one of us (S.I.G.) saw a youngster who had been on four different medications, the third one of which provided such severe agitation that she had to be hospitalized. It was rationalized that her hospitalization was due to her impulsive and agitative behavior. She had started off with mild symptoms of anxiety and inattentiveness and ended up being hospitalized twice for aggression and agitation. After a full evaluation and the realization that her behavior had changed for the worse with each subsequent addition of medication, she was gradually taken her off the medications and helped to get into intensive psychotherapy with the family involved. There were indications of a number of conflictual and anxious patterns that could be helped with this approach. She was a bright, verbal little girl who could participate to her advantage in a combination of individual and family-oriented therapeutic approaches. Within eight months she was functioning well in school and verbalizing her feelings. The family was learning supportive and constructive approaches rather than undermining and anxiety-causing ones. She continues to function well, both in school and with her peers. While she is not on any medication, other children sometimes do require some medication along with psychotherapeutic work.

This little girl is not an isolated circumstance, however. More and more children are being treated with medication or inadequate short-term therapeutic approaches due to a shift in the way professionals are thinking about human nature and human functioning. Pressures from HMOs and insurance companies for briefer and more "efficient" interventions are contributing to this trend.

The way the mental health system views human nature influences how all of us view ourselves, our children, and our families. During this same period, between the 1950s and 1990s, the diagnostic system became more research oriented, with the major changes occurring in the 1960s and 1970s. The goal was descriptions of mental disorders that could be verified more readily. What got lost was an accumulated wisdom for the prior 75 years on the internal workings of the mind. While the role of defenses, coping strategies, anxiety, and conflict, are still addressed by some psychotherapists, their removal from the diagnostic system led the way for a dramatic shift in how we think about who we are. It led us to think about human functioning as a series of behaviors and symptoms organized by different genetic and biochemical pathways. We need to understand human functioning not only at the biological level, but also at its psychological, social, and cultural levels. Many mental health professionals are attempting to reestablish this more balanced perspective.

One of the justifications for this overly narrow biological definition of human functioning is a misinterpretation of the role of our genes on behavior. Even though a child's unique biology (nature) may launch early parent-child interactions in a certain direction, modifying the child's environment by adjusting parenting styles (nurture) can influence the outcomes significantly. After all, a gene can't express itself, or have an influence, without its intimate partner—the environment. In addition, most recent research on how genes work in the body suggests that their expression or influence depends on their interactions with many different environments, including those in the cell, the body, and in the social and physical world; and that these interactions in part determine how we function. Nature and nurture thus appear to interact together seamlessly, in a developmental duet.

In spite of the considerable evidence for the importance of early experience, some argue that later experiences are equally important. However, they are not distinguishing the early essential experiences which help children relate, read social cues, and think (and take years of therapy to recreate even partially later on) from attitudes, values, and academic skills which are acquired throughout life. One-dimensional, catchy explanations like "It's all in the genes," "The bad seed," or "Biology is destiny" may tempt us with their appealing simplicity, but they often lead to poor solutions and worsening challenges when it comes to childrearing. The fascination in the media not long ago with the notion that peers influence a child's personality more than his parents is another such example of short-sighted thinking. Although peer relationships are important, they build on the early experiences that a child has with his parents. Children who haven't had the benefit of nurturing parental interactions early on have trouble even forming friendships, let alone negotiating the expectable ups and downs of peer relationships.

Overly simplified psychological, as well as biological, explanations can lead the public and professionals to believe that behavior can be controlled by simply rearranging rewards and punishments. This in turn can put the focus on discipline, rather than compassion, warmth, and love. Obviously, for healthy child care we need to have both guiding limits and loving, compassionate care. As we will see in Chapter 5, loving compassion helps children want to emulate and please the authority figures they love and admire and limit setting and structure helps them learn restraint when temptations are strong. While the proper balance is always being sought, we are seeing a worrisome imbalance: professionals and parents are embracing a back-to-discipline ethic that flies in the face of what we know about infants and young children. Some are advocating extremely rigid disciplinary measures even for infants and toddlers. Simplistic reward/punishment approaches to children's complex feelings and behaviors harkens back to earlier years when we were "taming the devil out of children." Such regressive approaches generally backfire producing one of two patterns—negativism and rebellion or fear, anxiety and passivity. Families, however, feeling overwhelmed and sometimes helpless, are attracted to simplistic, punitive, and harsh solutions. This is especially true when at a deep level families may feel guilty for providing insufficient nurturing care.

Why are we moving so dramatically into more impersonal ways of interacting with our children and in family life? After the first half of the century showing gains in our child care policies, why are we now going in the other direction towards a type of impersonal care that could undermine the ability of future generations to parent and nurture their young?

Perhaps we can get a glimpse of the reason for this worrisome downturn in care for children by looking at two sides of human evolution. We often associate human evolution with survival of the fittest, species competing with one another for survival. However, there is another trend, one that doesn't often get associated with evolution per se, but may be a very important component of our development as complex human beings. This aspect of evolution has to do with the human being's capacity to form families and co-operate in larger social organizations.

If you consider the level of social organization required to have an advanced economy, military, and government in order to survive in the modern world, it is staggering. Human beings have to be able to work cooperatively, compassionately, and empathetically with others in a group in all aspects of life. It takes cooperation and organization for family, community, or societal groups to function. This requires the capacity for empathy and compassion, for understanding and for coping with feelings in constructive and mature ways. New generations of children will be able to carry out these functions only if they are reared in nurturing empathetic families. Advanced societies, in order to compete economically and militarily and through stable government structures, require nurturing care for the children who will become the adults. In essence, behind the competitive advantage in evolution, lies nurturing care. The long period of dependency of human beings provides an opportunity for human beings to develop emotionally-based psychological capacities during a long childhood of protection and care. This is seen also in other mammals, but less in members of the animal kingdom where the young are out fending for themselves after only a brief period of nurturing and protection.

While nurturing care and competitive mastery are two sides of the same coin, we seem comfortable in focusing on the competitive survival side and do not seem comfortable focusing as much on the nurturing side. The theme of nurturance is associated with vulnerability and helplessness. Vulnerability, helplessness, and the need for nurturing care seem antithetical to the assertive self-sufficiency so embedded in the competitive ethic of survival. Could our need to deny vulnerability in ourselves mean that we have to deny seeing it in our children?

The question then becomes why now? Why should this conflict at present be even more apparent and more undermining to our child care policies? Perhaps the economic progress we have made so that most of us can take basic needs for granted has contributed to our neglect of nurturing needs. In the past, the nurturing role and the acceptance of vulnerability was often embodied in the maternal role. Women were expected to stay home with the children and gain their pleasure from nurturing others, not from competitive careers. Fathers and husbands were expected to take the reins of the competitive side of life. As education and economic progress has supported greater equality and moving beyond concrete rules, we are in a period of transition. A new balance has to be found. Women and mothers shouldn't be expected to embody the nurturing role while the fathers embody the competitive mastery one. We now know the great importance and long-term benefits of a father's close involvement in a child's life. But we haven't yet found a way to restore this vital balance in a new way.

Historically we have been able to deal with the balance between these two evolutionary trends through rituals and concrete rules, rather than reflective thought. In a sense, we may have never truly integrated these two trends in human nature, but perhaps now we must. An obvious solution is for men and women to share in both the nurturing and the competitive side of life. This requires a conscious reflective decision of families, recognizing the needs of the children. Meanwhile, to have both parents take hold of the competitive mastery side and farm out the care of children to others, which is what the last 30 years have been about, is an experiment that now must be reassessed in light of what we know that children require.

During this period of transition, when conscious reflection and decision-making replaces rules and rituals, we need to have a clear picture of the basic needs of children around which families must organize themselves. If we can't meet the needs of children, we may compromise the capacities of future generations to sustain families and provide economic and political stability.

To this end, we have identified seven irreducible needs of infants and young children and their families. These seven basics provide the fundamental building blocks for our higher level emotional, social, and intellectual abilities.

In the chapters that follow, we will consider each of these irreducible needs in terms of their implications for family life, child care, education, the social service and welfare systems, the criminal justice system and the health and mental health systems. We will attempt to formulate recommendations for changes in our policies with regard to each of the needs.

In doing so, we hope to challenge the status quo and provide recommendations for enlightened policies in the 21st century.

1

The Need for Ongoing Nurturing Relationships

Although consistent nurturing relationships with one or a few caregivers are taken for granted by most of us as a necessity for babies and young children, often we do not put this commonly held belief into practice. The importance of such care has been demonstrated for some time. The films of René Spitz and the studies of Spitz and John Bowlby revealed to the world the importance of nurturing care for the physical, emotional, social, and intellectual health of children and the dire consequences of institutional care. Other pioneers, such as Erik Erikson, Anna Freud, and Dorothy Burlingham, revealed that to pass successfully through the stages of early childhood children require more than a lack of deprivation; they require sensitive, nurturing care to build capacities for trust, empathy, and compassion.

More recent studies have found that family patterns that undermine nurturing care may lead to significant compromise in both cognitive and emotional capacities. Supportive, warm, nurturing emotional interactions with infants and young children on the other hand, help the central nervous system grow appropriately. Listening to the human voice, for example, helps babies learn to distinguish sounds and develop language. Interactive experiences can result in brain cells being recruited for particular purposes—extra ones for hearing rather than seeing, for instance.[1] Exchanging emotional gestures helps babies learn to perceive and respond to emotional cues and form a sense of self. Brain scans of older individuals show that experiences that are appropriately emotionally

1

motivating and interesting harness the learning centers of the brain differently from experiences that are either over- or understimulating.

Deprivation or alteration of needed experiences can produce a range of deficits. When there is early interference with vision, for example, difficulties have been observed ranging from functional blindness to problems with depth perception and spatial comprehension.[2] Emotional stress is also associated with changes in brain physiology.[3]

In general, there is a sensitive interaction between genetic proclivities and environmental experience. Experience appears to adapt the infant's biology to his or her environment.[4] In this process, however, not all experiences are the same. Nurturing emotional relationships are the most crucial primary foundation for both intellectual and social growth.

At the most basic level, relationships foster warmth, intimacy, and pleasure; furnish security, physical safety, and protection from illness and injury; and supply basic needs for nutrition and housing. The "regulatory" aspects of relationships (for example, protection of children from over- or understimulation) help children stay calm and alert for new learning.

Research with newborns by one of us (T. B. B.) shows that a newborn baby will attempt to keep himself under control in order to look and listen to cues around him.[5] He will put together four midbrain reflexes—tonic neck, Babkin hand to mouth, rooting, and sucking—in order to stay alert. If he cannot succeed, and loses control, he will use the human voice or touch to reinforce his effort to regulate his "state" toward alertness.

By eight weeks of age, this same research shows, he will be able to distinguish and respond differentially to his mother's versus his father's versus a stranger's voice and face. He is quietly alert to his mother, ready for a playful interaction with his father. Each of these important people will have learned his rhythms and cues and he will have created an expectancy to react appropriately with them. These are the ingredients for a strong sense of self-esteem in the future, and for the motivation for learning later on. In addition, this learning is fueling his ability to maintain impulse control for the future. The most important learning in the early years is provided by human interaction. Objects and learning devices do not compare.

One of us (S.I.G.) has shown that relationships and emotional interactions also teach communication and thinking. Initially, the infant's communication system is nonverbal. It involves gestures and emotional cueing (smiles, assertive glances, frowns, pointing, taking and giving back, negotiating and the like). From these, there emerges a complex system of problem-solving and regulating interactions that continue throughout the life of the individual. Even though this nonverbal system eventually works in conjunction with symbols and words, it remains more fundamental. (For example, we tend to trust someone's nonverbal nod or look of approval more than words of praise, which are sometimes misleading; and we shy away from a person with a hostile look even if the person says, "You can trust me.")

When there are secure, empathetic, nurturing relationships, children learn to be intimate and empathetic and eventually to communicate about their feelings, reflect on their own wishes, and develop their own relationships with peers and adults.[6]

Relationships also teach children which behaviors are appropriate and which are not. As children's behavior becomes more complex in the second year of life, they learn from their caregivers' facial expressions, tone of voice, gestures, and words what kinds of behavior lead to approval or disapproval. Patterns are built up through the give-and-take between children and caregivers. Importantly, along with behavior, however, emotions, wishes, and self-image are also coming into being. The emotional tone and subtle interactions in relationships are vital to who we are and what we learn.

Relationships enable a child to learn to think. In his interactions, the child goes from desiring Mom and grabbing her to saying "Mom" and looking lovingly. He goes from "acting out" or behaving his desires or wishes to picturing them in his mind and labeling them with a word. This transformation heralds the beginning of using symbols for thinking.

Pretend or imaginative play involving emotional human dramas (e.g., the dolls hugging or fighting) helps the child learn to connect an image or picture to a wish and then use this image to think, "If I'm nice to Mom, she will let me stay up late." Figuring out the motives of a character in a story as well as the difference between 10 cookies and 3 cookies will depend on this capacity.

The ability to create mental pictures of relationships and, later, other things leads to more advanced thinking. For instance, a key element essential for future learning and coping is the child's ability for self-observation. This ability is essential for self-monitoring of activities as simple as coloring inside or outside the lines or matching pictures with words or numbers. Self-observation also helps a person label rather than act out feelings. It helps him to empathize with others and meet expectations. The ability for self-observation comes from the ability to observe oneself and another in a relationship.

We have thus come to understand that emotional interactions are the foundation not only of cognition but of most of a child's intellectual abilities, including his creativity and abstract thinking skills.[7]

This recognition of the role of early emotional interactions in intellectual functioning is not the same as Howard Gardner's important idea of separate, multiple intelligences, or Antonio Damasio's research on the brain which suggests that emotions are important for judgment but somehow separate from academic capacities or overall intelligence. We do not see these as separate. Jean Piaget, the pioneering cognitive psychologist considered the child as a causal thinker once he can learn that pulling a string brings the sound of the ringing bell. However, this is not the child's first opportunity to learn about causality. A baby's first lesson in causality occurs many months earlier, when he learns that a smile brings a responsive smile of delight to his parent's face. The child then generalizes this emotional lesson to the physical world. We have been able to identify how affective or emotional interactions lead the way at each stage.

Emotions are actually the internal architects, conductors, or organizers of our minds. They tell us how and what to think, what to say and when to say it, and what to do. We "know" things through our emotional interactions and then apply that knowledge to the cognitive world.

For instance, when a toddler is learning whom to say "hello" to, he doesn't do this by memorizing lists of appropriate people. Experience leads him to connect the greeting with a warm friendly feeling in his gut that leads him to reach out to other people's welcoming faces with a verbalized "Hi!" If he looks at them and has a different feeling inside, perhaps wariness, he's more likely to turn his head or hide behind your legs. We encourage this kind of "discrimination" because we don't want our children to say "Hi!" to strangers. We want them to say hello to nice people like Grandpa. If a child learns to greet those people in this way, he will quickly say "Hi!" to a friendly teacher or to a new playmate. He carries his emotions inside him, helping him to generalize from known situations to new ones, as well as to discriminate or decide when and what to say.

Even something as purely academic and cognitive as a concept of quantity is based on early emotional experiences. "A lot" to a three-year-old is more than he wants; "a little" is less than he expects. Later on, numbers can systematize this feel for quantity. Similarly, concepts of time and space are learned by the emotional experience of waiting for Mom, or of looking for her and finding her in another room.

Words also derive their meaning from emotional interactions. A word like *justice* acquires content and meaning with each new emotional experience of fairness and unfairness. Even our use of grammar, which the noted linguist Noam Chomsky and others believe is largely innate and needs only some very general types of social stimulation to get going, is based in part on very specific early emotional interactions. For example, we found that autistic children who did not use proper grammar and repeated only nouns, like *door, table,* and *milk,* could learn correct grammatical forms if we helped them first become emotionally engaged and intentional. At the point where they learned to experience and express their desire or wish (for example, when they pulled us to a door to open it), they began properly aligning nouns and verbs ("Open the door!"). Infants and toddlers without significant challenges engage in these purposeful emotional interactions routinely; perhaps because they are so routine their importance for grammar and language has been missed.

Not only thinking grows out of early emotional interactions, but so does a moral sense of right and wrong. The ability to understand another person's feelings and to *care* about how he or she feels can arise only from the experience of nurturing interaction. We can feel empathy only if someone has been empathetic and caring with us. Children can learn altruistic behaviors, to do "the right thing," but truly caring for another human being comes only through experiencing that feeling of compassion oneself in an ongoing relationship. We can't experience emotions that we never had, and we can't experience the consistency and intimacy of ongoing love unless we've had that experience with someone in our lives. For some it may be a grandmother or an aunt, or it may even be a neighbor, but it must be there. There are no shortcuts.

An ongoing, emotional, nurturing relationship with a baby and toddler enables us to engage in interactions in which we read and respond to the baby's signals. This basic feature of caring relationships between a baby and a caregiver who really knows her over the long haul is responsible for a surprisingly large number of vital mental capacities. These "reciprocal interactions" teach babies how to take initiative. As pointed out earlier, they do something and it makes something happen. This is also the beginning of learning to think purposefully or causally. A sense of self, will, purpose, assertiveness, and the beginning of causal logical thinking all occur through these wonderful reciprocal interactions.

By 2–3 months, a baby and her parent will have been through 3 levels of learning about each other. In stage 1, the parent learns how to help the newborn infant maintain an alert state (1–3 weeks). In stage 2 (3–8 weeks), in the alert state she will produce smiles and vocalizations which are responded to by the adult. In stage 3 (8–16 weeks) these signals are reproduced in "games" (Stern) in which vocalizations and/or smiles are reproduced in bursts of 4 or more, imitated by the adult, in a series of reciprocal bursts or "games." Rhythm and reciprocity are learned in these games.

By 4 months, the baby will have learned to take control of the game, and to lead the parent in them (Margaret Mahler called this "hatching"). Thus, autonomy comes to the surface within these games.

Something else is also occurring. Through these reciprocal interactions the child is learning to control or modulate his behavior and his feelings. We all want children who are well regulated or well modulated, that is, who can be active and explorative some of the time, concentrate and be thoughtful and cautious other times, and joyful yet other times. We want children who can regulate both their emotions and their behavior in a way that is appropriate to the situation. We admire adults who are able to do this.

The difference between children who can regulate their mood, emotions, and behaviors and children who can't—for whom the slightest frustration feels catastrophic, whose anger is enormous and explosive—lies in the degree to which the child masters the capacity for rapid exchange of emotions and gestures. When a child is capable of rapid interactions with his parents or another important caregiver, he is able to negotiate, in a sense, how he feels. If he is annoyed, he can make an annoying look or sound or hand gesture. His father may come back with a gesture indicating "I understand" or "OK, I'll get the food more quickly," or "Can't you wait just one more minute?" Whatever the response is, if it is responsive to his signal he is getting some immediate feedback that can modulate his own response. He gets a sense that he can regulate his emotions through regulating the responses he gets from various environments. We now have a fine-tuned system rather than a global or extreme one. The child doesn't have to have a tantrum to register his annoyance; he can do it with just a little glance and a little annoyed look. Even if his mother or father doesn't agree with him or can't bring that food right away, they are signaling something back that gives the child something to chew on while he is deciding whether to escalate to an even more annoyed response. Even if he does escalate to a real tantrum, this extended sequence is preferable to going from 0 to 10 in one second. All the different feelings, from joy and happiness to sadness to anger to assertiveness, become a part of these fine-tuned regulated interactions, in a pattern of subtle nuances rather than an all-or-nothing pattern.

If a child is not learning to engage in this fine-tuned interaction, he doesn't expect his emotions to lead to a response from his environment. The emotions consequently exist somewhat in isolation and simply get bigger. The child is driven to use more global responses of anger or rage or fear or avoidance or withdrawal or self-absorption. Very young babies are prone to these more extreme reactions in the early months of life. When they cry, they cry very hard and loud because they are frustrated until we help settle them down. This has certain similarities with what has been described as the flight/fight reaction, which is a more global reaction of the human brain. But children are not limited to flight-or-fight reactions. They can have a variety of global reactions: global rage, avoidance, withdrawal, self-absorption, fear, or impulsive action.

By the time a child is talking at age 2 and 2 1/2 he should already have the capacity to be involved in long chains of interaction (reciprocal interactions) involving his different emotions, feelings, and behaviors. These are built on the earlier patterns laid down at 2–4 months. Children without this capacity operate in a catastrophic or extreme manner, having extreme meltdowns or tantrums or getting carried away with their excitement and joy, or anger or sadness, or even depression. Often, these extreme reactions are out of proportion to the events of the moment. They suggest that some parts of the child's feelings, mood, and behavior didn't have a chance to become regulated through reciprocal interactions. Families have different capacities to get involved in negotiations around certain behaviors and feelings. Some interact well with one another around assertiveness and anger, but not as well around sadness or sense of loss. Others are just the reverse.

The earliest patterns of parent/infant communication lay the groundwork for the later patterns. As children learn to regulate their behavior and feelings they can then go to the next level and problem-solve with the feelings and actually try to change what's happening in their environment. If something feels unpleasant, they can do things to change the situation and the feeling. If it is a pleasant feeling, they can change their environment to bring on more of those feelings. So by 18–20 months children already have lots of experience in trying to lessen those conditions that make them feel sad or angry and to increase those conditions that make them feel happy. Then, as they progress further up to age 2 or 2 $1/2$, they can form images in their minds—what we call symbols or ideas—and actually label the feelings that have come under fine regulation. We see this in the pretend play of children when they create scenes where there is anger, happiness, or sadness. Children who are well regulated have more details in their dramas. There is more subtlety to their feelings. Children who are more extreme in their reactions, in contrast, have more global patterns in their pretend play. At yet at a further level, they can begin reasoning about their feelings, figuring out why they are happy or sad or joyful. This occurs between ages three and four. As they get older, they can reflect on these feelings and understand them in the larger context of their peer relationships. They can recognize the gray area of feelings. As they become older this capacity for reflective thinking about feelings gets stronger and stronger.

Interactive emotional relationships, therefore, are important for many of our essential, intellectual, and social skills. This type of interaction is also central when we are trying to help children with special needs. Often, creating opportunities for long, empathetic, nurturing interactions around the child's different feelings can go a long way to helping a child learn "regulation" even when it isn't there in the first place.[8]

The notion that relationships are essential for regulating our behavior and moods and feelings as well as for intellectual development is one that needs greater emphasis as we think about the kinds of settings and priorities we want for our children. The interactions that are necessary can take place in full measure only with a loving caregiver who has lots of time to devote to a child. A busy day-care provider with four babies or six or eight toddlers usually won't have the time for these long sequences of interaction. Similarly, a depressed mom or dad or an overwhelmed caregiver with five children or parents too exhausted at the end of the day may not have the energy for these long patterns of interaction and negotiation.

Discussion

Early Relationships

TBB: We first learned the power and importance of interactive relationships while using our neonatal assessment.[9] When we started, nobody thought we should interact with the baby. In the past, we just let the baby lie there and observed him. That allowed us to believe that "babies don't see or hear"—crazy notions. As soon as we began interacting with the baby, holding him to alert him, cuddling him to soothe him, we saw that you could reinforce the baby for doing fantastic things. We saw "Here is an interaction that the baby stores." Then along come the mother and the father, each treating the baby differently, and he stores those differences and reflects them back by six to eight weeks with different responses. These emotional responses grow from ongoing interactions with consistent caregivers and are the key to future development.

SIG: We can now make a case that it's this early reciprocal dialogue with emotional cueing, rather than any cognitive stimulation like flash cards, that leads to the growth of the mind and the brain and the capacities to reason and think. Both emotional and intellectual development depend on rich, deep, nurturing relationships early in life, and now continuing neuroscience research is confirming this process.[10]

TBB: The preparation for this begins before birth. We studied seven-month-old fetuses using ultrasound to visualize their behavior. When a moderately loud buzzer was held 18 inches from the mother's abdomen, the fetus jumped with a massive startle. At each subsequent buzz, the startle diminished. By the fourth or fifth stimulus, the fetus stopped moving and brought her hand up to her mouth, as if to comfort herself. This diminishing response is called habituation to an otherwise intrusive, disturbing stimulus. Then, we used a soft rattle next to the mother's abdomen. The fetus alerted and pulled her hand away to turn toward the rattle. We were able to repeat this evidence of making a choice for the soft stimulus in the visual area. We saw her habituate to a strange operating-room light after four or five times. A pinpoint light on the abdomen caused her to alert and to turn her head toward it. We felt that this evidence of hearing and vision in the fetus was coupled with the ability to shut out disturbing stimuli and to alert to an attractive one.

I'd like to see this evidence in utero of complex responses utilized to distinguish stressed from nonstressed fetuses. If the fetus were stressed, the responses might be more automatic and less available to modulation and choice. If the fetus could demonstrate such behavior, it could be used as evidence that important learning and shaping were proceeding in utero. If there were impinging reasons for stress, such as undernutrition or exposure to toxins such as alcohol or drugs, the obvious conclusion might be that this learning would be impaired.

SIG: Yesterday, I was consulting on a two-month-old and watched him flirt with his dad with a tiny grin, getting his dad to light up and grin back. We've also studied babies who, because of family patterns or biological problems, aren't able to easily signal with their emotions. Often, however, they can learn. You've demonstrated these early two-way signals in your films and videos. What we need to emphasize is how this occurs in the early months of life, much earlier than at eight months or so, when a baby acquires motor skills. Then you can pull on a toy, but you can signal pleasure and sadness earlier. The affect system develops earlier than motor control. At every stage of cognitive growth there's an earlier stage in the affective sphere that predates interactions with the physical world. This emotional system is a baby's first way of getting to know the world and it gets the cognitive milestones started.

A sense of self begins here as well. You can't have a sense of self without a boundary between your emotions and emotions that come back from outside. This is strictly dependent on interpersonal relations. You can't have reality testing without a sense of self. That also starts in the first year, but then a baby plays it out in the second and third year symbolically by using words that have affective meaning: "Give me that" and "No, you can't have that." Every interchange like that has a "me" and a "you" and creates a symbolic boundary.

TBB: I think even intentionality begins back in the womb. Neonates are intentional. Years ago we observed the four stages of affective reciprocity in the first four months.[11] The first stage is when the mother teaches the baby to be calm and achieve balance within, in order to pay attention to outside signals.

Then she teaches the baby to prolong her attention and to wait for signals from a parent. The next is trading smiles and vocalizations and then the beginnings of reciprocity. These are matching the baby's smiles and vocalizations in timing, rhythm, and quality. The baby feels responded to and matched. The fourth is when the baby moves into what Margaret Mahler called "hatching," turning away from the mother and controlling the situation herself. This gives her the feeling *she* is in control—a sense of self-esteem. Within that, I think you're seeing the first stages of cognitive awareness. Also, by the time the baby knows the mother's and father's smells, voices, and faces, by six weeks, you should be able to tell by any part of the body and the heart rate whether the baby is interacting with the mother or the father. She knows what to expect from each familiar parent, and she knows it's different. Now, isn't that based on an expectancy, an awareness that is both cognitive and emotional at the same time? To try to tear them apart as early as that is impossible. At six to eight weeks, this awareness of differences in each important interactor is the first reliable sign of cognitive development.

SIG: I think we can say something even stronger: Emotion is not just part of cognition; it precedes it as far as we can see. Early on the baby has much more control over his emotional system. According to all current cognitive theories, the baby has to use his motor system to some degree to explore the world. But the child's emotional system probably matures much earlier and the baby can do many more complicated things with emotions. In a smile, there is a motor component, to be sure, but it's the emotion driving the smile (the facial muscles). The ability to manipulate the world, using your gross motor movements as opposed to your facial motor movements, comes a little later. Even a baby with low muscle tone can show affect with a twinkle in the eyes or maybe in the movement of his tongue. We have to tune in to that. Emotions, motor ability, and cognitive ability are, of course, part of one big whole. But instead of the traditional way of looking at the development of intelligence through manipulating and exploring the world, we can say that the child first uses the expression of emotion as a probe to understand the world. It's through his first affective interchanges that his sense of causality is established Later, through pretend play and interaction with affectively meaningful words (as opposed to reading them in a book), the child gets a sense of reality testing and becomes logical and learns how to reason.

A Baby's Waking Hours

TBB: Back to these early relationships: Parents often ask how much time with parents babies need.

SIG: At a conference in Wisconsin of speech and occupational therapists, psychiatrists, psychologists, and so on, I asked the audience if they could answer that question the president asked at a White House Conference: "How much time, then?" The consensus was that about half of the baby's waking time should be clearly very interactive, having fun with the baby and not just in feeding or cuddling. I'd go further. Most of the baby's waking time should be spent either in direct face-to-face interactions with caregivers or with caregivers being in sight and frequently facilitating the baby's exploration of the world. While awake, babies shouldn't be out of sight.

TBB: This is an issue that needs to be explored at many different levels. When I was in Cambodia, there were 24 and 26 babies in certain nurseries with only one or two teenaged survivors to take care of them. There would be 2–4 babies who would alert if I stood at the door and said, "Hi, how are you doing?" or walked over to speak to them. The other 20–22 showed no response whatever. If I went over and tried to play with them, they'd gaze-avert and turn away. Those 4, however, did interact. Then I would be told, "Oh, they're the ones the caregiver carries around on her hip." I don't know how much time she would spend interacting with those babies, but she was there for them. Maybe the question is not so much time, but simply being there for the children.

SIG: I agree. The challenge is that in today's busy society we may not be having enough intimate contact with our babies.

TBB: But the cream on a baby's dessert is when the parent responds to him in his own way. When he says, "Goo," she says, "Goo." When he smiles, she smiles. But if we say, "half a baby's waking hours," I think we'll scare the daylights out of parents. In 15-minute sessions, that would mean 16 episodes of 15 minutes each. That's a lot. But we'd find it difficult to answer any less, wouldn't we? Maybe we need to emphasize that there are many types of closeness and intimacy. Just being there is so important. In the highlands of Mexico where I have done research, mothers rarely, if ever, interact with a baby face to face. But they carry the baby in a serape all day long. They breast-feed the baby up to 70–90 times a day. That's being "there" for the baby!

SIG: This time together can surely be spent in a variety of different ways. One way is with the child and the parent playing direct face-to-face or interactive games or cuddling or rocking together. A second way is helping the child explore by being available: "Oh look at this!" While the parent is available sometimes the child may play on his own and other times the parent facilitates. The third is the child playing on his or her own while the parent is in sight on the phone or reading the newspaper or cooking. How much do we want of each? It may be different for each baby. Babies who are more "laid back" or motorically active and independent often need more of the direct, nurturing holding and face-to-face time.

TBB: Babies are so different as individuals; they are of different temperaments. My first book, *Infants and Mothers*,[12] was written about three very different babies: (1) a quiet, sensitive one; (2) an average, middle-of-the-road baby; and (3) a very active, almost insensitive baby. Each of these had very different needs for being parented, and each created a different environment by affecting their parents differently. I'm pretty certain that when a parent can be in tune with her baby's individual temperament, when there is a "goodness of fit" (à la Winnicott)[13], a parent senses and even reads the baby's individualized need for which kind of "being there" is indicated and how much is enough to fuel that baby's sense of self-esteem and motivation for learning. "Being there" isn't a rigid requirement; it's sensitively geared to each baby.

SIG: When I talk to parents who aren't stressed and who have the time (they're not overloaded with work), where one parent is home or they're sharing working and home life, the sense I get with most children and families who are doing well is that most of the time is divided between the reciprocal play, direct face-to-face interaction, and holding or cuddling, and the facilitated play, as well as being "in sight" (talking on the phone, cooking, etc.) and available.

TBB: If parents try to use this as a yardstick, will they get nervous or run away from it? It would be fascinating to do a time study and see what is actually going on. In the 1960s, William Caudill studied the 24-hour experiences of children in Japan. Beatrice and John Whiting collected data like that for some time in Africa, as did HanUs and Mechtilde Papousek. Back in 1900 in this country, Millicent Shinn studied her niece hour by hour. These studies led to conclusions about the way children were being raised in various cultures. These are familiar time studies on which major assumptions about the quality of parenting are based. All of them showed, though, how little actual face-to-face time there was. Maybe it wasn't as necessary as just being "there," hanging out. The baby is aware by visual and auditory cues that the parent is available.

SIG: Dolores Norton from Chicago did a study using a video camera that was turned on 24 hours a day.[14] Among the points she stressed is that there were not many long sequences of interaction. There were short little bursts, but not nearly what we're talking about here. The National Institute of Child Health and Development is looking at the quality of care in home and day care settings, and they are finding that it's the sensitivity and quality of the emotional interactions between babies and parents or caregivers that is important for language, cognitive, and emotional capacities.

TBB: Most other cultures don't put their children down to play by themselves as much as we do. They carry them around all the time as they go about their business. In Korea they carry the babies on their backs. They don't interact with them that much in those positions, but their goal is perhaps different. Instead of making the children into independent individuals, they want stable, quiet, informed, happy citizens who are aware of others around them.

SIG: Here, we expect some autonomy quite early. A healthy eight-month-old baby who's learning to crawl around in a responsive household will begin to initiate a lot of interaction. This leads to even more. He's going to get a lot of reciprocal interaction because he initiated it—with other siblings in the family, relatives, or whomever. When we're talking about reciprocal interactions, we're not talking only about the care the mother gives. We're talking about the father, the siblings, nannies, baby-sitters, and other family members.

Emotional Interactions

It's those emotionally vibrant experiences that set the stage. The baby has to want something. Mobilizing this intent and weaving it into an interaction gives a combined emotional/cognitive experience. Every experience, by definition, has some affect and cognition in it, but in terms of valence, those that are highly emotionally meaningful to the child are the ones that capture his desires and promote his intelligence.

TBB: Newborns, and I have this on film, have a different set of facial expressions for a human face versus an object right after birth. Observers watching only the baby's face can tell whether or not he is looking at a person or an object. This is built in at birth, and new parents are sensitive to this very slight difference even when they aren't consciously aware of it.

SIG: This is a perfect example of how a baby begins to categorize experience based on affective meaning. But if he doesn't like the human face or if the face doesn't bring any pleasure or excitement, it is unlikely he'll form that differentiation.

TBB: Tiffany Field did some studies showing how smiling is increased by smiling back at the baby and how vocalizations are increased by vocalizing back to the baby.[15] In other words, if you produced what the baby was producing, you significantly increased the chances of a response. A baby seems to light up: "Hey, they're doing back to me what I just did." We did studies looking at this from the other direction: If the baby smiled, what was the chance that the mother would smile back. This turned out to be around 80 percent of the time, versus touching back or vocalizing back or doing something else. The chance of a sensitive mother or father doing back what the baby did is enormously high.

SIG: Yes, these are the key ingredients of all the reciprocal play we've been talking about. A good additional theoretical argument for the importance of emotional interaction for cognitive as well as social and emotional growth is that when affect is involved, it appears to activate many different parts of the brain, often integrating left and right as well as different components. The whole affect system is involved and branches out into all parts of the cortex. There are connections to the visual, the auditory, to the spatial systems, and so on. So emotional experiences may be creating much more synthesis. I bet that if we could get PET [positron-emission tomography] scans while babies were playing, when they were emotionally invested and involved, you'd see many areas lighting up.

TBB: Remember this diagram I've often used to show the fueling of the central nervous system—the two circles, the external feedback system and the internal one? (See Figure 1.)

It seems to me that when you reproduce what the baby has just done, you're fueling the internal feedback system as well as the external. You're saying to him, "That's great! You just did it!" I would think that would pertain in the same way to the object and the human face, with the object fueling just one system, but not the whole mass of systems you mentioned. There is no acknowledging of what the baby's just done. The next step, after reinforcing the baby's productions, is waiting until the baby expresses herself and makes a demand. I'm again thinking about the idea of "hatching" and how if the mother respects any initiative the baby takes, it becomes a very valued stimulus for the baby's ego development. If she doesn't respect the infant's demands and rides over the baby's attempt to "hatch" and to become separate, that kind of growth could be arrested. Now we need to see how much is lost in instances when the baby's productions are not valued and responded to.

SIG: When you read the baby's signal and you're sensitive, it becomes a truly reciprocal interaction, incorporating the baby's initiative. The first games we play are generally ones to entertain the baby, making funny faces or getting the baby to look at us. But as the baby gets further along in the first year and the motor system gets organized, if we gradually shift to letting the baby take the initiative, we can get some interaction going. As we do that we're respecting the baby's uniqueness and individuality in subtle ways, not by just letting the baby crawl away instead of running after him and scooping him up into our laps, but by challenging his initiative and getting many circles of communication going.

TBB: I think that starts as early as two months when the mother waits for the baby to do something, then does it back. The setup is already there. It may not be as overt. Waiting and then reproducing it may reinforce it.

SIG: Yes, it starts very early. The more you respect the baby's initiative and respond to the baby's overtures, especially those early emotional expressions—the little grin or look—the earlier the process begins. This takes place as you're forming the relationship. Individuation, differentiation (i.e., the rhythm of back and forth), and relating occur as part of the same process. Babies learn to love while being respected as unique.

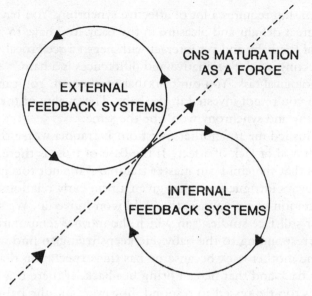

FIGURE 1   Three Sources of Energy for Development

TBB: At this early stage a parent is also respecting the homeostatic system. The baby builds up to an excited peak and then is allowed to go back down. Playing with a small baby means respecting his physiological system, as well as the motor, the affective, and the cognitive systems.

SIG: In other words, this earliest relationship needs to be one that has a fine degree of synchrony between the systems of the baby and those of the caregiver the mommy, daddy, or other person.

TBB: What we're saying in defining this irreducible need is that the relationship between the baby and his caregivers is a unified system. That's what we tried to show with our TV show, "What Every Baby Knows." I was really trying to teach people to pay attention to their child's behavior as a language and to respect it as such. If we can urge parents to pay attention to this behavior, to respect it, and to respond appropriately to it, we will be on our way to enhancing early brain development.

SIG: An even more profound message you were giving is that a parent's emotional relationship with a baby, in which that language is embodied, is the first step in development. It's not to be taken for granted. This is the cornerstone and the foundation piece. Reading the baby's signals and building the relationship requires a lot of affective synchrony. You have to take great delight and pleasure in the baby. You have to feel part of the baby and yet interact with her in a reciprocal way. Respecting a baby's initiative and differences is a hard psychological task. You can't do that on the run. You can't do that if you're not invested in the baby. The quality of the empathy and synchrony won't be the same.

TBB: This led me to another question: Is trauma worse than withdrawal or lack of affect? If the base of trust is there, it seems that the child can master trauma, if it's not too great. It's always intrigued me that given a firm early relationship, an expectation of a response, the child won't give up. We see this in our still-face studies,[16] in which the mother temporarily stops responding to the baby. He keeps trying to find ways to get the mother back because he has this expectation that she'll come back and that he can bring her back. If there is a mother who is too depressed to respond, however, and the baby hasn't ever really gotten her to interact very often, he gives up after 3 tries rather than, say, 15. This may be critical. It's really the baseline, the secure foundation that a parent is setting up. Once this is in place, the baby can become more resilient and enterprising.

SIG: The worse thing for a baby is not having a loving person in her life or being uncertain about that person. If one is missing entirely, for example, in an institutional setting, or if a caregiver is ambivalent or inconsistent, the need we're defining here is not satisfied. The worst situation is not having a relationship at all or being unsure. Children will cling to an abusive parent rather than being moved to an unknown situation. The greatest fear for a child is the loss of a primary relationship. In talking about this positive, nurturing relationship, we're not talking about a Shangri-La without distress, anger, annoyance, defiance. From a few months on, we can see all those emotions in a baby. A parent who sees that as part of the relationship, who has a realistic notion of relationships, can be more nurturing. When the caregiver shuts down and pulls away if the baby is angry, the baby experiences the sense that anger results in loss, detachment. If parents can stay nurturing and try to soothe the baby through the anger, recognizing the change in their tone of voice ("Oh, you're mad at Mommy. I'm going to see if I can make it a little better"), the baby gets the message that lots of different emotions are part of the relationship. There's pleasure and trust, but there's also anger, annoyance, frustration, defiance, negativism. The baby learns he can be annoyed or defiant and the parents will still be there.

TBB: My colleague, Joshua Sparrow, has a word for that. He calls it "testing the tolerance for negative affect." I think it's interesting that a baby tests that tolerance all throughout the second year.

SIG: The baby needs to feel confident he can turn away or feel bad and Mom or Dad will still be there. If he can count on this, he can experiment with separation, anger, defiance, and excitement. If he has to look over his shoulder, he has to be much more cautious or hold onto you with his negativism.

TBB: The "vulnerable child" syndrome is just the opposite of this. The mother never lets the child be in control or lets him out of her sight. By overprotecting the baby, the mother takes away his own internal feedback. He becomes too dependent on her for signals and for control. He never learns to trust himself.

SIG: When a caregiver marches to her own drummer, not following the baby's lead, it's a relationship of a kind, but not a balanced relationship, where she's really empathizing with the child.

TBB: A parent needs to hear that. She needs to know that the baby can manage the negative side and that she, too, can manage it. It becomes a balance of mutual expectation and trust in which each member of the dyad values the other.

SIG: Then the relationship becomes an integrated experience early on. In psychoanalysis we talk about ego splitting and polarized affect states. I tend to see this in the second year when caregivers are unable to nurture toddlers through angry states. The baby keeps anger and love as separate. When nurturing occurs even during anger and other strong emotions, the baby begins to learn that these different emotions, like love and hate, can be connected with one another.

TBB: In our Touchpoints training,[17] I always point out that there's bound to be a feeling of negative aggression in the baby and a feeling of negative aggression in the parent. All passion is both positive and negative, not just positive. Without the negative, it isn't passion. I think this needs to be brought out.

SIG: These negative emotions need to be distinguished from traumatic experience. There's research on trauma, showing the physiological and emotional reactions of children who are highly stressed. This kind of extreme stress is seen in babies who haven't the pleasurable secure base. When an experience is overwhelmingly scary, like in a child who's been sexually or physically abused, you get the stress system taking over. Babies who are abused can get vigilant and hyperfearful. These physiological patterns are not necessarily irreversible. If you again provide nurturing warmth and expose the baby to security and comfort, although it takes a lot longer, the baby will often integrate those negative experiences as part of relationships and do quite well (if the stress hasn't gone on too long or if it hasn't derailed motor development, cognition, or several developmental phases). But an ongoing, warm, intimate relationship needs to be there in the first place; it's the tool one can use to help a baby recover from stress. Of course, where stress has been chronic, the recovery process can take years.

Divorce and Custody

TBB: How can we maintain this strong primary relationship in a divorce situation? What about joint custody and visitation rights? I get asked about the joint custody all the time. We need to think more about visitation rights, overnight rights, as well. How early would you let a baby go overnight?

SIG: If divorcing parents live near each other and both are good parents, I recommend that they keep the relationship with the child as similar as they can to when they were married. The ideal situation is for both parents to see the child every day. That would lead to security and comfort with both parents. If both parents spend lots of time with the baby and can help the baby feel secure (i.e., he will let either one comfort him when he is upset), then you can have sleepovers early on.

It's more typical, though, that the baby is with Mother most of the time and spends only a little time with Daddy or vice versa. Then I'm uncomfortable having a sleepover before the baby is three years old. Even then, it would depend on the circumstance of the baby and whether or not the baby is ready or feels comfortable about the situation. Although you always have to take individual circumstances into account, generally the primary caregiver should have the other parent come over frequently and play with the baby. The more the other caregiver plays with the baby and comforts and feeds and is a "secure" person, the more quickly the sleepovers will become a real possibility. If the other caregiver is seeing the baby, say, four times a week, it may be a natural transition.

I was called in on a situation with a four-year-old child where the father wanted to take the child for two weeks on a summer vacation. I suggested he take the mother and have a whole extended family vacation, but he shouldn't just take the child away that long from his mother. The most this child had ever been away was three days. It was too much to stretch from three days to two weeks. They could work up gradually, but not all at once. We worked out a compromise.

TBB: Three years old seems to me the time to begin trying out overnights. If the child is resourceful at night and is able to sleep alone, these would also be signs that the child is ready. But it should be geared to the child's temperament and his response to separation from the live-in parent.

SIG: Would you say to the judges that for a two-year-old or an 18-month-old, who doesn't see a lot of the daddy, if the daddy wants three-day weekend overnights, the answer would be absolutely not?

TBB: In all likelihood.

SIG: To take the baby for a week or more in the summertime would also be an absolute no? Yet we see case after case where separation from the primary nurturing caregiver is mandated by the court. In one instance, in my practice, it took two months to help the child recover and feel secure with his mother after an overly long visit with the father before the child was ready. Lots of day visits are a great way to establish security with the other parent.

TBB: In terms of joint custody, we need better guidelines.[18] The main issue in joint custody is whether the parents can handle their anger and competitive feelings in a way that leaves the child out of it. The best predictor for the future children of divorce is whether they are spared the antagonistic feelings of parents. For a divorced child always feels it is his fault, that if he had been a better child his parents wouldn't have split and fractured the family. The other fear is that of abandonment: "If one parent will leave me, maybe the other will, too." Visits by the parent who does not have custody must be predictable and reliable and must not disrupt the child's routines. A routine becomes a reliable source of reassurance for the child. Overnight visitation and separations need to be taken seriously as potential threats to the child. And yet, the noncustodial parent needs to be available to the child. A lot should go into each decision: the stage of the child's development, the child's adjustment to the divorce, the reliability of each parent in keeping promises to the child. Regular visitation of the noncustodial parent is ideal as long as it doesn't disrupt the family's routines. The child's well-being should come first. At present, family court judges have recognized the absent parent's issues, but not yet the child's adjustment, as paramount. [See the family court guidelines at the end of this chapter.]

SIG: One situation a number of parents have implemented is the child staying at home and the parents taking turns with the child there. The parents who do this feel that the children should have the security of their own room and one home and that they, the parents, should move around. If the families are well-to-do and can afford to keep the original home and have apartments for themselves in this arrangement, each one would spend half the week in the home and half the week in the apartment. Obviously, this is really complicated, and logistics have to be worked out.

TBB: If we gave parents what to look for and some basic guidelines for when moving from household to household or overnights are too early, when they would interfere with the child's development and so forth, they could make their own decisions.

SIG: As we said, there's still the problem of separating kids from the primary nurturing parent for a week or two in the summer or long weekends before the child is ready. A three- or four-year-old will usually not be ready for a two-week summer vacation away from the primary nurturing caregiver. By the time they're five, six, or seven, children are often ready. If the separation is done gradually and the nonprimary caregiver comes over on a daily basis, the transition will happen more quickly.

The second principle I look for in a divorce is easy access to both parents. It's best for parents to live close to each other, whether or not they share the same house, so that when the children get to be school-aged, they can bike or walk to one house or the other. They can go to the same school, no matter which house they live in, and they can have friends over to either house. This puts the children a little more in control of access to Mommy and Daddy. It's always best when the child can take initiative to seek closeness. This has worked very well for some children. But it takes very mature parents who put the children first.

I tell parents who are divorced that whatever happened happened, but that now, because of the children, they're related for life. They're relatives and are in the same family, whether they like it or not. It's a question of whether or not they're going to get along and be civil, on behalf of the children, or whether they're going to undermine the children. They can't not relate to each other. The children need both parents. Some parents need ongoing therapy. Some parents are able to work it out on their own.

TBB: We are still assuming a very nurturing primary caregiver in the first place, somebody who takes full responsibility for the child and is the primary caregiver.

SIG: Ideally there would be two primary nurturers from the beginning. But that is not widely practiced now. The goal of using the left and right hand together—having two primary nurturers—that's not something that most parents who are together think of. They get caught up in having one primary and one secondary nurturer. When there are two primary nurturers, all these decisions come more easily, but that has to start early. In most situations it's not the case. How can courts assess the situation?

TBB: Courts are overloaded. They haven't enough time. They don't have any backup for evaluating the situation with the parents and child. If they had all that information ready, then maybe, with the time they have for each child, they could make a more informed decision.

SIG: But policies now are based on faulty understanding of children, for example, the notion that two-year-olds can be separated easily from a nurturing parent.

TBB: At the same time, there's a need to recognize fathers. This has come about to some extent. Up to now it's all been mothers and the mother got everything. She got custody; shared custody was rare. More recently, courts came to the realization that they ought to try to keep fathers in on it, for both financial and other reasons. So they began to make big efforts to keep fathers involved. This led to shared custody, but also to some crazy decisions. The parents of a seven-month-old called me, saying that a judge had decreed that the baby should spend half a week with each one of them. One of them lived in

San Francisco and one in Chicago. They came to consult at our unit for a few days. Eventually they were able to agree on a better decision and took an active role once someone had taken the time to explain the child's needs to them.

The other thing that's interfering right now with good decisions is too much emphasis on family solidarity—trying to keep families together. Trying to keep families together at all costs may be very destructive. I think what we need to fight for is a thorough exploration of the child's development and needs and of each parent's capacities. From that, courts could help parents work together for their child's best interests.

Day Care

SIG: If parents have options and are able to provide high-quality care themselves, I find it best not to have infants or toddlers (in the first two years) in full-time, 30–40-plus-hour-a-week day care. Current research and my own clinical observations suggest that most day-care centers do not provide high-quality care. The quality of interaction between caregivers and babies is often less than optimal. Also, the current ratios of four babies per caregiver in the first year and six in the second year, coupled with high staff turnover, minimum wages, insufficient training, and the expectable change of caregivers each year, make it difficult to provide high-quality, ongoing, nurturing care in those early years.

The question is, are parents able to shift back to caring for their babies and using day care less?

TBB: I would prefer if day care for babies and toddlers weren't necessary, but I think that there is a large portion of the population right now who can't take the full-time care of their infants.

SIG: Is one reason why parents can't do this a difference in the way people are growing up these days?

TBB: Expectations are changing. It's like what is happening to marriage in a society where the divorce rate is going up to 50 percent. The expectations for marriage have changed. I think the same thing is happening to the way mothers perceive staying at home. In an earlier generation, most mothers were expected to stay at home, and it was easier for them to do so. Now we've changed that expectation entirely, and it's hard to reverse it.

SIG: From the child's point of view, however, let's look at the first year of life in full-time day care—40 or more hours a week. How do you think babies develop relationships in this circumstance?

TBB: Babies can make multiple attachments that are meaningful. Certainly I would hope that the parents come first and the baby makes secondary attachments to everybody else. I visited a day-care center recently at a time when all the mothers were there. After a while, only one mother was left and all the children gravitated to her. I turned to the very talented day-care people there and said, "They really seem to desert you, don't they?" They said, "When there's a mother here, we don't even exist." The children were already differentiating among caregivers. It doesn't even have to be their mother; it just has to be a mother.

SIG: That's not so great. In a number of day-care centers, when the children are mobile, I see a lot of emotionally hungry children. Children come up to any new adult and hang on. Some of that reaching out for any mother is simply reaching out to anyone who will give them some attention. It's a little indiscriminate. We see that in institutions such as orphanages where there is emotional deprivation. A minute here and there of reciprocal interaction, sometimes around feeding or diapering, is not enough to provide the needed security and sense of being cared for.

  If we are going to give parents flexible options, we need both to improve day care and to reduce the number of hours per week children spend in day-care situations.

TBB: Again, I think it needs to be a case-by-case decision, weighing this or that, rather than simply telling people what to do. Some parents are better parents if there is an outlet for them. But we do need to provide the child with an optimal secondary caregiver.

SIG: When I talk to college students, I often ask them how they see their lives in terms of having children. As they think about a career and getting married, are they taking into account child-rearing, as well as the demands of a profession? Are they engaged to a neurosurgeon or are they going to be neurosurgeons themselves? Are they planning on having several children? Having two neurosurgeons in the family along with four children may be more difficult and demanding than they can possibly imagine. On the other hand, if two people are getting married and both want careers, and one of them is a writer and the other a psychologist, they may have more control of their time. Each one could work two-thirds time or one could work halftime and they could get child care for the limited remaining hours. But a lot of these potential parents haven't thought this out. They want children and a good career and see no problem. What they're being led to believe now is that full-time day care in the first years of life is as good as if not better than what they can provide: "I'll have a baby, take a two-month leave of absence, put the baby in day care, and I'll be a lawyer and my spouse will be a lawyer. We'll work until 8:00 at night. We'll pick up the baby, come home, and play for an hour." In families like this I see children not getting their basic needs for nurturing met.

TBB: When I see a family like that I see a lot of grieving. That kind of treatment of the child is ignoring the child's interests to such an extent that there must be a lot of denial. Something is so painful that these parents have to hide behind defenses.

SIG: But do we support this type of denial or help parents out of it? As new parents make their decisions early on, some parents intuitively plan for the flexibility to be home more; sometimes it's the mom and sometimes it's the dad who stays home. The parents who are more ambivalent and tend to use denial often look around for guidance. But they're getting a lot of misinformation. They're told it doesn't make a difference. If parents-to-be knew more about this need for a continuous, close relationship, they might plan more realistically. They would see how hard it is to have such relationships with two full-time jobs and full-time day care. If parents see the options, they could make choices. If they have a caregiver at home and pick well, they have a greater likelihood, if they can afford it, of having the same caregiver being with them for a number of years. In day care, by design, the caregivers change each year. Turnover is so great, though, that there may be another change or two changes even within one year. There may be three changes of caregivers by the time a baby has had a year of day care. Minimum wages, lack of training, and so on contribute to this. The caregiver in a day-care setting is not like a *meta peleth* in a kibbutz in Israel, who is a stable person in a child's life, with him for four or five years. It doesn't have to be the mother. It could be the father or the grandfather or grandmother. The child needs a caregiver in his or her life who's going to be there for the long haul.

TBB: To improve day care, I see three babies per adult as the absolute maximum for the first year of life. But now the norm is four babies per caregiver. Imagine a mother with triplets and how hard it is for her to care for all three babies at the same time.

SIG: Would you recommend, Berry, that a baby should keep the same caregivers for the first three or four years? One group of caregivers, for example, would follow a group of children who started as infants on up through their toddler years.

TBB: This would work as long as the caregiver really liked each baby, but suppose she didn't like one? Couldn't it be moved to another caregiver's group? Caregivers and babies, like parents, could be evaluated for "goodness of fit" between them. Also, when you go up into the second and third years, and taking care of four children becomes possible, a fourth child will be added to the group of three. The fourth baby wouldn't necessarily get the same caregivers.

SIG: The extra children in the group might come from outside, perhaps from home. To make this work, you'd have to have expanding entry into day care at the second and third years, with each class being larger than the last. More children are in day care by age three than in the first two years of life. Then we have to create incentives for the staff of day-care centers to stay on, giving better wages and training.

TBB: We have to increase wages to a decent level, and we need to improve their status. At present, they are thought of as "baby-sitters" with some scorn.

SIG: That's what we need to correct. We need to get across all that's involved in meaningful care of a child: creating ongoing dialogues, reflecting and accepting a variety of emotions. You can sometimes find people who are warm and nourishing and emotionally responsive, even though they haven't been given a chance to educate themselves. Sometimes you can find young people who want to get experience with children and who are naturally sensitive and flexible.

TBB: Day-care staff need constant refueling. It's a demanding job, taking care of somebody else's children. If parents and day-care personnel could handle their natural, inevitable gatekeeping, parents could become peer "fuelers" of the day-

care personnel. The team (of parents and child care worker)
could share the child's optimal development.

SIG: We need to see all this from the point of view of prevention.
It's a public health issue.

TBB: When Congress was talking about that $22 billion for
improving child care, I got a chance to go down to
Washington, and told them that if they just turn the money
over to the states, it will all get eaten up. You'd do better to
give the money to states tied to choices based on the quality
child care that we know how to produce, and to let them pick
their choices. When it came to laying out choices that will work
for the child, they said, "Oh, we have to do some research." I
told them there was already plenty of research. What we need
now is just the will to put the research into practice. They asked
if I could tell them what programs work. I said not by myself,
but I certainly could gather a bunch of colleagues who could
tell you which ones we guarantee would work.

State governments can eat up revenues for child care at the
top, if we're not careful. The one sector that could make a real
difference and could afford to, and might be motivated to if we
were smart enough, would be big business. If we could get
them to set up a center in every business site that would contain
preventive health care, child care, after-school care, and elder
care, then maybe we could begin to reach a lot of people. I
don't think we need to use the schools for this, but Ed Zigler at
Yale has a model he calls the "School of the 21st Century," in
which all these caregiving situations are gathered into school
buildings that are not in use and made into centers for families
in their communities. (See Organization list in Appendix.) In
our Touchpoints model, we are recommending that parent
centers be established in every community where parents could
receive child care, preventive health care, after-school care, and
elder care. Parent resource centers, such as Family Support
America, could be established for peer resources. (See
Organization list in Appendix.) Parents could then begin to feel
a sense of community around them.

Our Touchpoints model has been developed at Children's
Hospital in Boston to train multidisciplinary representatives from
communities that are ready for change in an outreach, relational
model. (See Organization list in Appendix.) We want to improve
preventive health care and child care with several goals. At each
visit of parents and child, the provider (child care or medical care)

identifies the strengths versus the failures of the parent. The child's development is the language between professional and parent. The parent is valued as the expert in the child's development. In this way, the passion of the parent is fostered. The relationship is transactional versus top-down. Each visit becomes an opportunity for sharing the child's new achievements and encouraging the child's development, both physical and psychological. Twenty-five centers have espoused our ideas, and they are changing communities to become parent-friendly. Our goal is to offer preventive outreach for the present 40 percent of underserved. We do know what to do. Can we do it?

Foster Care and Adoption

SIG: Besides the children of working parents, we need to think of children in foster care, or in institutions of any kind. We've seen what happens in certain Eastern European orphanages, where there weren't primary caregivers invested in each child. Here in this country we have kids going from one foster home to another foster home and changing caregivers frequently. We have institutions where children stay until they're placed in foster care. These aren't necessarily run with a nurturing caregiver really invested in the baby or child.

TBB: William Weld, the former governor of Massachusetts, appointed a Foster Care Commission in 1992 consisting of some 20 of us to improve the Department of Social Services.[19] We looked at 100 random cases, pulling out the records. Not one of these cases had ever really been worked up in the first place. Nobody knew what the child was going to bring to the foster care situation. Nobody knew what he needed and nobody paid attention to matching the child with a family that was going to work. Of course, that meant that children went from one family to another to another. Whatever problems a child started with were being compounded.

SIG: What percentage of the 100 children had been in multiple placements?

TBB: Most all of them. The governor paid attention to our report. We got a new manager who brought in expertise and set up tracking systems for these children. As soon as the department began to track them, it became clear that the children were being shoved around. They were able to cut down significantly on how many moves the children made. We made recommendations that these children get an initial workup so that everyone knew what was going on with them in the first place—whether they were abused or neglected or came from families that never paid any attention to them. In that way, we would start off knowing where they stood psychologically and emotionally. As soon as we did that, the children began to get foster placements that fit and that they stuck with. In the years since then, we've significantly changed the picture of foster care in Massachusetts.

SIG: Once you worked up somebody's background, what then was the practical solution that helped the state make better foster care decisions?

TBB: Up to that time, all they were doing was putting on Band-Aids. We began to know a lot more about the foster care families, because they had cared for other children and information had been gathered about them. By identifying what was in the child, the agency could go to a foster mother, say, who had two children now and wanted a third and explain that this child has such and such a temperament and is like this or that. She could then take some responsibility for the decision. The other thing our work did was to encourage agencies to focus on getting these children adopted. The dream that they were going to reconstitute the original families was too often a dream. Adoption was being postponed year after year in the vain hope that parents could be rehabilitated. The children suffered.

SIG: Should there be a change in the state and national laws that require holding off on the adoption of children? Given what we know about the importance of early and ongoing relationships, making families wait to adopt isn't best for the child.

TBB: In Massachusetts, you have to wait at least a year to see whether the mother is going to want her child back or not.

SIG: That is where the parents want the child back or have a fantasy about wanting the child back. But what if the parent is willing to give up the child?

TBB: In that case, adoption is now possible. The need to have babies adopted earlier was why I really started the NBAS.[20] You couldn't adopt a child under four months old in Massachusetts because nobody could identify whether the child was normal neurologically or not. I started working on the NBAS to identify children who could be adopted early on and to change the law from four months to zero. You can now

adopt a child from birth if the parent gives up custody. But I
don't know that the NBAS is still used all that much. I wish it
were. In some cases you can adopt a baby without its having
been examined. In Korea, adoption agencies require that the
foreign mother come to Korea for a month to get to know the
child.

SIG: By not working with the mothers, agencies certainly prolong
the time in foster care. The laws give too much time for
reclaiming a baby, which delays adoption in many cases and
interferes with it. This runs in opposition to what we
recommend that every baby needs. Every baby needs a solid
continuing relationship. By prolonging foster care and putting
off adoption, we're creating unnecessary stress on the baby.
Instead, we should be trying to get to know the mother and the
baby and try to help the mother make a decision that's good for
her. She'll often need help, whether she takes the baby back or
gives it up. The states and the courts have to realize that many
current laws are working against the baby's interest. We have to
create legally shorter time intervals plus mandating support for
counseling to help mothers make a decision in a shorter period
of time.

TBB: There are also situations where the parents who are going
to adopt get to know the birth mother during the pregnancy.
Does having the birth mother in the picture interfere with
intimate relationships?

SIG: I don't think so. In many cases, if it works well, the
mother is less likely to contest the adoption. In cases we've
worked with, the mother often feels like part of the extended
family.

TBB: But there's the danger that the adoptive parents can feel
secondary in some way. They may worry that the mother will
decide all of a sudden that she wants the baby back. Remember
the baby who was given back to the birth mother after the
adoption had actually taken place, Baby M? The birth mother
had already nursed her baby in the neonatal period. Of course
she wanted her back.

SIG: Is there a point of time that we want to recommend, for an
adoption, a time when we would say it's too late to reunite the
baby with the biological parents?

TBB: Clearly we need to set a period of time after which we can
say that the baby's rights take precedence. The mother certainly
has rights, but do courts recognize a baby's rights?

SIG: When would we say that the child should not be separated from a nurturing caregiver? Should we say that after a certain amount of time we can't do this to the children?

TBB: I would say that it ought to be based on the particular child.

SIG: At four months, we might recommend that the transition be made gradually. The adoptive mom needs to first visit and reestablish a relationship. Then she needs to be supportive and nurturing and let the birth mother or foster mom visit so there's not a lot of separation anxiety. A foster mom can even be like a grandmother or an aunt and remain a part of the child's life. You would need to create a transition with a lot of contact. The longer the time, for example, the harder for the baby to change. Once a baby is with someone for six months or more, you're going to compromise that baby's relationships and development.

TBB: Why would you go to six months? I think that four months should be the cutoff time because at four months the baby is showing the first signs of autonomy. I would expect this to go underground if the baby were traumatized by taking it from one environment to another. So the whole basis for the child's autonomy would be at high risk. I would want to require that a biological mother who took her child back would have to be closely supervised to be sure she is making it with that baby. The baby's issues should come first.

I would want a safety net system of nurturing for a birth mother when she took a child back at any age. I think the reasons she gave up the baby have to be explored. Was she depressed? Is she out of her depression? Is she ambivalent? Is she still ambivalent? Some sort of assessment would be essential.

SIG: The basic idea is that as the baby gets older and more related to the caregiver, separation gets to be less in the baby's interests, even if it's the biological parent who wants the baby back. The psychological parent is the real parent. We've been overdoing the biological rights of the parent and underdoing the baby's rights. The further out you get, the more compelling the reasons would have to be to get the baby back. The missing piece in the legal system is the neglect of the baby's rights. We have to be able to explain to parents and judges what's going on with the baby. The baby is forming a picture of who he is as a person, and a sense of trust and nurturing, all through a relationship with a nurturing caregiver. To break this up, you run a grave risk. There's a lot of suffering. People don't realize the amount of suffering that children go through when you pull the rug out from under them in this way.

TBB: We have to establish and make clear to parents and those who make decisions about children what we think happens in the first three years. There are three key developments. One is a clear sense of self-esteem in the child; the second is enough confidence to be altruistic and care about other people; and the third is motivation for learning. Those three, at least, are endangered when anything serious happens to a child's main relationship in the first three years.

SIG: Those three are absolutely endangered. In addition, the baby is forming the basis for learning about intimacy. By forming a sense of self based on intimacy, trust, and relating to others, he's learning warmth and compassion. The baby is also learning—through reciprocity—how to be intentional, purposeful, and willful. That leads to learning how to be logical and organized. He's learning that he can have impact and force things to happen. In the second year, the growing sense of self helps babies pull together the little pieces into a person. Preverbally, they're learning how to be scientific problem solvers. Then they're learning to use ideas and form a sense of self in terms of who they are as people. This is when we begin to see altruism. We usually don't think enough of all that happens in the first three years when we put children at risk. We're endangering the child's entire cognitive and emotional development when we play Russian roulette with foster care and adoption and custody. By spelling out these necessary developments, we could make a strong case for shifting the emphasis toward what's best for the child.

TBB: We should also be thinking about assessing adoptive parents and preparing them. Many adoptive parents are bound to be vulnerable, especially if the reason for adoption is infertility. One parent feels like a failure. The other has had to accept it. Then, they make a decision to adopt. In the waiting period, their hunger and anticipation for the baby builds up. They want to be ideal parents for this baby. When the baby arrives from another setting or another culture, he's likely to be hypersensitive and overwhelmed by the change. No matter how poor the previous environment has been, because of his adjustment to it, he's bound to grieve. At four months, I would expect one month of grieving and readjustment. At a year, at least two months. Because of his hypersensitivity, the baby turns away from these eager new adoptive parents. He won't look at them. He won't accept their overtures. He won't eat. He is withdrawn or fragile. The parents' vulnerability is reinforced. Then, because we know so much about intrauterine influence, they may begin to see the baby as already damaged by such intrauterine exposures as deprivation. They begin to expect failure. We could prepare adoptive parents for this adjustment period. We can prevent such failures in adoptions.

Mothers in Prison

TBB: What about moms in prison? In the first year, the chances of rehabilitating the mom on the strength of the child are so good, and the chances of the baby being hurt by being with the mother in prison are so slim, that I would recommend it.

SIG: That makes sense if the mother has a chance of being out in a year or two. If the mother is going to be out in two years, they should make the program a two-year program or make every effort to have the mother go into a halfway house. You don't want the child to be with the mother for a year, then separate mother and child for a year, and then put the child back with the mother. If the mother is sentenced to prison for one year, I recommend that the baby be with the mother. This might work for a mother who was pregnant and gave birth in jail. This is not so in the case of five- or six-year-old children.

TBB: Jean Harris started a program like this down in New York State [Sing Sing] and it's worked very well.

SIG: If a mother got a 10-year sentence for a serious crime, that's a complicated issue. Perhaps, the baby could be brought up by the grandmother right off, visiting the mother all the time.

TBB: I would still rather have the child with the mother for the first year. That would be so therapeutic for the mother.

SIG: Definitely therapeutic for the mother, but what about the baby?

TBB: If the child can then go to a grandparent, it might work. But if there's nobody in the family who can take that child over after the first year, it should be decided right up front what would be in the child's best interests, which indeed might not be to be with the mother at all. At any rate, the earlier the decision, the more stable the environment we could offer the child.

SIG: If the mother is going to be in for a year, two or three, and the mother does real well, you can get her in a halfway house so she can be with the baby. A program would have to make every effort to keep mother and child together until the mother gets out of prison, not just for a year. Do it right, don't just do it halfway. But if the mother is in for 10 years, and there's no grandmother, I agree it's in the baby's best interests to be adopted. In circumstances where you have a grandmother or aunt to care for the child, the question is whether it is better for the baby to be with the mother in prison for the first year and become related to Mommy and then to form a new relationship with the grandmother or better for the baby to start off with the grandmother and then just visit Mommy.

TBB: It's better to have loved and lost than never to have loved at all.

SIG: But the baby could fall in love with the grandmother or the aunt.

TBB: The chances of good care for a baby are good with somebody who is incarcerated. Do you remember that old Skeels/Skodak study[21] where the women were in institutions and did such wonderful jobs with the children? They were women with severe problems, but they were in institutions and didn't have anything else to do but play with the baby. They probably had 50 percent of the waking time with the baby. I think this needs to be considered. Perhaps because she's incarcerated, she'd be a better mom than she ever might be if she were not incarcerated. This would give the baby a decent start. Then the grandmother could take over. But when women have done so terribly in society, I also worry about what kind of grandparents we are assigning the babies to.

Orphanages and Group Homes

SIG: Related to that is the question: What kinds of institutional care do we have now, rather than foster care? There's a transition period where foster care doesn't start immediately. There are group situations before a child goes into foster care.

TBB: But there's been a real revulsion against orphanages in this country and I don't know how many there are left.

SIG: Some group homes are like foster care. The problem with institutions as large as orphanages is that they tend toward impersonal care. Small group homes may work better because they are more personal.

TBB: If we are expecting to provide nurturing caregivers, hadn't we better consider what kind of nurturing we can offer the caregivers themselves? Burnout is right around the corner when you're working in such an institution. And it can take many forms, such as neglecting children, mistreating them, even hating them. Could we suggest that institutional caregivers be provided with weekly peer groups and supervision, that they have a mentor to refer to for their own issues, that they be evaluated from time to time for their own adjustment and problems, as well as for their performance?

We've been struggling with these issues for those who work with drug-addicted teenage mothers. They've done well and I kept wondering why. Then I thought—these caregivers have a motive. They have a real motive: to get these girls off drugs. Maybe what we need to do is to give caregivers in institutional settings a clear motive, to spell out what it is we're trying to achieve with these children. Are we trying to get them to develop in specific ways—affective, cognitive, motor? Maybe we need to be very clear about goals. We're not just asking caregivers to be good-hearted, sweet, and safe, because that burns out. But we can say we want to see these skills, these activities, these responses they can try to meet, and we'll have ways to measure progress.

SIG: In all the settings, including day care, we do know the kinds of interactions children need to be involved in. When we encourage "play" or "reciprocal interactions" we know what that means. But we have to spend a lot more time on education and training. The entire orientation and value system of settings for children need to be reconsidered in light of what we now know about the importance of consistent nurturing care and sensitive emotional interactions. Training, ongoing support for staff, and regular observations of how they are doing in the context of specific standards are needed. In fact, all the needs we are discussing in this work should be part of a program.

TBB: I like to think back to the 10 nurses we trained when we first started Touchpoints. We brought in 10 nurses from around Boston who together had been in outreach care for a combined total of 180 years. They were wonderful women, dedicated nurses. Halfway through the week of training, they said they couldn't take anything else on. They didn't have the time.

"We're being asked to see more and more patients, not fewer," they said. "There's no time." When we asked what they were spending their time on now, they said the mothers had them listen to all the reasons that their lives were terrible and how much abuse they had to live with. I asked if they were going to change any of that and they said no, all they could do was give the mothers support. I said they could do that, but that they also had something very special in their hands. They had a child's future. If they spent 10 or 15 minutes out of their time with the mother talking about the child's development and capturing her passion for her child, they could give her a sense of hope that they couldn't otherwise. Well, their eyes lit up. At the end of the week, they said that they didn't know how close they had been to burnout. Some even wept. They hadn't had any guidelines. I think guidelines are what caregivers need most.

SIG: You were helping the nurses feel that they were doing something important. Now what about the orphanages around the world where they're taking the unwanted children, in terms of the importance of relationships and nurturing. What do we want to say to them?

TBB: The orphanage in Seoul that I was in just last week has very young babies who have all been left on the doorstep. I asked why they couldn't get the babies adopted and the answer was that they didn't know who their parents were. These children would be much better off adopted rather than waiting a year or two, but they couldn't do that.

SIG: Does their legal system say you have to know the parents before you can adopt the child?

TBB: You have to keep trying for a year to find out who the parents are before adoption. There were many families who wanted to adopt these children.

SIG: Somehow there needs to be an awareness of what we are doing to the child by waiting a year.

TBB: I get worried about trying to do things across cultures or countries because I think there are so many ethnic problems we don't understand. When I was doing cross-cultural work, it would take us a year to understand what all the variables were. All we can do is lay out the values that *we* think are important in our culture and then say that we hope that these are translatable, adaptable across countries. I don't think we should try to do it ourselves. In some cultures, the child probably bears a stigma if his mother left him on a doorstep.

SIG: The challenge is to create truly nurturing settings so that children don't lose ground in an impersonal institutional setting, and to initiate processes within different cultures, including adoption, that help children become part of a family as soon as possible. In Russia, they have tried a program in which the mother, as she gives birth in the hospital, spends a certain amount of time with the baby right with her, breast-feeding and bonding, and so on. This has cut down by half the number of babies who were abandoned in the hospital, which originally was very high.[22]

TBB: When Melvin Konner and his wife, Marjorie Shostak, went to the Kalahari Desert they trained with me on my Neonatal Behavioral Assessment. When they got back I was dying to hear what the Bushmen's newborn babies were like. They said we only saw 50 percent of them. Apparently, grandmother and mother go out into the bush to deliver a baby. They decide right at birth which ones they're going to bring back. This is a nomadic culture, living very close to the edge of nutritional and other requirements of survival. Every new baby upsets the balance of the tribe, so they can only afford to raise a few each year. The ones they bring back are the more eliciting, well-put-together babies. You can see that to get into cross-cultural recommendations is tricky.

SIG: Here in the United States, if a baby has to be in an institution or group home because there's no foster placement, that's where we can set guidelines. For instance, there should be one nurturing caregiver who is assigned to that child and not more than two others and that caregiver should be with that child for as long as she's in the institution. They should also try to create a transition with caregiver visits once the child is adopted or goes into foster care. We also need guidelines for interactive play, for physical handling of the baby, and for how much time the baby should be left alone.

TBB: What about care with relatives?

SIG: I think we have to be flexible and provide the best care for that baby. There has to be enough flexibility, and people with time to assess whether the system is being exploited or abused. Say you're looking for a foster home and the grandmother says, "I'll take the baby, but I can't afford to without the same help you give a foster mom. I'm more familiar with the baby and love him." If you find this to be true, then it's in the child's best interests. But in another circumstance, if you can see that the grandmother isn't going to provide very good care and is in it for the money, the baby might do better with a foster parent.

The missing piece that runs through all this is what's good for the child. The child comes first. Then you have a basis to make some decisions.

TBB: I think we can give courts and agencies guidelines and even some yardsticks for making decisions. A lot of the poor decisions made for children in the courts are due to a lack of assessment and a lack of time. You can't expect judges to take that time, but you can expect them to have able people attached to the court who do take that time. Family court judges are really, really important. [See King's County, Washington Family Court Guidelines at the end of this chapter.]

Introduction to Recommendations (S.I.G.)

A Child's Day

To put the recommendations that follow in context, the following pages outline an optimal structure for a child's day. Through the hours of the day, the nurturing relationship that we have discussed would play itself out in the following way.

Babies and Toddlers. We can divide up the types of involvement caregivers have with their babies in the first few years of life into a number of broad categories. One type (inappropriate for toddlers or infants who are awake), would involve being in the house with the child, but not being in sight of the child because one is in a different room. Another would be presence in the same room, or the next room if there is a large opening between the rooms, where the child can see the parent and the parent can see the child, and they can readily hear one another but are not necessarily involved directly in any play, interaction, or facilitation of use of toys or materials and so forth. The parent and the baby would each be involved in his or her own activities. The baby might be simply sitting in an infant seat or attempting to entertain himself on the floor with the parent cooking, cleaning, or otherwise being occupied. The third type of involvement would be where the parent or caregiver, available intermittently, is facilitating the baby's interaction with his environment. This might be looking at pictures together or the parent helping the baby explore a toy or helping a toddler explore his surroundings. The caregiver or parent might be helping the toddler look, touch, examine, vocalize, and eventually verbalize about the experience. The fourth category of experience would involve the parent directly interacting with the child. Here, the parent would be following the child's interests, such as in making sounds or funny faces or handing objects back and forth or, for a preschooler, being involved in joint pretend play where the parent is pretending to be a dog or a cat and hamming it up in a drama of the child's choosing. In this fourth category of experience, the parent is directly involved with the child, and the parent, in essence, becomes the play object or the toy or the object of interest. It could involve holding, cuddling, comforting back rubs, hugging and kissing, caressing, imaginative play, and so on. For the verbal child, this might involve direct conversation or negotiation about toys or books or bedtime or decisions regarding foods, activities, and so on. What characterizes this fourth type of engagement, which we [S.I.G.] refer to as "floor time"[23], is following the child's lead and the direct, continuous communication between the child and the parent or the caregiver. Many of our most prized and precious magic moments with our babies and toddlers are part of this category.

In deciding how to divide the child's waking time into these kinds of activities, it is important to note that an infant who is sleeping 14 hours a day might have 5 or 6 hours available when feeding, diapering, and simply calming down are not guiding the interactions. During feeding and diapering activities there can and should be lots of warm nurturing interaction with exchanges of vocalizations and gestures.

In the hustle-bustle of ordinary life the three types of activities in which the caregiver is within sight may occur in many different settings: in the kitchen, in the play area, in the supermarket, in the car. Also, these activities will merge into one another. What we are talking about here are approximate ratios or guidelines. Although it is ideal to set aside special times for the third type of interaction during which there are no distractions, these three types of involvement can really ebb and flow with one another. During facilitating time the child might be the parent's sidekick at the supermarket or in the kitchen or upstairs in the bedroom. Sometimes the child is helping parents do chores or simply learning about how Daddy puts on his socks or figuring how the buttons on the washing machine work as Mommy is putting the clothes in. In the supermarket, the child is looking at the interesting bottles and cereal packages, helping Mommy take one off the shelf, learning to restrain herself when she wants the bright colored candy and

Mommy has to say, "No, no," and the like. Some of the time Mommy is busy checking her shopping list and making sure she has all the items she needs. But a minute later she might be helping little Johnny take his favorite cereal box off the shelf. We will call this type of availability informal facilitating, because the parent is there to help but it really occurs intermittently around the child's interest, curiosity, and initiative.

For many parents we recommend this relaxed, seamless flow, which has a natural and warm quality to it. Parents or caregivers who tend to get preoccupied and structured with their tasks may need to set aside more and more special times for the facilitated or direct nurturing interactions. At a minimum, there should be four 20-minute or longer opportunities for direct interaction simply because these kinds of interactions help babies learn to have an emotional dialogue and eventually an intellectual dialogue with their caregivers over longer stretches in time. They facilitate focus and concentration, depth of engagement, preverbal signal reading and problem solving, and, at the preschool level, the creative and eventually the logical use of ideas. The 20-minute or longer periods are highly desirable, but again they can be interspersed with shorter periods of time that are part of the routines of the day. During diapering, feeding, shopping, cleaning, and cooking we can take breaks for facilitating a child's interaction with his environment and for direct one-on-one interaction. The goal to work toward is for the completely independent time to be less than one-third of the time and the combination of direct interaction (floor time) and facilitating time to be at least two-thirds of the time. As one reviews one's day one can get a sense of whether one has a relatively appropriate balance. This would apply in different forms to all ages.

It is also important to emphasize that the lion's share of the baby's time needs to be with caregivers who are going to be an ongoing part of the child's life and have the child's trust. The depth of one's intimacy and feelings for others depends in part on the depth of feeling one experiences in ongoing relationships. Therefore, not just any caregiver will do. Each child requires caregivers who will be a part of his life throughout his infancy, childhood, and adolescence. Becoming dependent on primary caregivers who disappear does not breed in a baby an inner sense of security and consistency. Child care arrangements where children are spending most of their day with transient caregivers should not be viewed as optimal or chosen by design.

Preschoolers.   During the preschool years children require nurturing, warm relationships with their parents just as they do during the infant and toddler years. Now there will be more time playing with peers and other relationships that can enrich their lives. During the preschool years, the four types of availability can also be used to characterize children's time. They are likely to be spending time in a preschool program, other group activities, and peer play. Therefore the available waking time for interactions with caregivers may be somewhat less than in the infant and toddler years.

There may be brief periods of time when children will be in a different room from their parents, looking at a book, playing with their toys, or simply relaxing. It is best, even during the preschool years, however, to have the child within earshot and eyesight. Connecting rooms are fine, but being in a different part of the house is not. Therefore, during these years, time available apart from preschool or group activities should still be spent mostly in the three types of availability discussed earlier, which include being available but involved in your own activities (less than one-third of the time), and (more than two-thirds of the time) available to comment on or help with the child's activities, and available for direct, one-to-one interactions. One-to-one peer play, in addition to a preschool program, should be an almost daily experience (i.e., four or more times per week) for preschool children.

Early Grade School Years.   For the early school years, Grades K through 4, children are generally able to spend more time out of sight, although it is still good to have them in hearing range and to be quickly available to them. This not only increases a sense of security but also reduces the likelihood of dangerous behavior.

The days of a grade school child are composed of schooltime, peer play, and homework, as well as family time. For most children the pattern of available family time will be from the late afternoon into the evening. The evening is left for a combination of homework; family time, including play with siblings; and getting ready for bed. There should be a minimum of three hours of available family time—let's say from 6:00 to 9:00—divided into independent time, time available for facilitating, and direct interaction time. This can mean direct interactive imaginative play for early-school-age children and interactive games and activities for the older-school-age children. In addition, conversation during dinner or during transition times is another wonderful way to connect. Now there are many opportunities to be involved with the children's learning about their world. This includes help with homework and hobbies, as well as teaching them things that are important to the parents, for example, about holidays and values (including religion) or simply being a helper in the carpentry area or in setting the table. Children this age can do a number of things relatively indepen dently, but with parents available. That might involve homework on their own without help, hobbies, time on the computer, or watching TV.

Sibling play with and without parent involvement can be part of the afternoon or evening. Time when the children are playing with Mom or Dad together can be a high point of an evening and weekend.

These parameters are not intended to suggest that the time be broken up into neat intervals with X minutes for homework and X minutes for learning about the world and X minutes for direct play, either with siblings or with parents. Often, as with the babies and toddlers, there will be a seamless back and forth. The child may be doing homework for 20 minutes and then need a break and get involved in a hobby or go down and find Daddy and help him make something or help Mommy in the kitchen or do some imaginative play and then go back to finish the homework. A child may be having fun telling jokes during dinner and then ease into talking about something happening at school or current events or exploring some new pictures that have been hung in the kitchen. Here, direct interaction and facilitated learning about the world may occur in a seamless back-and-forth manner. Here, too, more than two-thirds of the available time should be available for these type of relating.

The reason why it is optimal to protect some 20-minute or longer intervals for direct interactive joyful play with younger school-aged children and fully involved interactive games (e.g., sports, dance, music) with older school-aged children is that these times create a special closeness and intimacy with parents. The relaxed informality allows for the sharing of ideas. In this atmosphere, the child can express what's on his mind indirectly through imaginative play, or through games. The child who is angry and demanding, for example, will demand to play only by his rules and will be reluctant to give in to anyone else's rules. The child who is scared and frightened may, in his imaginative games, play out scenes of hurricanes or calamities or illness. Empathizing with the child's perspective and offering a lot of warmth and nurturance as one tries to help the child broaden her perspectives can be very valuable.

Relaxed Availability, "Hanging Out Time"

Even when children are working on projects or games independently, parents should be available. Children should feel secure
that they can leave the parents to go off to their bedroom or to
do something else and come back and find the parents there. The
parents are hopefully, therefore, not totally involved in their own
computer Internet searches or in long conversations on the telephone. Rather, they are reading the newspaper, chatting with each
other, and the like. The children sense a calm, relaxed availability
that doesn't have to be measured. Many parents who are very
busy will complain, "Well, I've made myself available and now the
kids don't want to talk to me or tell me about school or get my
help with their homework or play with me." It's as though the
parents are measuring every second of time away from work or
the computer. The point is that children need to feel a relaxed
sense of availability. They have to be able to take parents for
granted. When they do, they have the security that when they
come and go, there is a base to come back to.

As children get older, parents also need to be skillful in enticing
children into activities that are going to be fun for both. With a
3-year-old, pretend play and special games and activities the child
enjoys will get the child's attention every time. By the time children are 7, 8, 9, and 10, however, activities can be a little more
challenging. The children will have their special interests, and parents need to join them, whether it's in sports, dancing, or playing
with action figures from a favorite TV show or special games that
they and their peers at school are all enjoying. In the teenage
years this relaxed interaction becomes even more difficult. Often
driving teenagers places is a great chance for an extended dialogue.

When Time Alone Is Excessive

Sometimes children are left to do things independently for long periods of time before they are old enough. For example, some parents will plop their toddler in front of the TV so they can get their
housework done. A few minutes in front of a *Sesame Street* video
might be fun, but two hours in front of the TV screen is more undermining than helpful for a toddler. Similarly, some parents will
feel that because their eight-month-old is an "easy baby" who
seems content to sit in the infant seat and look around the kitchen,

he can do that for a couple of hours at a time while they are catching up on phone calls or other work. The child, however, is not receiving enough interaction during these times, and simply because the child is not demanding involvement, interaction, and attention doesn't mean the child wouldn't benefit from them.

Some very easygoing children can get lost, in a sense, because they make it too easy to let them do their own thing. Sometimes 18- or 24-month-olds will entertain themselves wonderfully with puzzle pieces or blocks or with little trucks and cars. Not infrequently, they get involved playing more repetitively than creatively with these objects if no one is playing with them. If they are warm and sweet children and have nice language development, their parents may not worry that anything is going awry, feeling that they have a wonderfully self-sufficient, easygoing, "laid-back" type of child. Why not do the housework, return those phone calls, or get on the Internet and get some work done?

The fact is that too much time in the independent mode in the first 3 $\frac{1}{2}$ years is not the optimal way to be with a child. As an outer limit, no more than one-third of the child's waking time should be in this completely independent mode, and it should be divided up into short periods, for a few minutes here and there (e.g., 15 minutes). Being available for facilitating informally usually means an ebb and flow between some independent time and some facilitating interaction. A child who seeks out Mom or Dad or siblings or another caregiver will create this rhythm on his own. But many children won't lead their parents and may give up.

Until the age of three no more than a half hour a day should be spent in front of the TV set and, for a child who is over age three, no more than another half hour working with the computer. By and large, however, parents will find that life goes best when they are in that informal facilitating mode available to their children to help them explore and learn about their environment while the parents are doing some of the things that they need to do, like shopping, cooking, cleaning, or having the child accompany the parent while the parent is involved in hobbies or interests.

At the same time, as we pointed out earlier, parents need to tune in to their child's interests. Here, it is ideal to have a number of these 20-minute or longer periods where the parent marches to the child's drummer. The caregiver joins the child in his or her world in directly interactive one-to-one play. Or perhaps the child wants to explore and the parent follows the child's lead, be it in the supermarket, out in the back yard, or simply as a parent helper in playing with those pots and pans. The key is availability for 20–30 minutes at a time at various points during the day.

Relationships in Day Care

It is also important to consider now how these same principles can be applied to other contexts where children may find themselves, such as family day care, makeshift baby-sitting arrangements, as well as institutional day care settings and care by relatives. These same standards for the nurturing care of children growing up in families apply to these other settings. In other words, a child in a family day care or day care center should spend most of her time in facilitated activities or direct one-to-one interactions. However, in observations of day-care settings we found it rare that there were long interactive sequences between the caregivers and the babies.

Since it is so hard for caregivers to have long, nurturing interactions when caring for four or more babies (standard in most institutional day care), and because of the staff turnover that is characteristic of most institutional day-care settings, as well as the tendency to have staff change each year as children move from the infant room to the toddler room to the preschool room, we believe that in the first two years of life full-time day care is a difficult context in which to provide the ongoing, nurturing care by one or a few caregivers that the child requires. Part-time day care, on the other hand, may be quite helpful in giving mothers and fathers a chance to do other things and may not compromise either the security of ongoing nurturing care or the types of experiences we have described. But 35-plus hours a week for infants and toddlers makes it very difficult to have the consistency of caregiver and the depth of nurturance required, or the amount of facilitating interaction with the environment or direct interaction that we believe is healthy for infants and toddlers.

Because some families will need full-time day care in the early years, we must work to improve its quality. This means lower child/caregiver ratios, better training and salaries and maintaining the same caregiver from birth to roughly age 3. Although there is general agreement on the need to improve day care, improvements in the last 25 years have been modest. As we pointed out earlier, studies of the quality of available day care are not optimistic. We may be trying to rationalize a system that simply isn't providing the essentials of what children need. It may therefore be best to reconsider our assumptions. The best way these assumptions can be reconsidered is by each and every family having good and accurate information. With this awareness we believe most will make a wise and enlightened choice.

Recommendations

In making the recommendations that follow, we are both mindful of the fact that there are many circumstances where nonparental care may be highly desirable or absolutely necessary. Single parents working to put food on the table, even if able to provide high-quality care themselves, may have no choice but to use out-of-home child care for 40-plus hours a week. Here, the goal would be to find the best care available and to work with the child care providers as a team to provide integrated care for that baby or toddler. There may be families where there is emotional stress in individuals or family stress that makes it highly desirable to have 30-plus hours of care provided by others. On balance this will provide a much stronger support system for this particular baby or toddler. Each circumstance has to be weighed individually, and parents have to make wise and enlightened choices regarding their own particular situation.

Continuous Relationships

- In the first three years, every child needs one or two primary caregivers who remain in a steady, intimate relationship with that child.
- During the infancy, toddler, and preschool years, children should always be in the sight of caregivers. There should be no time, other than when they are sleeping, that they are out of sight of caregivers.
- No more than one-third of infants', toddlers', and preschoolers' time should be spent in fully independent activities. The time that is spent in independent activities should be spent for 10 or 15 minutes here and there rather than a longer period in independent activities.
- The other two-thirds or longer time should be spent between two types of activities: those in which the caregiver facilitates interactions with the environment and direct interaction, such as cuddling, holding, shared pretend play, and funny face games. Infants and toddlers need at least four or more 20-minute or longer periods of direct interac-

tive time. Preschoolers need at least three of these direct, interactive play opportunities. In a two-parent family, both parents should be part of these spontaneous, joyful games. During the facilitated time, caregivers are available to comment on, respond to, and help in the child's explorations, though also engaged in other activities, such as cooking or putting clothes in the washing machine. Some of this time a small child could be accompanying parents to the supermarket or being a junior chef.

- During the school years, when we consider available time, we are considering time minus schooltime, after school activities, and peer playtime. Here, too, we recommend that of the available time two-thirds be spent with the caregiver being available for facilitating or directly interacting. The "facilitating" time could be spent helping a child with homework, hobbies, or other activities. The times of direct involvement, which should include at least two 20-minute periods (each parent should participate where possible) might mean imaginative play, games or other activities in which the child can take the lead.

- We recommend that working parents both be available for at least two-thirds of the evening hours, from 5:30 or 6:00 to 9:00, and that, if possible, in addition, one of the parents be available in the late afternoon when the children are home, often playing with peers or siblings, or involved in after-school activities. Also, the parents should be available enough so that they or the children don't have to be measuring each moment of time and the guidelines outlined above can be taken for granted.

Parental Leave

We recommend a leave of most of the first year of life for one parent.[24]

Day Care

- We do not recommend full-time day care, 30 or more hours of care by nonparents, for infants and toddlers *if* the parents are able to provide high-quality care themselves and *if* the parents have reasonable options. We also recommend improving day care considerably by lowering ratios, improving training and wages, and, for children in full-time day care, having the same caregiver remain with the infant she cares for for three to four years. Those families that require day care will then have options for higher-quality day care than is now the case.

- In the first three years, a primary caregiver should be assigned to each child and should remain the same from year to year.
- For the first year there should be no more than three babies to one adult.
- For the second year, there should be no more than four toddlers to one adult.
- For the third and fourth years, there should be no more than five to eight children to one adult.[25]

Group or Institutional Settings

- Various types of institutional arrangements, including children in group situations, need to follow the same guidelines outlined earlier for the family. Ongoing nurturing care with one or a few constant primary caregivers should include direct or "facilitated" interactions for at least two-thirds of the available time. In-service training, growing financial incentives with experience and training, and support structure to facilitate nurturing attitudes are all important components of satisfying this requirement for ongoing nurturing care in group or institutional settings.

TV

- In the first three years, no more than one half hour per day should be spent watching TV. After age 3, an additional half-hour of TV or computer time could be shared with a parent.

Mothers in Prisons

- Efforts should be made to keep babies with mothers and foster that relationship, if there is a reason to believe the mother will soon be able to return to society and take care of that baby herself.

Adoption

- Adoption regulations need to be reviewed and more attention needs to be given to the needs of the child. Children's development is undermined by long periods of time in different types of care with different caregivers. In contested situations, when the foster parent is willing to adopt a child, but the biological parent is ambivalent, social service support should attempt to work out an extended-family type of support system for the child that meets everyone's needs.
- A birth mother should be allowed no more than two months to make a final decision about adoption. Every mother who is ambivalent about a pregnancy should first receive counseling. If she decides to carry the pregnancy to term, she should have counseling to learn about her options, and to help her decide whether or not to keep the baby.
- Newborn infants should have a thorough neurological and behavioral assessment before adoption. The results should be made available to the adoptive parent.

Foster Care

- Every child who is a candidate for foster care should have a detailed assessment, which should be discussed with and explained to foster parents to help them make a decision.
- Foster care for children needs to be focused on the care from the child's perspective. This means incentives for foster parents to stay with the same child, even if difficult, including greater social service support and training opportunities. A higher remuneration should be available to foster parents based on amount of training and experience and the ability to stay with children until adoption.

Custody

- The legal system needs to review guidelines in cases of divorce and separation to take into account children's needs for ongoing nurturing relationships. Children should not be separated from the primary nurturing parent for overnights until the child is age three unless the child sees both parents many times a week and feels very secure with both parents. Daily or very frequent visitation, at least weekly, by the noncustodial parent should be encouraged to facilitate an ongoing nurturing relationship with both parents in a divorce or contested custody situation. Longer visitations, such as vacations, should be adapted to the age of the child and also to the degree of security the child feels with the noncustodial parent. Unless the child sees both parents many times a week, overnights should be started gradually between ages three and seven, beginning with one overnight and then perhaps a number of months later a second overnight, and then longer visits, gearing the recommendations to the child's comfort and security level. Some sample guidelines follow.

King County Family Court (Washington State)[26]

Visitation Guidelines: Shared Custody

No model of visits fits every family.
Infant (0–1):
- Consistency of physical and emotional care.
- Close relationship with nurturing adults.
- Disruption can be serious, cause regression.
- Visitation: Frequent, but not more than 1–3 hours at a time; same home.

Toddler (1–3 $\frac{1}{2}$):
- External disruption can be critically damaging.
- Visitation: Frequent daytime visits 4–8 hours; overnight only when child familiar with nonresidential parent's home; by 3, an overnight or weekend.

Preschooler (3 $\frac{1}{2}$–5):
- Increase visits with siblings or other children.
- Visitation: Weekly, day visits; minimum two weekends a month; extended visits 2 weeks at a time, but with contacts with residential parent.

Early Elementary (5–9):
- Visitation: Two weekends a month; up to 4–6 weeks' extended visit.

Parenting Plan

A good parenting plan developed for a family should be based on the following considerations:

1. The development needs and age of each child.
2. The psychological attachments of each child.
3. The way the child-rearing tasks were shared during the marriage.
4. The preservation or development of a close relationship with each parent.
5. A consistent and predictable schedule that minimizes the transition between the households.
6. Each child's temperament and ability to handle change.
7. Parents' career demands and work schedules.
8. The need for periodic review of the plan, noting trouble signs and revising as each child's needs and circumstances change.

Assessment

A. Interview and test respective parents.
B. Observe and examine minor child(ren) in interaction with Parent-1.
C. Observe and examine minor child(ren) in interaction with Parent-2.
D. Examine minor child(ren) individually.
E. Review record and make collateral contacts.
F. Score and interpret test data; integrate findings and formulate opinions and recommendations.

2

The Need for Physical Protection, Safety, and Regulation

This irreducible need for physical protection, safety, and regulation, like the need for ongoing relationships, is self-evident to many parents and policymakers. The extent to which it is not met, however, may not be so self-evident. In many countries of the world, due to wars, famine, or poverty, adequate food, housing, and medical care are not provided for large numbers of children. In spite of a number of impressive health and nutrition programs, it is clear that the United States and its allies and the United Nations all working together could do significantly more to protect the world's children.

In the United States and many other countries, meanwhile, where there are stable and successful economic and political systems, nonetheless we are not doing a very good job of providing physical protection and care for our children. Far too many are exposed to unnecessary risks and are born with low birth weight and with preventable physical, learning, emotional, and social difficulties. Increasing rates of early abuse and neglect make many babies vulnerable to alterations in their central nervous system. Prenatal and postnatal exposure to alcohol, tobacco, lead, mercury, and other toxic substances, as well as childhood and adolescent substance abuse, are also undermining healthy central nervous system functioning. Growing violence toward and among children and teenagers also compromises physical safety and protection. In addition, emotional and social stress, as well as the still unresearched impact of the overuse of TV and computer games in lieu of human interaction, provides an additional hazard to children's health.

In terms of providing physical protection and care for our children and providing protective environments that can guarantee healthy development beginning with the inception of life throughout childhood and adolescence, we must face the fact that we are not making adequate progress. For a country with remarkable economic health and growth, the United States does not compare favorably with many other industrialized nations. It could do much better, especially among the poor and certain minority groups, with its prevention, screening, and intervention programs to improve prenatal and childhood health care for all, reduce infant mortality and low birth weight, and protect children from violence, abuse, and neglect.

One of the most important preventable challenges to our children's physical safety and protection is toxic substances in their environment. Debates regarding how much of a particular toxic substance is necessary to harm a child (or adult) tend to obscure two facts that demand our immediate attention. Many toxic substances that affect the central nervous system (some of which are also associated with cancer and with immune and reproductive system dysfunction) are in drinking water, soil, air, and areas inside the home. Children, because of their smaller bodies, rapid growth, and expectable pleasure in playing on the ground, floor, or rug while exploring with their hands and mouths, can absorb many of these toxic substances in relatively higher proportions. In addition, where products are tested, the federal government establishes safety standards on the basis of the weight and physiology of an adult male.

The urgency of this challenge to children's physical protection is illustrated by recent studies on human breast milk (one of the few remaining symbols of purity and health). These studies have found that breast milk can be contaminated by high levels of dioxin (the chemical found in Agent Orange), levels that are significantly above the allowable limits for cow's milk. In the United States, the average dioxin level of 17 is almost three times more than the upper limit set for cow's milk in countries like Belgium, France, and the Netherlands. Data from the International Agency for Research on Cancer show that the range goes from 45 in Jordan to 3 in Thailand, with industrialized countries like Germany and the United Kingdom at levels similar to that in the United States. Remarkably, in most countries, human breast milk could not be legally sold. Though more data have been collected on dioxin,

breast milk can also be compromised by PCBs and other chlori-
nated compounds such as DDT and chlordane.

Although the American Academy of Pediatrics and the World
Health Organization conclude that the benefits of breast-feeding
are enormous and far outweigh the risks, it is nonetheless alarming
that something so beneficial is being contaminated.

Protecting our children from exposure to chemicals like dioxin is
a far greater challenge than we might imagine. Exposures occur
prenatally through what the mother has ingested and breathed, and
then continue after the baby is born through breast milk or
through general environmental exposure. We have to consider that
these substances may be contributing culprits, along with other factors, in the increasing incidence of learning, attentional, and several
developmental problems.

Where data are being collected, they show alarming increases in
the number of children with severe developmental problems presenting for evaluation and treatment. In California, for example,
there has been a 270 percent increase in children presenting with
autism over the last 10 years.[1] Additionally, there has been over a
1000 percent increase in California (although some argue this is a
result of better and earlier identification and diagnosis) in children
presenting with autistic spectrum disorders involving social, communication, and thinking problems not quite severe enough to
meet the criteria for autism.[2]

There are many of categories of toxins commonly found in the
environment. In addition to the well-known risks of lead, alcohol,
and tobacco by-products, as well as patterns of substance abuse, a
number of toxins can be found in products used for lawn care (e.g.,
herbicides), insect control (e.g., pesticides), and house-cleaning
and painting products (e.g., volatile organic compounds). As stated
earlier, children, because they enjoy playing on lawns, carpets, or
floors and sometimes explore with their mouths, can take in
through skin, breathing, or eating much more of these toxins for
their size relative to adults. Yet sufficient studies have not been
done to establish safe levels of these toxins for children from the
prenatal through the childhood years. The Environmental
Protection Agency has identified more than a dozen categories,
ranging from lead to nitrogen dioxide (from poorly vented gas
stoves and heaters), on which parents need to be better educated.[3]

The fact that toxic substances have contaminated breast milk, water, soil, and air should be cause for alarm and collective corrective
action. Although there are a few things that parents and children

can do in the interim, such as limiting the amounts of animal fats in the diet (animal fats tend to store these chemicals), not eating fish or shellfish from polluted bodies of water, and avoiding pesticides, herbicides, and other toxic substances (especially in relationship to where children are playing), a major goal must be to reduce and remove this major health hazard.[4]

Concern about these toxic exposures and other threats is compounded by the fact that even modest damage to the functioning of the human central nervous system can result in an escalating cascade of learning, intellectual, emotional, and social problems. For example, the children who are exposed to toxic substances (e.g., alcohol, tobacco, drugs, lead) in utero have a high likelihood of being born with nervous systems that are either over- or underreactive to basic sensations such as touch and sound. They also have a higher likelihood of difficulties with auditory processing and language or visual-spatial thinking. They also tend to have difficulties with motor planning and sequencing, i.e., planning and carrying out actions. Any one of these factors can increase the tendency toward learning problems, impulsivity, antisocial behavior, and difficulties with forming peer relationships, reading social cues, and even organizing thinking and sustaining a sense of reality. The effects can be seen early in infancy with babies having difficulty calming, orienting, and carrying out single actions like putting their hands to their mouths or collaborating in a warm cuddle. In situations where these compromises are coupled with even modest degrees of family or environmental stress, there is a much higher likelihood of severe problems by the time the child is an adolescent. If the early compromises to the central nervous system result in underreactivity to touch, sound, and pain and therefore lead to sensory craving, increased activity, and risk taking and this pattern is coupled with neglectful, punitive, or abusive environments, there is a high likelihood of antisocial behavior (often beginning with conduct problems during childhood). Successive failures with each environment—preschool, school, peer groups, and eventually career opportunities—only further consolidate anger, impulsivity, and disregard for others.

In such situations of double vulnerability, corrective environmental experiences—which would provide sustained nurturance and empathy; persistent gentle, but firm, limits; and lots of work at planning and organizing behavior and anticipating consequences of actions and reflecting on feelings—are often simply not available. Such programs are labor-intensive and require enormous skill. We

have identified the elements that can make such programs successful. But society has not yet made a commitment to such needed efforts beyond some demonstration programs. For children who are
already in this pattern of successive developmental failures, such
programs are absolutely essential.

Chaotic environments, in and of themselves, can also affect the
way the nervous system operates. In one study, one of us (S.I.G.)
observed babies who were born with excellent capacities to calm
down, focus, attend, and regulate but were in chaotic environments. By one month many were very hypersensitive to sound and
touch and had poor motor planning and sequencing capacities.
Those who were neglected developed low muscle tone and became
apathetic and listless. In the extreme, we see this pattern with babies who develop failure-to-thrive syndrome. Due to emotional and
physical neglect babies lose weight and become listless and self-
absorbed, evidencing low muscle tone and poor cognitive as well as
language skills. As we pointed out earlier, these extremes are also
seen in institutional settings where children are deprived of human
affection. These alterations in the way the nervous system works
appear to occur in a continuum, with only the most extreme ver-
sions having gotten our attention in the past.

Not all threats from the social environment are so clear or extreme. A recent study by the Kaiser Foundation revealed that children were spending five plus hours a day in front of TV or computer screens.[5] We have not sufficiently studied the impact of such
passive, repetitive perceptual activities on children, but from what
we know about the human nervous system, it is reasonable to
raise serious questions about their impact on attention, learning,
and coping. In contrast to "screen time," dynamic interactions
with other children and adults seem to enhance learning and development.

The goal is to prevent such cascades of failure from occurring in
the first place. Trying to do so means approaching the situation at
two levels: preventing the physiological insults and improving the
family and physical environments children grow up in.

As we attempt to prevent the insults that make children vulnerable to behavioral and intellectual problems, we need to be aware
that the human nervous system, which is growing quickly in pregnancy, continues to grow very rapidly during the first five years after birth. Furthermore, new brain-imaging studies suggest another
rapid growth spurt of the nervous system through the adolescent
years of development. This means we have a vulnerable, rapidly

growing system that can be influenced by physical factors and experiential factors anywhere along its journey.

Just as with a car going rapidly along a road, for which even a mild push on the side can lead it to alter its trajectory or have a serious accident, the fast-growing human nervous system can be influenced by even subtle challenges.

Many parents, physicians, teachers, and policymakers are asking: Why are we seeing more children with problems of attention, impulse control, language, learning disabilities, unstable moods, and pervasive developmental disorders affecting relating, communicating, and thinking. Our inability to identify a single specific factor suggests a cumulative risk model. That is, if we look at the possibilities, we can identify a list of factors, each one of which may contribute in combination with some of the others and genetic susceptibility. For example, exposure to toxins or extreme stress may make children more vulnerable to middle ear infections or allergic or autoimmune reactions, which may increase the risk for developmental problems, especially in genetically susceptible children. Many of these factors have in common their effect on aspects of central nervous system regulation involving reactivity to sensations (sound, touch, movement, pain), the capacity to process and comprehend those sensations (e.g., language, visual-spatial thinking), and the capacity to plan and sequence actions (e.g., problem solving, executive functions). When any of these regulatory capacities are compromised, the child's behavior may stress his or her caregivers and create the potential for a cascade of worsening problems as described earlier.

We therefore have to consider how to wage a successful public health and education campaign on the familiar suspects as well as to conduct more research on some of the newer probable suspects.

When we consider what's at stake in terms of the future and the cost to individuals and society for every child whose nervous system is not functioning well, we realize that we must take a much bolder approach than we have been using. The physical protection and care of infants and young children and families have not been a high enough priority. To be sure, we give lip service to this goal, but on the national and international agendas it has not been in the top three of our priorities. A child's basic right to physical protection and care must be the foundation on which all our other efforts are built. Not to do so speaks so clearly about our lack of concern for children that its continuation is sure to demoralize any other efforts we might attempt.

The first step in guaranteeing physical protection and care for a baby is support for the mother during pregnancy, through the delivery process itself, and during the child's early years. Nurturing support means understanding the needs of each family and working with them, for example, in being able to find help and satisfaction in prenatal care, in the delivery process, and in well-baby care. The families that don't come in for prenatal care are often the most worrisome, and we haven't had ambitious outreach efforts. Selected demonstration programs have shown that these can be helpful and effective.[6] We need to make them routine. Medical school and residency training programs, especially in obstetrics and pediatrics, need to spend considerably more time on the psychosocial factors that will often determine the health or illness of patients.

In addition, there are many models of care for the delivery process involving psychological and physical support. One particular innovative model, which involves a specially trained individual (i.e., a *doula*) to provide psychological and physical guidance during the delivery process, has been found to improve the status of many babies and parents.[7]

Postnatal care is especially important because of babies' rapid growth and changing needs. For multiproblem families, the challenges to early development are enormous because of the many problem behaviors in the family interfering with appropriate care. Many programs have demonstrated success.[8] Yet in most communities, these most-in-need families are largely neglected.

All parents want know if their baby is doing well and what to do if there are challenges. Are the old standbys such as weight gain, motor milestones (such as sitting, crawling, and walking), and some cognitive and language milestones (e.g., sounds and then words) sufficient? We can now do much better. We can monitor a baby's intellectual, social, and emotional development at the same time and identify developmental, learning, or behavioral challenges earlier than ever before.

In order to do this, however, requires a broader concept of well-baby care. The Touchpoints model developed by one of us (T.B.B.) creates a context of nurturing support and guidance as well as careful monitoring of a baby's growth and development.[9] [See Appendix for more information about the Touchpoints model and program.] The Developmental Growth Curve developed by one us (S.I.G.) allows us to look at how a baby is using motor, sensory, emotional, social, language, and cognitive skills together to master his or her "functional developmental capacities."[10] (See Appendix for the growth chart and questionnaire.)

The goal is to promote healthy development and identify problems early, if they are present, and provide needed guidance to overcome them. The most difficult decision for parents and primary health care providers is when to wait and see, and when to do a full evaluation and, if needed, begin an intervention. Significant family or parental difficulties at any time warrant helpful care and, if needed, appropriate treatment. In our recommendations we outline some of the developmental signs in babies that indicate a full evaluation is warranted.

Discussion

SIG: The need for a safe and secure environment starts well before birth. Many babies are put at risk before they are born. They're exposed to all kinds of assaults that endanger the growth of their nervous systems. Smoking, alcohol, and other toxic substances undermine the growth of a healthy nervous system. We're seeing more and more of the ways in which they can interfere with later ability to process sensations (sights and sounds), as well as organize thoughts and plan and implement appropriate actions.

TBB: In regard to the intrauterine experience of babies, I think that education has had a powerful influence on mothers' behavior. It hasn't reached down yet to poor, stressed, or depressed women, especially in some of our cities, but it's had a powerful middle-class and I think even working-class effect. Mothers now know that if they smoke or drink it's going to affect their babies and so they generally refrain. It is very encouraging that education can do that—change habits.

We now know a lot about the effect of a variety of substances that hurt the fetus. We can also recognize stress in the fetus by six and seven months of pregnancy. The day may come when we can pick fetuses that are really stretched beyond their capacity and get them out of the uterus where we can do a better job than in utero. I'd like to see a scale like my Neonatal Behavioral Assessment Scale developed for fetuses. We could expose them to external stimuli like auditory or visual signals, or rocking, or stimulating them and seeing how complex or rich their behavioral responses were. French scientists J.P. Lecuanet and M. Busnel are working on visual responsiveness in the fetus and there has long been research on auditory response,[11] but there is much more to learn. I'd like to watch the capacity of the fetus both to shut out or respond positively to a stimulus. I've seen it by seven months in fetal responses on ultrasound.

In other words, by seven months, we can recognize whether a fetus needs protection or not. I think we're on the brink of more and more technology that will help us. The Japanese, for example, have a three-dimensional ultrasound that allows you to look at the whole fetus, which we don't have yet. With that, you can see not only how complex the baby's movements are, but also how alert its responsive behavior is and how much it can maintain attention, stay asleep of it's asleep, how it uses habituation. All the things we've learned from newborn assessments could apply in utero and that would give us a lot more capacity to pick out which babies are stressed.

In the studies of habituation in seven-month-old fetuses using ultrasound that I mentioned earlier, we identified behavior that shows a healthy responsiveness. Certain complex responses could be utilized to distinguish stressed from nonstressed fetuses. If the fetus demonstrates such behavior, it's evidence that important learning and shaping is proceeding *in utero*. If the baby were stressed, we expect that the responses would be more automatic and less available to modulation and choice. If there were reasons for stress, such as undernutrition or exposure to toxins such as alcohol or drugs, this could be a way of finding out whether learning is being impaired.

But there's a big question here: How early do you have a right to protect the baby-to-be? Can we jail mothers who take drugs to force them to withdraw from their addictions? For certain mothers, is abortion the answer? When people write to me to ask if I believe in abortion, I say I do, not as a woman's right, but as a baby's right. A baby has the right not to be born into an unwelcoming, nonnurturing environment. I've seen enough babies deprived and enough child abuse to never want to see that kind of life for a baby. Along with the question of abortion goes the issue of how much to monitor pregnancy. In any case, there is great need for better programs to support parents and to offer the baby a life free of abuse and neglect.

SIG: In terms of helping parents protect their fetuses from drug abuse, alcoholism, tobacco, there is indeed a problem of how much should be mandated and a part of the legal system? Can you have child abuse of the fetus? In some high-risk communities, 50 percent of fetuses are already damaged by substance abuse and alcohol. When you begin creating an impact on a nervous system that's going to be lifelong for that child, that's very serious. Once the baby is born, we are very concerned about abuse of children that's relatively mild compared to what alcohol and other toxic substances in utero will do to the unborn child.

TBB: We found this with lead poisoning, too. Before we abolished lead gasoline, we could tell whether or not a mother lived near a major highway by the behavior of the baby.[12]

SIG: We are only beginning to have the science or clinical experience to say how chemicals currently in the environment are negatively affecting the growth of the nervous system, as well as the immune system, both prenatally and postnatally. Many studies were conducted regarding cancer. Newer studies have shown that the risk to the nervous system in terms of integrative functions and the risk to the immune systems occur at levels less than for cancer risk. We need to look at these toxins in terms of risk for babies. Theo Colburn did the pioneering work that showed how life in the Great Lakes is being affected by pesticides and the potential dangers to human health.[13]

TBB: It seems that this can affect childbirth. Peter Nathanielsz has shown that an anesthetized fetus is already at high risk for not participating in active labor.[14] The uterine contractions depend on an active fetus. With an underactive baby, contractions come to a stop, and brain damage to the fetus is much more likely. He postulates that a fetus that has been affected by intrauterine toxins, drugs, or anesthetics is already at higher risk for cerebral palsy. My neonatal assessment is being used with these studies. Back in 1983, Greta Fein at the Merrill Palmer Institute in Detroit showed that DDT sprayed on the grass that cows ate, and the milk that pregnant women drank from those cows, affected the babies significantly at school age in terms of IQ.[15] We have to have that sort of information available to use.[16]

SIG: We need a much greater understanding of the damage that can be done to the nervous system by drugs, alcohol, and environmental toxins. The biggest denial is coming in terms of pesticides and other toxic substances. We all recognize severe mental retardation and autistic symptoms and the problems they bring. There is less awareness that when you challenge that nervous system in an unhealthy way through poor nutrition, toxic substances, smoking, alcohol, and so on, the majority of babies are not going to be mentally retarded; they will have more subtle problems, difficulty in coping with things like sights and sounds. At birth, these risks may not be obvious. They're going to get overloaded easily. They're going to be very distractible. They're going to be overactive and they're going to have the symptoms listed for attention deficit disorder. A lot of them will also crave sensory input, be underreactive to pain, and will end up with disorders involving antisocial behavior and aggression. When they can't process what they hear or see or comprehend it easily, a lot of them are going to have school problems. They'll have trouble comprehending math or being able to read. They'll have trouble entering the high-tech world of employment and being a wage earner and tax contributor. Perhaps most important, they'll have trouble regulating their emotions. That's a very high-level function of the nervous system. The regulation of feelings is vital for being a parent and developing the skills to work in groups so we can better ourselves in future generations. These are some of the risks that we are taking.

TBB: Much of this damage indeed takes place at a very early stage. Our chance to protect emotional and neurological development is very high. The effects of alcohol and drugs are powerful in the intrauterine stage, lessen after birth, and recede as the child moves to age three or four. The loading factors, so to speak, and the preventable factors are way up here to begin with and then drop down. The earlier you start, the more you can do.

SIG: The CDC [Centers for Disease Control] in Atlanta is planning an epidemiological study of autistic spectrum disorders. Clinicians around the country are reporting that there are more and more children with atypical nervous system functioning—some with autistic features, some with frank autism. In terms of individual differences, there appear to be a lot more children at the extreme, maladaptive end of your scale. How far do we want to go using the legal system to protect babies?

TBB: I can see a backlash: turning people off, creating resistance to being supervised with prenatal care, and so forth. I worry about a punitive approach. I would rather do it through education and by positive incentives—using the passion that people bring to their pregnancy to try to capture them at that point.

But there is another question. Joshua Sparrow at Boston Children's Hospital has been working on the influence of these technological advances we've made (ultrasound, amniocentesis, etc.) on what mothers' perceptions are of their babies and themselves.[17] When we're assessing whether the fetus is OK or not OK, it seems as though we are asking whether the parents are OK or not OK. This can be felt as judgmental, an attack on people's privacy. Fetal assessment to decide whether the baby's stressed or not means that somebody is judging whether or not the mother is carrying the baby in an acceptable way. We'd better take these concerns seriously. We really have an obligation to protect the mother and her own ego, so that she'll be able to nurture the baby when it does come. We have to involve her in our efforts, helping her see the meaning of this diagnostic work. We can make it useful to her as she learns to nurture the new baby. With our Touchpoints model, we try to reach people in pregnancy so as to capture them for the work that they need to do. It's a magical time for the mother and father.

SIG: While giving the mother physical care, we should be doing much more to support her and the baby's father psychologically. From the physical care standpoint alone (taking the mother's blood pressure, blood tests etc.), we help save a certain percentage of babies. The psychological side of prenatal care, which may be an equally important, is much less expensive. A well-trained nurse, a mental health professional, or a counselor could provide a lot of it. Childbirth classes can be very helpful. We may want to consider advocating an optimal program for this social and psychological support prenatally.

TBB: The goal is to build up the mother's and father's capacities for nurturing whatever baby they get. Right now the system is set up to optimize the physical or genetic outcome of that baby. We're finding that when we demonstrate fetal behavior, mothers respond and feel closer to the baby. When you show the mother her newborn's capacities, you're talking her language.

Prenatal visits can accomplish so much. I always ask the expectant mothers to tell me about their two babies in their dreams—the perfect baby, and then the imperfect baby. "I never dream about an imperfect one." "You don't? Most people do." "Oh, they do?" Then mother will then tell me about the one they dream about but can't face. Then I can reassure them that we can deal with that one, too. This presents an opportunity to explore with the parents, in a nonjudgmental way, their questions and past experiences with impaired babies. If they can share their concerns with me, I will help them nurture whatever baby they get. I have parents keep a log of a 24-hour day of sleep/wake cycles, and I have them time the uterine wall turbulence during the day. From the patterns they lay out, I can tell them that we can tell that the baby sees, hears, and responds differently to different kinds of stimuli." Then even the most serious mother comes alive and says, "Oh, tell me!" I begin to tell her and she nods and recognizes that if she goes into a noisy room, the baby becomes more active, and that in a quieter room, the baby calms down. The mother knew all these things already. All you're really doing is confirming what she knows and helping her make this initial attachment. The earlier you start, the more solid the foundation. Ideally, the pediatrician, nurse practitioner, or family doctor undertakes this prenatal visit with the parents-to-be. If not, we should be preparing other kinds of therapists to join parents at this time. A baby deserves a mother and a father who are ready to nurture. By joining them in a supportive relationship before delivery, we can give them back what we've lost in our culture—the feeling of being surrounded by a protective extended family.

SIG: Can we do more with childbirth education?

TBB: At present, the childbirth education curricula are aimed at preparing the mother for labor and delivery, not necessarily helping her become a better nurturer. Marshall Klaus and John Kennell have studied the role of a doula, who remains with the mother during labor and birth. They have shown a significant reduction in need for medication, in duration of labor, and in complications of labor from consistent support in labor.[18] A supporting person (father and/or doula) also enhances the mother's readiness to attach to whatever baby she gets. The father's presence at birth certainly has been shown to increase his own capacity for attaching to the new baby.

We also try to show mothers-to-be a newborn assessment, since there is so little time in the shortened hospital stay, hoping that they will see what a newborn is like. Then when they see their own baby during this shortened hospital stay, they say, "Oh, there it is in my baby." It is more meaningful to them because they have already seen the amazing abilities of a baby.

SIG: What would we advocate in terms of education about health practices, smoking, alcohol, and also how to nurture a baby through pregnancy and after, in terms of providing this physical protection and care? When should we begin this education? Should it begin in grade school, high school, colleges?

TBB: All of the above. Sally Scattergood's program in Philadelphia, which has brought babies into first grades, is wonderful.[19] In this program, first-graders have an opportunity to diaper, to feed, and to observe developmental progress in small babies. Since most children are not in large families today, this gives them an opportunity to see the baby as a "person" and to experience a role in handling and nurturing babies. As far as I know, the long-term effect on such outcomes as teenage pregnancy or the ability of these students to nurture their own babies has not yet been studied. But we can bet that it might be one variable in affecting their image of themselves as able to nurture another.

SIG: Perhaps human development in all its stages should be a part of the curriculum just like history, English, and biology, from the first grade on. Right now, children are learning more about frogs and other nonhuman species than they are about human beings. They learn about human beings only indirectly through learning history and literature. It used to be that that was the only way of learning about human beings, because we didn't have a science of human development. We didn't know much about how children grow and develop. But now that we know about human beings directly, why not offer history, literature, and a course on human development. I don't see a lot of resistance here other than tradition. Imagine if children, starting in kindergarten or first grade, had a track on human development along with biology.

TBB: I'd include some hands-on learning. All of the programs we know of that have been so successful use that approach. In some pregnancy prevention programs on the West Coast, teenagers have been exposed to handling babies and having to diaper, feed, and watch their stages of development. Actually, the chance to watch human behavior in a child smaller than you are is a marvelous way to engage the interest of a child of any age.

SIG: The resistance may come from people's concern about our getting into family and religious issues. But if we could get this cooking, imagine what it would be like for kids to know about human development the same way they know about math. Average children in junior high school knows adding, subtracting, multiplying, decimals, and fractions. If they knew the fundamentals of how babies and children grow, they would not only be better baby-sitters, but when it came time to being parents, instead of reading Brazelton for the first time while waiting for the baby to come or after the baby comes, they would have an intuitive sense and a lot of hands-on experience.

TBB: We have to remember that pregnancy is a heightened period for learning. But such classes could be a chance to develop the concept of relationships, of altruism, thinking about other people besides yourself. I would use it as a way of reaching out to children and letting them see the mechanisms within them that parallel what's going on with the child they're playing with. Then you could say, "Now you see, because you were aware of how you were as a baby, you are so good with that baby." If you did it that way, I think you'd open people up for relationships rather than just concentrating on parenting.

SIG: Along those lines, I routinely have siblings come in when I see a child who has challenges, and I help the parents coach the sibling in how to play with the child. Once we get the sibling involved with the child who has difficulties, there's such joy and pleasure and mastery. The children are usually avoiding the sibling because they don't know how to make it work. I find that when children baby-sit, they're naturally intrigued with other children. This is opening them up, dealing with the softer, more vulnerable core of themselves. This hands-on experience indeed works better than anything else. It opens up that nurturing side of humanity. Some people have that already intuitively, women more than men, sometimes, but men do have a nurturing side as well. Some close it off and run away from it. But many seem to want to express that side if you give them the opportunity.

Sure, there'd be resistance because you're encroaching on the emotional side of life. But, if by the time they hit their 20s they had an intuitive feel for child care and the development of children, what a good start that would be, compared to where people start now. What I find is that many parents run away from it because it's new and scary. Some run back into their professions. They're frightened and don't know what to do.

TBB: I think we have to separate it somehow from incursions on the politics or religion or authority of families. When I go to testify in Washington, my appearance is often followed by a parent in an intact family who says, "If you do as Dr. Brazelton suggested (regarding day care, preventive care, health care, parental leave), you're taking away any choice in our family." There is such a very powerful bias in this country, that families ought to be self-sufficient and not allow others to interfere with them. In the curriculum, I would emphasize relationships and children learning about themselves. Teaching them how to become parents later on is too politically dangerous. Opening them up as parents need not be either partisan or political.

SIG: What kind of changes in societal attitude do we want to promote? While we want to discourage teenage pregnancy, if a mom feels she's done a terrible thing by getting pregnant, she's going to deny it or cover it up, keeping it a secret as long as possible. Then she may go on taking her drugs as long as possible. This holds true for the father as well. What would be a healthy societal attitude about teenagers getting pregnant in the first place?

TBB: First, there's the question of whether or not the mother even has to have the baby. If she decides to, I'd rely on the fact that mothers want to give their babies a better chance than they had in life. We could say to them, "Wouldn't it be something to look forward to if this baby had the best brain in the world? And the only way he's going to have a good brain is if you stop smoking or drinking or whatever else." Then you could instill a sense of hope.

SIG: We need to do more about prevention. A child development curriculum could discuss "When are you ready?" "What kind of support does a baby need?" "Should you wait until you're older?" Once someone's pregnant, even due to an accident, if there is a clear desire to carry the baby to term, then we need to convey an unambivalent message that the baby should be cherished. We should promote the healthiest baby and the best nervous system possible. The mother has to feel supported herself—that she's the belle of the ball and is carrying this precious, future-president-of-the-United-States inside her. If not, she's not going to take care of herself. If she feels she's carrying this embarrassment, she's going to be ambivalent— sometimes wanting to hurt it and sometimes wanting to help it. If we can make each mother feel valued and cherished, without, at the same time, promoting pregnancy in teenagers, that's what we want. I think a societal shift is needed. We need to convey that every baby is a baby of the world and of the larger society. We want you to wait and do it when you're ready, but if it happens and you are going to keep the baby, you are now doing something wonderful and we will help you as much as we can.

TBB: I think we're doing a lot of that although we may not be doing as much in the places that matter. For instance, we aren't reaching many Latino mothers with any of this. Other minorities may be just as neglected as they are, but this is a clear need. Infant mortality in the first year (reflecting vulnerability in the newborn) is directly correlated with prenatal care and the opportunities for intervention it offers. The infant mortality figures seem to imply that either we aren't reaching Latino pregnant woman, or our approach does not fit in with their cultural values. Or both. We need to organize our outreach system to respect the cultural beliefs and practices that minorities bring to this passionate job of parenting.

SIG: While we're looking at social attitudes, we might consider malnutrition in other parts of the world. Is there anything we can say beyond the obvious question of why that continues? Why do we have so many babies dying? We think of ourselves as a human species with some degree of shared humanity. What we're saying here is relevant to most industrialized countries, but there are worldwide issues in terms of these irreducible needs. The world is more similar than dissimilar now.

TBB: In Kenya, where we have visited clinics, we see families with too many children to feed in relation to the yield of the land they have. They are using up their resources. They are close to the edge in terms of the environment and malnutrition. We saw the same vicious circle of malnutrition and then failure in attachment and nurturing in these overloaded parents that we'd seen in Guatemala.[20] We could distinguish newborns whose mothers were eating only 1,400 calories a day from the offspring at birth of women who had adequate calories (2,000 a day). The neonates were more alert, more responsive, could control their behavior to pay attention and to utilize habituation to shut out interfering stimuli. These babies at birth were ready to play their role in bringing their mothers and fathers into a firm attachment with them. The undernourished infants were too guarded, turned away from social stimulation, and presented their new parents with negative responses. When we stayed in their homes in the perinatal period we saw that parents of these deprived babies fed them only on demand (often only three to four times a day, at a time when a new baby needs six to eight feedings a day). The effects of intrauterine deprivation were compounded by extrauterine deprivation, and the cycle of future failure and poverty was set up in infancy. These undernourished babies were 10–15 points below in IQ at school age. There are a lot of other factors that go into worldwide poverty and malnutrition as well, but these are ones for which we will search for answers.

SIG: People assume a certain degree of civilization and shared humanity. There isn't sufficient worldwide concern about saving babies. What allows us to shut our eyes about situations in the world that we would not tolerate here in the United States? Are we in denial? Do we not care? Or are we overwhelmed with our own problems and feel powerless? Can we identify the factor that interferes with greater collective action?

TBB: I think we feel a lack of control. As you and I talk about this, I feel a lack of ability even to begin thinking about the problems. When we worked in Kenya, Guatemala, and southern Mexico, we learned a lot, but we sure didn't influence anything one way or the other. Maybe we can ask for an international agency that would look after children's rights, just as we have peacekeeping forces.

SIG: Such an agency could at least keep track, so that we could judge nations by how well they provide for these irreducible needs. Just as there's a worldwide effort to foster democratic values through incentives like trade and loans, we need to elevate the care of children to a higher level.

TBB: There are so many things that dominate people's treatment of children. For instance, one reason France, Sweden, and other European countries are so far ahead is that they're eager for more children. They're trying to encourage people to have children. In Africa, that's not the case. In the Japanese islands we visited, the people who lived in the countryside wanted more children, so they would do a lot of things the people in the city wouldn't do to foster their children's development.

SIG: By developing guidelines for certain basic irreducible needs of children—for example, being born with a healthy nervous system (and all that requires)—we could make this a criterion for world opinion. There is an ethical aspect here, an opportunity for international agreement.[21]

TBB: Closer to home, there are some safety issues that we haven't addressed. There are what I call touchpoints in safety that need paying attention to. For example, to begin with, parents should

know about turning down the hot water to a reasonable level in
a house with small children. When the child becomes mobile at
eight months, every family should have a list of safety measures
that they put into action if they haven't already. I recommend
that parents get down on their hands and knees and go around
the house looking up to see what it is that the child is going to
be seeing so they can be sure they have everything protected.
The next touchpoint is when the child runs away from the
mother in the grocery store, out into the street, or in the yard.
What do you do about that? Another one is when, at age four
or five, they begin to be attractive to pedophiles. When do you
start to institute education for how a child takes care of himself
in the face of kidnappers, and so on. I personally think that four
and five is not the right time. That is when children are making
their own assessment of adults and they deserve all the energy
they have to identify with and imitate important adults. If you
take that away from them, you may be doing the child as much
harm as good by setting up distrust of other people. It's really
entirely up to us to protect them up to about age six or seven.
After that we cannot control everything. At that point, you can
start to talk about what to do when a stranger talks to you or
makes an advance to you and/or you don't feel comfortable.
You ought to be able to turn to an adult and say, "I don't feel
good about this," and get the adult's help. Little children
should not be in a position to have to run away from strangers
and avoid them. They should be protected and meet others in
the company of trusted adults. By six or seven, they can be
prepared and learn when to run away or whatever.

SIG: Kids who have a good nonverbal communication system in
place with their parents tend to react more strongly to verbal
commands and body language and often stay closer than
children whose nonverbal communication skills are not as well
organized or children who are hyperactive. Parents can learn to
recognize whether their child is a good responder to their
nonverbal cues and is ready to go into a busy place.

The whole concept of physical safety, protection, and safe
environments depends on awareness of individual differences.
We don't think about this when we send children off to
preschool. These differences make a big difference in the kind
of dangers a child gets into. The individual vulnerabilities of the
central nervous system are part of the need for safety and
security.

TBB: The unpredictability of negativism and autonomy issues in the second year makes for particular dangers. Some very healthy children can shoot off like a rocket. And yet, the danger of too much restriction and control might be that the child's natural inquisitiveness and negativism might be suppressed. Harsh punishment is not the answer. A parent who knows when and how to set sure limits quickly passes this on to the child. We call it *referencing*. A toddler knows when her parents mean no by the tone of the parents' voices, or by nonverbal behavior. This is the first important step in keeping a rambunctious child safe and secure.

SIG: Yes. In the early years, the kids who are tuned in nonverbally can sense that when your voice goes up there's danger. They are going to be safer.

TBB: Unless there's something else going on, like the urge to get away from Mommy. The main thing is that parents need to be reminded that this is still their issue and they need to know what needs to be done to protect their children.

SIG: We can see a good example of the nonverbal system at work in three-year-olds. Very few three-year-olds, even if they get into the living room, if they're otherwise doing well with nonverbal and emergent verbal communication and they're pretty well regulated, will take their paint and spill it over the living room carpet and chairs. It doesn't happen that way. Often, when parents say, "I can't control him," I notice that they're not changing their voices very much and giving the child enough feedback or they're not very involved with the child. I ask them, "How come he's not spilling paint on the living room carpet?" "Oh, he would never do that!" "Why not?" "Because he knows I wouldn't stand for it!" Then I say, "How come he doesn't have the same feeling about pinching his little brother or sister?" Often you can watch two parents and see conflicting feedback. One might be tense and disapproving with looks and head nods and the other might be giving a secret chuckle or saying sweetly, "Please don't do that." A child can sense permission to go ahead and do what he or she wants.

TBB: In terms of safety for the child, it would be useful to look at the kinds of things we have accomplished, like car seats, airplanes, and airbags. Our efforts here could be a model for other problems that our society could take a role in, for example, passive smoking and guns.

SIG: Here we get into controversies about what's education, what's legal, what's the family's right to decide. Again, if we can make them part of the educational processes, starting in grade school, they can become a part of a person's way of thinking. They become internalized. Belief systems will already have been primed so later, as adults, they won't have to be convinced.

Recommendations

Making Children a Worldwide Commitment

- A worldwide effort with much greater commitment and higher political priority of the industrialized countries is needed to provide protection from starvation, illness, and violence for the world's infants, children, and families.

Exposure to Toxic Substances

A. Before birth: A fetus must be protected from exposure to alcohol, drugs, tobacco, and environmental pollutants.

B. After birth: The special vulnerability of children, especially of the nervous system, needs to be taken into account in all regulation of food and environmental safety. In particular, children's health needs should be the basis for regulatory safety standards rather than those of an adult male whose vulnerability is far less. To this end, Senator Barbara Boxer has introduced the Children's Environmental Protection Act in Congress, but it has not been passed. The presence of dangerous toxins in breast milk is a human rights issue and deserves immediate national attention.

Public Awareness Campaign

A. To bring about protection from toxins we need a systematic and persistent public education campaign on the effects of various substances, illegal and legal, on the human nervous system and healthy behavior. At a minimum, this campaign should teach parents how to reduce exposures to chemicals by following four simple principles: Avoid the purchase of toxins, ventilate

the house well, lock up household toxins, and reno-
vate with nontoxic products, especially in the baby's
room. Parents must be made aware that in addition to
such well-known problems as lead, common household products (such as pesticides, cleaning products,
paints, and varnishes) contain toxins and that there are
alternatives that accomplish the same purpose that do
not contain toxins. Federal leadership and collaboration between the federal government, industry, and
citizen's groups is needed to improve regulations for
toxic substances in the environment whether seeping
into the soil or water supply or released into the air.
(For further information, see www.checnet.org.)

Basic Security

• Babies need to be secure in their world, need to be born
into families who want them. Society must see that unwanted births are prevented. Information on contraception
and reproductive health should be available to every woman
of childbearing age.

• For very young children, physical safety is entirely a parent's
responsibility. Children under six or seven should not be
frightened by being told not to trust strangers or being
warned of danger and abuse. However, positive constructive guidance—"Always hold Mommy's hand in the shopping mall"—can be helpful as soon as children are verbal
enough to understand the reasons for concern. This guidance should be gradually matched to the child's ability to
discuss these issues. At the appropriate age, these threats
need to be taught gradually and with calm reassurance.

Support in Childbirth

• In addition to medical care, laboring mothers and the fathers need consistent psychological support during the entire process of childbirth, whether from a doula, midwife,
or other childbirth professional.

Early Pediatric Care

Early pediatric care should include:
A. Regular sharing of information and assessments.

B. Guidance to promote healthy development.
C. The early identification of challenges or disorders.
D. Early and comprehensive interventions, if required. Examples of the developmental signs in babies and children that should indicate a full evaluation is warranted include

- By two months, no signs of looking or listening (e.g., turning toward sights and sounds).
- By four to five months, no signs of relating to caregivers with joyful smiles and sounds.
- By eight to nine months, no signs of back-and-forth communication (e.g., reaching for a rattle in Dad's hand or initiating and reciprocating different emotional expressions and sounds).
- By 12 months, no signs of multiple circles of communication in a row (e.g., back-and-forth exchange of emotional gestures sounds and even a word or two), copying Mom's or Dad's facial expressions or sounds.
- By 16 months, no signs of complex problem-solving interactions (e.g., taking caregiver by hand to help get toy or food).
- By 24 months, no signs of beginning pretend play (hugging a dolly) or understanding or using words to get needs met ("Give juice").
- By 36–48 months, no signs of the logical use of ideas with caregivers and peers (e.g., answering where, when, and why questions as part of conversation lasting at least a few minutes) or in pretend play with dolls, action figures, or stuffed animals.
- At any time, signs of serious family or emotional difficulties in Mom or Dad or other family members.

(See also Appendix for Functional Developmental Growth Chart and Touchpoints program guidelines.)

Support for Multi-Problem and Multi-Risk Families

- Comprehensive programs with extensive outreach and center-based components would include providing much more ambitious social, and postnatal psychological and family supports than existing prenatal and postnatal programs. (See Chapter 6.)

Protection from the Inappropriate Use
of Psychiatric Medications

A. Medication should not be used without a full mental health evaluation, including a review of presenting problems and current functioning, a developmental history, a clinical interview (including play) with the child, observation of child-parent interactions, and discussions with caregivers of family relationships and patterns.

B. Medication, if required, must consider safety and efficacy studies for the age group and problem area and, unless there are special reasons, should be used only as a component of a comprehensive program that often will need to include clinical work with the child and his or her family and consultation with schools.

C. Side effects need to be considered very carefully for their long-term effects on development, learning, and personality, especially subtle ones such as mild agitation or increased aggression, as well as decreased sense of humor and emotional range and expressiveness. The use of multiple medications, with one attempting to offset the side effects of another, should be reviewed with extreme concern because of the potential risks.

D. Schools and other educational settings should, if appropriate, discuss with parents the indications for an evaluation. They should not, however, make a recommendation on the use of medication. There are many causes for specific challenges. These can best be understood—and treatment of them considered—in a full clinical evaluation.

Public Education and
Human Development Literacy

• An organized, federally led educational effort mandating education in human growth and development is needed in grade schools, middle schools, high schools, and colleges.

• A human growth and development curriculum should have the same level of importance as History, English, Science, or Math, and include readings, hands-on experience and discussion appropriate to the child's age and the issues relevant to that age. Physical, psychological, and social factors, and expectable emerging capacities and challenges should be considered. The goal is human development literacy.

Three Levels of Community Programs

Community programs should include:
- Public education campaign on children's development including school programs.
- Family support guidance, including peer support
- Early intervention for at risk children, with professional follow-up and assessments shared with the parent.

The Need for Experiences Tailored to Individual Differences

What if we could figure out how genes and physical influences during pregnancy express themselves early in life? What if we could identify each baby's strengths and vulnerabilities and his special way of dealing with the world? Could we then help a baby or a small child overcome challenges in paying attention, regulating mood, learning to talk, control impulses, read, or do math? Could we strengthen children's capacities for trust, intimacy, resilience, perseverance, and coping? We are much closer to these goals than one would imagine. Our reluctance, however, to accept children's unique differences is slowing us down.

We have traditionally expected children to fit the expectations of parents and society at large. To some degree, this is absolutely correct. The expectations we have for children to become socialized, for example, to learn to curb their aggression, and to be empathetic and kind to others are very important. On the other hand, in the last 50 years we have learned that expecting children to live up to our expectations is a two-way street. The degree to which we can tailor experiences to each child's unique qualities increases the likelihood of that child's growing up physically, intellectually, and emotionally healthy and thus able to meet the expectations of family and society.

Historically there has been an ebb and a flow between wanting to fit children to our expectations and trying to tailor our care to children's needs. Back in the 1940s, for example, children were on fixed schedules of feeding and sleeping. It was believed that structure was needed if children were to adapt to their environment. This worked for some children who had very flexible coping capacities (based on a flexible central nervous system). Other children, however, didn't do well in such settings. They became more irritable, self-absorbed, distractible, or depressed or aggressive.

In the 1950s and 1960s, individual differences in children became better understood. The temperament research of Stella Chess and Alexander Thomas became the most visible expression of this new view of children.[1] It showed that parents had different perceptions of their children in such basics as activity level and outgoingness. Therefore, perhaps parents should adapt their care to their perceptions of their children. Other investigators, such as Sybil Escalona, Lois Murphy, and Jean Ayres went beyond notions of temperament and showed that babies were not just perceived as being different but actually had physical differences, such as some babies' being more sensitive to sound or touch than other babies and therefore requiring different types of early environments. The work of one of us (T.B.B.) advanced this understanding of children a huge step farther with studies of individual differences and the widely used neonatal assessment scale.[2] He showed that newborn babies can be systematically assessed and their unique characteristics identified. Many aspects of their physical differences—the way they respond to touch, sound, and sights, the way they organize their movements—can help parents to get to know their babies.

This research revealed the way newborns alert to interesting visual and auditory cues, and shut out (or habituate to) repeated uninteresting ones. They vary in their ability to control states of consciousness (sleep, awake, alert, fussing, crying) in order to pay attention. Some will fix on and follow the human face and voice at birth, using active facial behavior and suppressing interferring movements in order to pay attention.

We have been able to determine which babies were affected by toxins and undernutrition by their behavior at birth. Using their behavior, we can gear our auditory, visual, and tactile behavior to elicit an optimal response in each newborn. If we talk too loud, touch too abruptly, or pick up too suddenly, a fragile newborn will gaze avert, hiccough, or spit up. They can defend themselves. But if an observer uses gentle touch, one modality at a time, she can reach out for and capture almost any newborn. Demonstrating the newborn's behavior becomes a technique for demonstrating the baby's temperament at birth to new parents who can see an answer to their question "How will I ever learn to nurture my new baby?" The answer: "Follow your baby's behavior." A provider who demonstrates and shares the newborns individual behavior characteristics with new parents is helping to cement their relationship.

One of us (S.I.G.) and his colleagues then showed that these individual differences were an important part of healthy, normal development as well as various types of emotional, social, and learning problems throughout childhood.[3] They developed specific interventions tailored to these individual differences that can be used preventively as well as for early intervention and treatment.

Understanding how to work with individual differences has led to a fundamental change in our understanding of how nature and nurture work together. It's not a horse race between nature and nurture, in which intelligence or social skills or temperament can be said to be X percent nurture and X nature. Rather, we have now come to understand that nature is expressed in part through the child's particular way of taking in sensations, comprehending sensations, and organizing and planning action. Nurture, the interactions we provide for our children, then works with nature much as a key does in a lock. The right experiences can open up the lock of nature and help children realize their potential.

Many personality traits derive not from any single, overriding genetic characteristic, but from the complex interplay of multiple factors. Newborn babies do not exhibit innate overall traits of temperament such as introversion or extroversion. Rather, we have observed that both babies developing normally and those with challenges show a great variety in physiological traits such as sensitivity to sound, touch, ability to plan or sequence movements, and the capacity to understand sounds and words and figure out patterns in physical space. Can an infant easily get his hand to his mouth when he wants to suck? When he is older, can he copy shapes such as triangles and diamonds? Does he pull away from even a gentle touch, hold his ears when the vacuum cleaner is turned on, or shut his eyes in strong light?

Children also differ in how they comprehend their world. One might confuse sounds but be a whiz at figuring out how things relate to each other spatially. Another could be just the opposite. Some children have low muscle tone, so that even holding up their heads or turning to look in one or another direction requires extraordinary energy, whereas others may poke Dad in the nose when they intend only to touch him gently.

Such physiological patterns can have many causes, including heredity as well as by factors in the prenatal environment, such as drug use while pregnant. Though contributing to temperament or personality or to tendencies toward illness, they are intermediary influences and can express themselves in different ways. Many children at risk for autism, for instance, often seem self-absorbed and underreactive to sensation, but the same traits can be seen in many healthy children.

An optimistic aspect of our observations is the fact that children with certain physical traits need not be limited by them. Caregiver response may have greater impact than previously thought. Oversensitive children, for example, can become outgoing and confident. Children with weak auditory processing and delayed language can become verbally gifted. Parents can go beyond simply finding a "fit" with their children. With special methods of care, to varying degrees they can help their children change the way their nervous systems operate and thus their personalities. Although there are general personality tendencies that are in part determined by physiological characteristics, these can fall anywhere on a continuum from disturbance to health depending, in part, on how caregivers interact with the child. Many of the most important personality traits, such as the capacities for relating to others, trust and intimacy, empathy, and creative and logical thinking, are largely determined by how we nurture a child's nature.

There is continual feedback in all this. A child's way of processing sensations and organizing motor responses influences the caregiver's reactions, which in turn triggers a new round of processing and response in the child. A well-coordinated, vigorous infant might try to grab a toy from her father's hand, initiating a game of tug-of-war, whereas the parents of a flaccid baby may give up when she scarcely touches a proffered ball or teddy bear. Each child leads the response of those around her. Since the caregiver, through innumerable small actions, serves as the chief intermediary between a baby's developing mind and the environment around her, the baby's own behavior therefore helps shape the world she comes to know.

The book *Infants and Mothers*[4] first brought an understanding of individual differences, and the baby's role in shaping his or her world, to parents. It describes three different babies and their temperament, and helps parents identify their individuality.

A parent's response to particular kinds of behavior can also vary. Some mothers and fathers tend to reach out, whereas others wait for the children to act. Some talk a great deal, whereas others use facial expressions to convey meaning. Some are cheerful, others more serious. Some are laid back, others intrusive; some woo their children energetically, whereas others are more passive and easily become discouraged. These parental patterns, in turn, exert their own influence on babies. Patterns established by the caregiver can alter tendencies to a certain kind of behavior enormously. Self-absorbed infants can become outgoing by age two and cautious infants may become bold toddlers. Through the interactions between the baby's physiological traits and the caregiver's behaviors there emerge personality characteristics.

With caregiving geared to their individual differences, many youngsters born with even serious challenges can do better than expected. In a recent review of over 200 children diagnosed as having autistic spectrum disorders, most enjoyed significant improvement in their mental and emotional functioning when their parents and a therapeutic team were able to work with individual differences and find suitable "keys."[5] This work shows that physiological traits in themselves do not necessarily limit or define a child's potential. Moreover, the more compromised a child's endowment, short of massive and incapacitating damage, the more powerful and decisive the influence of the nurturing he receives. So few children grow up in truly optimal environments that we have no idea of what the parameters of development really are.

Parents have long known and accepted that each of their children is different. We can now provide tools to confirm this intuitive impression, but more important, to systematize it so that parents can use their insights to promote healthy development in each of their children, not just the ones who fit more easily into the expectable family patterns.

In clinical practice and research one of us (S.I.G.) has pinpointed styles of caregiving that can support or counteract particular physiological patterns. The same combination of biological traits can be developed into such valuable gifts as empathy, courage, leadership, curiosity, creativity, determination, self-discipline, self-confidence, perseverance, and originality; or, alternatively, they can serve as the basis for the development of self-indulgence, recklessness, cruelty, hostility, rigidity, detachment, irrationality, and fearfulness. Whether these certain physiological patterns become talents or problems depends, in short, on how the child's nature is nurtured.

Of growing concern to society are violent *antisocial* children, adolescents, and adults who treat others as objects rather than as fellow human beings. Poverty, abuse, and emotional deprivation have largely taken the blame for this dangerous and troubling pattern. John Bowlby's classic paper "Forty-Four Juvenile Thieves"[6] described children neglected in early life who became highly antisocial. The intuitively obvious connection between a lack of warmth bestowed on a child and his subsequent inability to feel it toward others convinced many at the time the paper was published in 1944 that environmental influences were all-important in contributing to or preventing delinquency.

Nature, however, cannot be discounted. Among children severely deprived of nurturing affection in the early years of life, including those in institutional care, two tendencies have been observed. One group of children became withdrawn, depressed, or apathetic. Some stopped developing physically, failed to gain weight, and even became quite ill and did not survive. Those in the other group sought out sensation, becoming aggressive, promiscuous, and indifferent to others, relating to them only to fill their own concrete needs. In other studies, a higher than expected degree of subtle difficulties in the functioning of the nervous system has been found among antisocial children and adults (problems in perception, information processing, and motor functioning).

Antisocial behavior cannot be explained by either the deprivation model which looks to social causes such as poverty, family breakdown, trauma, decaying morality, and lack of authority, nor the physiological model, which cites inborn differences in the function of the nervous system. Rather, it is the interaction of neurological deficits with environmental stresses, which in turn combine with certain types of early parent-child relationships, that increases the likelihood of antisocial behavior.

Caregiver patterns involving extra nurturing, practice at modulating activity, increased opportunities to engage in pretend play with empathy, and gentle but firm consistent limits often lead to positive development. In contrast, punitive limits and hostility or avoidance, neglect, and inconsistency often lead to increased antisocial patterns.

There are many ways to describe variations in temperament or physiological patterns in children. One of us (S.I.G.) has described five common types:[7] the *active, aggressive child*; the *highly sensitive child*; the *inner-focused or self-absorbed child*; the *strong-willed child*; and the *child who has difficulties with attention*. Each of these types of children requires parenting tailored to their particular tendencies and needs if they are to develop their particular strengths.

Such tailoring of interactions or teaching to a child's individual strengths can also help children ordinarily considered autistic or mentally retarded. A number of children diagnosed with autistic disorders with whom we have worked have ultimately developed outstanding cognitive, emotional, and social skills.[8] The fact that even some have responded so well reveals a prognosis far more hopeful than ever thought possible. Retardation is usually thought to result from pervasive biological damage so severe that children will necessarily be rated in the bottom percentiles on all their mental abilities, motor capacities, verbal and spatial abilities, and the like. A close look, however, reveals that these children, too, show a range of individual differences, with some weaker and some stronger in verbal versus spatial abilities or motor capacities and so forth. Working with these differences, playing to children's personal strengths while slowly remediating their weaknesses, has helped many do much better than ever expected.

The need to tailor experience to individual differences is particularly important in early education. For example, there is a percentage of children who have trouble learning to read and are then at risk for related learning failures in subjects that require reading, such as history and social studies, and then become discouraged, getting into behavioral problems and being at risk for dropping out of school and so on.

When children don't respond to the routine reading methods, even when provided with more systemization and intensity, it is often because they have difficulties with processing sound. They can't discriminate subtle sounds and therefore have a hard time relating the sounds that they hear to the letters that they see. Other children have trouble with the perception of the letters themselves, but the vast majority have difficulty with sound discrimination. For these children a phonemic-awareness-based approach, which helps them learn how to discriminate sounds first and then relate sounds to visual perception of shapes and letters, appears to work very well. In a variety of research studies this approach has been shown to help children who have found it difficult to read learn to read and in fact even enjoy reading.[9] Similarly, there are children who have difficulty mastering mathematical concepts, not so much because of inability to memorize their math facts as because of difficulty with visual-spatial processing so that they have a hard time picturing the concept of quantity. Here, approaches that combine strong emotional interest in particular objects, such as coins or cookies, with using the child's ability to visualize quantities or distances (or, for that matter, amounts of time) seem to provide the foundations for better math skills. As a final example, children who have difficulties with motor planning and sequencing have a hard time writing four or five sentences in a row that are all related to one another. Understanding the fundamental problem provides the road to remediation, rather than simply drilling the child in a memory-based way on grammar.

The current vogue for back to basics and extended school days is unfortunately moving education away from the recognition of individual differences and toward a one-size-fits-all approach. Simply doing more of what has not been working will not prove helpful, nor can you teach a child simply by testing him. Similarly, greater accountability without teaching innovations will also be unlikely to produce improved results, any more than (as the old saying states) weighing a cow over and over will fatten it. Assessment can be a very valuable part of learning if it lets teachers know how well their methods are working and lets students and parents know what is being mastered and not mastered. In the best types of assessment, the child is constantly learning and assessing, as a demonstration to himself and others of his mastery of the material.

When we focus on individual differences in education we focus on the core processes, such as auditory processing and language, visual-spatial thinking, motor planning and sequencing (often termed *executive skills*), and sensory modulation, as well as different levels of abstract thinking that children need to master to be successful academically as well as socially and emotionally. We often neglect these fundamental individual differences or processing capacities that underlie all learning and education while emphasizing memorization of facts. To those who say, "Well, at least they should know who Grant or Lincoln or Washington was," the answer has to be that that's the wrong approach. There is no "at least." If children are left with only a few isolated facts, they will still be poorly educated. They certainly need to know who Washington, Lincoln, and Grant were, but they need to know these names in the context of concepts of history. To understand concepts, they have to be solid readers, good visual-spatial thinkers, and advanced abstract problem solvers. There is no shortcut to these basic skills, which underlie all of learning. Back to basics, therefore, must mean getting back to the basic processes that underlie all learning.

For an educational system or an individual teacher to ensure mastery of these basic processes, six basic assumptions are necessary:

1. *The uniqueness of each child.* A child's experiences in large part determine what she learns. To facilitate learning and appropriate mental growth, experiences must be tailored to the child's "individually different" central nervous system. Children are different in their degree of mastery of early developmental capacities, such as their ability to focus and attend, the depth of their intimacy and relatedness, their ability to be purposeful and intentional, their capacity to solve complex problems, their skill in using ideas symbolically and creatively, and their capacity to think logically and abstractly. Family, cultural, and community patterns are also unique. Understanding these patterns makes it possible to construct educational programs based on individual differences in the child and his family and community.

2. *Families and educators working together.* An individual-difference approach does not mean testing, labeling, and then tracking children. Educators and parents should work together to review the child's development, observe his functioning, and describe his profile. The physical environment, the curriculum, and the type of relationships that will foster learning are then adapted to each child's profile. As a result, cognitive and social skills are facilitated and disorders are often prevented. This does not mean separate learning environments for each child or group of children. Children learn together and enhance each other's growth. Teachers can use different areas of the room and flexible modules to create optimal learning opportunities for each child. To implement such an approach, parents need to be partners in the governance of the school, and the school should be fully integrated into the community.

3. *Learning through dynamic emotional interactions.* As the child begins his formal education, dynamic emotional interactions are instrumental for learning. Abstract thinking, which is involved in reading, comprehending history, writing, science, social studies, and math, always involves two elements: (a) emotionally meaningful experiences with others and one's social and physical environment and (b) the capacity to reflect on and categorize interactions and expand on these experiences.

4. *No room for failure.* Children who fail a particular test or exercise need to be given an opportunity to redo that exercise. This can be during school hours, after school hours, on weekends, or in summers; nonetheless, the children can't simply be promoted nor held in first grade for 20 years. Neither approach will work. Rather, the approach to educating the child has to be altered until a road is found that enables that child to have some relative degrees of mas-

tery of that particular area. The child, for example, who is having trouble with math may take a long time to get the fundamental concept of quantity. Even if the goal for that child becomes simply competence in addition, subtraction, multiplication, and division before the end of high school, at least that goal would be well worth the effort. Therefore, a child redoes the exercise until he gets it, but each time new understanding of the source of his difficulties is achieved by the educators to provide a yet better approach to that child. For example, if the child is not able to do homework at home because there is no support or the child is unmotivated, after-school activities may have to be provided to do the work that ordinarily would be done at home. The child's motivation and the family structure in this individual-difference model are taken as individual differences, as variables in the equation, not as moral considerations that can justify letting a child fail. Rather, the child's motivation and the family disorganization can be seen as challenges to be met. Other services can be brought to bear to support the family if there is extreme family chaos or difficulties, or if the child is having severe emotional and social difficulties and is at risk for school dropout and subsequent delinquent behavior. Other community supports and help are suggested in Chapter 6.

A respect for individual differences does not undermine individual responsibility. Paradoxically, in this individual-difference model, individual responsibility is far greater than in any other model. Children are not allowed to escape into passivity, helplessness, or maladaptive behaviors. Their individual responsibility is challenged through extra help and structure. No one is getting off the hook here—not the child, not the educators, nor the families.

We (S.I.G.) have developed a developmental individual-difference relationship-based model (or the DIR model), in which children are understood in terms of their developmental capacities, their individual differences, and the interactive relationships likely to be helpful to them (as well as those that are going on at present that might be undermining their development).[10]

The D.I.R. model has become the basis for a new organization, the Interdisciplinary Council on Develomental and Learning Disorders (ICDL), with Regional Councils in most American cities, ICDL works to improve services for children (and families) with developmental and learning disorders and has recently issued *Clinical Practice Guidelines* for children and families with special needs, including autism and related disorders.[11] This type of approach doesn't necessarily reward the gifted student more than the slower student. It rewards them both for being part of the learning process. Each one can achieve a high level of self-esteem by having a relative sense of mastery in terms of where she started and what she has accomplished. In such an atmosphere, children will embrace an approach that helps them learn. The more we can individualize and the more we can help children work with innovative methods until they master particular material, the quicker we will get to a higher level of educational achievement and self-esteem for all children.

5. *Small groups.* This individual-difference model calls for children's being educated in much smaller classes than is now the case. Classes of 25 and 30 children are not conducive to learning. For the most part, only children who are capable of learning basically without the help of school learn well in such large classes. To help gifted students to reach their full potential, average students do better than they are doing now, and children with challenges to become competent requires small classes for all children.

6. *Foundationbuilding time each day.* We have stated already that each child has her own processing profile in terms of the way she takes in and comprehends information and communicates and thinks. These processing capacities are the building blocks or the foundations for reading, math, writing, and all types of academic, as well as social, thinking. At present, these building blocks tend to be dealt with informally as part of the processes applied to different subjects. However, because these processes are implicit rather than explicit, teachers and students are often not aware enough which of these processes come easily and which ones require extra work and practice. The fundamental building blocks we are talking about include auditory processing (the ability to take in and figure out what you are hearing), visual-spatial processing (the ability to take in and figure out what you are seeing and to negotiate the physical world around you—this is essential for math and science, as well as reading), sensory modulation (the ability to process information without being overreactive or underreactive in each of the five senses), and motor planning and sequencing (the ability to organize and sequence actions and thoughts—an important component of what's often referred to as *executive functions*). Because these basic processing capacities underlie the academic essentials, a quarter to a third of each school day (beginning in preschool and kindergarten and continuing throughout high school) should be spent on strengthening these foundation skills. Many gifted teachers and schools already imple-

ment some of these skills informally. The key is to make the practice more explicit and more systematic.

The concept of individual differences also has implications for our social service system. In providing supports for families it is important to understand the ways in which those whom we are working with take in, organize, and process information, as well as plan their actions. Understanding individual differences can provide insights into natural talents and needs for job training. Also, individual differences in family structure and support can provide valuable information about what's needed in a family support program.

The concept of individual differences is most important when we look at the interface between social service and legal systems and our approaches to children and families having extreme difficulties. In order to plan programs of rehabilitation, even when they are occurring in the context of confinement due to criminal activity, it is imperative that we understand the individual differences of the child and family. Each child's profile can provide a guideline for how to help that child. For example, in one program with potentially delinquent youth, an interested mentor worked with the children in a way geared to their particular needs around a new job, problems with their family members or the police, and learning to read or add or plan actions. The mentor was there on site with the children, providing ongoing nurturing support as well as instruction in areas of vulnerability or weakness, educationally and vocationally. After two years in such a program, eighty percent of the children were moving on to successful courses in their adult life, in terms of relationships, family, and career. Eighty percent of the children who dropped out of school and did not have access to such an individual-difference-oriented program wound up either in the criminal justice system or the mental health system.[12]

The individual-differences model is also important in our mental health system. In our approaches to mental disorders and mental health we have, to some degree, stepped ahead of our data. We have applied labels to patterns of problems and diagnosed syndromes when the evidence is not yet compelling that many of these disturbing behaviors actually fit into true syndromes. By treating various kinds of behavior as a syndrome, rather than patterns of behavior, we tend to develop interventions or treatments aimed at the syndrome rather than at the underlying elements that may be responsible for each type. A good example is a child who's unable to pay attention. If we focus on individual differences, we may find, for instance, that that child has problems with motor planning and sequencing. Special exercises to improve sequencing and planning actions may be very helpful. On the other hand, a child may also be overreactive to things like sound and noise and may get easily overloaded when further frustrated or anxious, and that reaction may intensify a tendency to react more to other noises and sounds as well as pursue impulsive activity. Reducing the noise and tactile sensations in the environment, working on self-soothing and self-regulating, and anticipating circumstances where overload and arousal are likely can help such a child organize, plan, and modulate his behavior. On the other hand, if these underlying processing differences are ignored and only the surface symptoms and "syndrome" are worked with (e.g., the child, because of his behaviors, is assumed to have attention deficit disorder), we may try a syndrome-oriented medication, such as Ritalin. In a particular child, it may backfire because of his overreactivity to the environment and his tendency, when overloaded, to go into exaggerated patterns of oversensitivity and impulsive action. In such children, we've noted that at times certain medications may tend to produce more agitation and more impulsive behavior and sometimes grandiose thinking. (Children who tend to be underreactive to sound and touch, on the other hand, we have observed clinically, often benefit from these medications.) Here, we have a very good example of how focusing on individual differences can help us plan more effectively for the individual child and the importance if we are going to try a biological remedy, of knowing what to look for early on to see if it's producing side effects or truly being helpful.

Similar patterns can be observed in children who are feeling sad and down on themselves. This can be viewed as a syndrome, childhood depression, or can be looked at in the context of the child's individual differences. We've noted that some children, for example, who from the time they were infants and toddlers have been very sensitive to subtle variations in their environments, instead of becoming active or impulsive tend easily to have hurt feelings. Some of these children tend to have weaker visual-spatial processing capacities and strong auditory processing capacities and are often very sensitive to even slight variations in touch or sound. Understanding this, we can provide them with extra soothing and nurturing care and also ways to verbalize and understand their reactions to their environments. When we are able to work with children in this way, their tendency to become sad and morose often changes as they develop flexibility based on understanding their individual differences.

During childhood the individual-differences approach has advantages even when biological remedies are being considered, together with psychosocial ones. The individual-difference orientation tries to identify each child's unique profile in its subtlety and infinite variations and tries less to group children together into labelled syndromes, particularly when, as indicated earlier, the bases for the syndromes are not as fully established as one might think.

In summary, the individual-difference approach to understanding human functioning has the potential to significantly change the way we think about children and families in our educational settings as well as in our social service and mental health systems.

Discussion

SIG: Our current child-rearing patterns, educational approaches, and social service, health, and mental health systems only rarely recognize or deal with individual differences. Also, for a variety of reasons that aren't yet entirely clear, maybe due to chaotic early environments or exposure to substances that damage the nervous system, more and more children seem to show extreme evidence of these individual differences.

TBB: We need to look more closely at these differences, both in terms of parent-child interactions and also in terms of the rest of the social world. The same contribution of the child goes across all lines—with parents, teachers, peers, day care staff, and so on. Each of these people has a chance to learn about a child and to pay attention to that child's particular needs.

Recognizing Differences Early

SIG: In your Touchpoints model, each child, as a part of a well-baby or education program, from infancy on up, is assessed periodically in terms of individual differences and developmental needs. This assessment requires cooperation between health and education departments and implies a new concept of what education means. From the principle that every child should be educated from age five on, we've moved down to preschool, Head Start, and now Early Head Start funding through the government for limited numbers of children. The next step is embracing the concept that these assessments need to begin at birth, perhaps through mandating insurance coverage (as part of well-baby care with appropriately trained developmental specialists in a pediatrician's office). We'd like to see the recognition that to do a decent job we've got to understand each baby and child. Resistance is predictable. Some will see it as encroachment on the family, or parental authority. But it ought to be seen as an extension of health care.

TBB: Yes, support rather than intrusion. We need to understand each family well enough so that we can help the child thrive. We have to give families a goal that is positive. If we march in, look down at them, pronounce what is wrong, and prescribe the things they need, this will be felt as encroachment. If we took a transactional approach instead and said, "We want to understand where you are and how we can support you and join with you in helping your child be strong and healthy and learn well," I think you'd have less resistance. You'd still have the far right to deal with, but I still think you'd have a better chance of reaching most parents—certainly the ones who are so vulnerable and hopeless. You'd have a better chance of capturing them if you had that approach.

I'd set up a positive model of outreach in which the child is your focus and your language, and in which you see parent and child periodically for health and psychological reasons to see how well they are doing, not to change or shape or anything like that. This is the focus of our Touchpoints program. We're also trying to change the way we train pediatricians, nurses, child care workers, and teachers. We need an outreach, understanding, transactional model, which I think is absolutely antithetical to all the training we're given. We need to ask ourselves, "OK, how often do we need to see a family and learn if they're going to make it on their own or need the help we can give them." On a curve of effectiveness, does the usefulness of the visits fall off? At these visits, professionals could meet with a family and assess developmental levels as well as individual needs. We could get a very good fix on how much people needed and how much they didn't need. Not everybody needs all this outreach, but a model would help us identify the differences.

At present, our model is based on the concept that you shove everybody together and the outliers become obvious and then you address them at a symptomatic level. That isn't going to work and it hasn't worked. The outliers can be identified early. Then we don't have to put all our resources into them. We work with them from the start. Stanley, the programs you have designed do the same thing. We can learn a lot from both the normative stream and the exceptional-child streams. But it's not going to be across the board, one size fits all; it has to be individuated right straight from the start. This means that we must train providers—child care and medical—to be aware of which families need what. We must also train them to set up a relationship with each family based on cooperation, with everyone working toward the child's best outcome.

SIG: Let's say we have nothing going on. How would we set up the system? How would you train and who would be trained?

TBB: Well, I'd train everybody. There are different levels of training. We train the trainers and they go out to the ones who are going to be providing the care. They offer community-level training. There's also specialist-level training. Specialists, like physical therapists and occupational therapists, just need the supplement to what they're already doing, a shift to a family-oriented and relationship-oriented approach.

In our program, nurse practitioners, pediatricians, physician's assistants, family doctors, and so on get universal training. They've sat together and talked about relationships—how you make them, how you use them, and how you look for them at each vulnerable touchpoint. They get a crash course in child development that they can use in their work with parents.

At the core of our program are these occasions that we call *touchpoints*. These are the vulnerable times like the normal regressions in a child's development that provide an opportunity for entering the family system and joining parents to understand the child's development.

SIG: Let's go back to what we were talking about earlier—every future parent getting educated, presumably in school. A couple decides to get married and they're thinking about having a child. In our ideal society, where do we start with them? Do we start that whole process with parents learning what having a baby means in the elementary school years? By the time this couple is thinking about having a baby of their own, they should have a certain amount of education in child development and rearing under their belts. Then we begin the Touchpoints prenatally with childbirth education and the obstetrician, nurse practitioner, and all the helpers. A system would be in place, beginning with pre-prenatal discussions.

TBB: Another key time is the home visit in seven days.
Postpartum depression is often missed with shortened hospital stays. It's not just the babies who need a checkup in seven days,

to see whether they're anemic or withdrawing from drugs or dehydrated. You're also concerned with whether or not the mother is extremely depressed. You try to include the father, too.

I'd start right from the first with a model like our Touchpoints program to reach out to people and try to bring them into the system. Then we could attend not only the baby's physical development, but emotional and cognitive development as well, with input into family interaction.

The first step would be prevention. The second would be assessment so we knew exactly what the child was like. If you have two or three assessment points along the way, you have what I call a recovery curve. This gives you a fix on the things that are going to go along right, no matter what you do, and also the things that never will change, and also those you may be able to help. Issues of fit between parent and child and attachment are the ones that are really open to intervention. But first we have to get families into the system—a preventive system. Part of this irreducible need for appropriate experience is a preventive health-care–child-care system that can spot mismatches and the children whose developmental level and temperament are not being recognized.

Preventive Services

SIG: We can produce a game plan, a community-based program of outreach, periodic assessments. For example, what do we need for a child who's not forming an emotional relationship with his parents?

TBB: Who are the people who are going to have to change what they're doing to achieve this? Should this all be embedded in a day care or school system? Which bureaucracy should handle it, or do we need a new approach?

SIG: By the time you get to school age, there are some services embedded in the school system. Should we ask the school to do more or should we ask the health department to do more? What sort of services do we need to prevent dire outcomes? Say we've identified a child at 18 months who has bad receptive language problems, who has low muscle tone, and he's in a chaotic family. What do we need to take care of this?

TBB: Everyone has to learn to speak the language of the child and to be concerned with his optimal development. Our concept of Touchpoints is not just for providers of day care or preventive health providers. It's for phone operators, school van drivers, and for everyone in the community involved with the child. I would say that we need to make the community child-friendly and child-oriented and parent-support-oriented. Then we go after the things we've already learned—childbirth education classes, later the kind of peer groups of mothers set up by the Family Resource Coalition.[13] I've recommended to our Touchpoints providers that they bring in mothers with babies the same age each visit so that they sit in the waiting room together and talk with each other about what's going on. In that way, they become a peer group that goes right straight through the child's development.

SIG: Do we recommend that these services be provided via hospitals, as in childbirth education classes, or get switched to something else, for example, education?

TBB: When early intervention services are indicated or developmental problems show up, then you have to include other disciplines. They've got to be available to you. These, as well as pre-prenatal education, probably need to come under the umbrella of health. Other disciplines need to be retrained to look for relationships rather than didactic information.

SIG: The ideal education that would enable parents themselves to recognize their child's development and individual needs starts with the pre-prenatal education and then pregnancy and would continue through childhood and adolescent years with periodic reevaluations. The question is: What sort of support services do we need to do all this? Let's say that you discover that a mother is very depressed, thinking her baby is not going to make it and she's not going to make it. Daddy is fed up and there are a lot of marital problems. Once we've teased that out it's more than just listening and understanding.

TBB: In our present system, a mother might get a few sessions with a social worker if she really pushed for it. I'd rather have a group of people who work together, like an infant mental health clinic. This would involve a social worker, a neonatologist, a family therapist, and a psychiatrist or child development specialist who could identify problems. You need to have all these people available to call on, and they need to be used to working in a team.

SIG: If a mother had other psychiatric problems or was clinically depressed, she would need a mental health professional to work with her and her husband. If there were just typical anxieties, then being a part of a group with other prenatal moms and dads might be enough. This would be under the health system. And here we get into the other questions: What do we mandate? What should be covered by Medicaid, health insurance, or HMOs? If there were federal guidelines that said that to do business HMOs had to cover these services, they would cover it. If it weren't mandated, they wouldn't do it.

TBB: Before you do that you have to change the whole view of health care toward a preventive, outreach approach. Unless you do, you're not going to get an HMO or anybody else to pay for it. Our medical care at present is made of expensive Band-Aids once there are problems. We haven't proven that prevention is going to save a lot of money at the other end, which is what will motivate change.

SIG: We would need to define here what is needed. It's easy to talk prevention and it's hard to do prevention.

TBB: Well, for instance, right after childbirth, in the hospital, I think that everyone caring for mother and baby should be trained on my NBAS scale and should share the scale with the mother. This is a matter of only 10–15 minutes. We've cut down the expectation of the time needed for the scale to spread its use more widely.

SIG: Are you recommending that this be done by a *doula* or some nurse in the hospital? Would you also be including the kinds of things that Marshall Klaus and John Kennell recommend in terms of the birth process, with the period of attachment and the skin contact?[14]

TBB: I'd give people choices. Some mothers want the baby right away and some don't. The same thing about a *doula*. They can be an enormous support, but I wouldn't be rigid about it. I think the main thing is to give people choices and really explain their options, not just "Do you want this?" or "Do you want that?" and "If you do, sign here."

SIG: I agree. That's exactly the way to do it. The concept of individual differences extends to family choices as well as babies. If we use the concept of tuning into individual needs and differences right at the point of birth, for example, we can see that there are a lot of experiences that are helpful to many moms and babies, such as the ability to have a labor companion or a few minutes with the baby on the tummy after birth. These things need to be explored prenatally with moms as part of the

prenatal Touchpoints outreach. Then the hospitals should be
flexible in making these experiences available, tailoring
experiences to individual differences.

TBB: Some of these choices are not ones that all women could
afford unless they were mandated and covered by insurance—a
doula, for example.

SIG: We have to identify those things that we believe are
especially helpful and should be part of the options. We might
also advocate that the assessment of individual differences begin
prenatally, looking at a baby's activity levels. A mother needs to
know that she can tell a lot by the baby's cycles and states in
utero. We may eventually learn that if the baby is very inactive
prenatally, it may be a sign that the baby is at risk for certain
kinds of difficulties. There may be things we can do that will
help the baby be a little more active. Feedback from the uterine
experience has not been explored yet. This would be a
wonderful study for someone to do—to identify babies who are
inactive prenatally and to try a certain series of physical exercises
with Mom and see if they make a difference. Then, when the
neonatal assessment was done at birth, if there were a difference
between those who received prenatal interventions and those
who didn't, that would open up a big area.

TBB: There's much else needed. We have to have a lactation
consultant available. We've mentioned the home visit at five to
seven days by a nurse who's trained in the neonatal assessment
and who could demonstrate how to tune in to the baby's level
of development and temperament. Then again, at three weeks,
there should be another visit.

SIG: I think at this point we need to brainstorm a little more
about the backup services needed. As we identify the outliers or
the extreme cases, we need that team we were referring to
earlier made up of the different disciplines. The intervention we
have now is not adequate. Let's say a baby is identified at six
months with low muscle tone, which puts him at risk for
language, cognitive, motor-development, and social and
emotional problems. If the baby is in a hospital follow-up
program for preemies, he or she maybe gets some physical or
occupational therapy related to the program. If the child gets
referred to an early intervention, a 0–3 program, in many places
all that's likely to happen is a home visit once a week or once
every two weeks This person may not have been trained in
physical or occupational therapy but gives the mother some

ideas about how to play with the baby. This may not be a great deal more than the mother can read in a book. It's highly variable right now and the chances of that baby's getting a full program are minimal. A baby with low muscle tone is going to need a couple of visits a week. A specialist will be needed to work interactively to discover how to reach that low-muscle-toned baby. Right now that's nonexistent. We don't have a lot of trained people to do that kind of work. There's not even sufficient awareness that once you identify a physical risk, you're also at jeopardy for interaction problems and delays in emotional and intellectual development. If a baby is not interacting, he's not learning to be purposeful and intentional and he is not vocalizing back and forth. You need to monitor language, social, emotional, and cognitive development to see if further work is needed as the baby gets a little older. It may be necessary to bring in a speech pathologist to work on oral motor skills because the baby can't make sounds even though the interactions are getting better.

We also need to identify whether the cause of the problem is elsewhere. Perhaps there is a mother addicted to drugs who won't bring the child to physical therapy, or the child has low muscle tone because of emotional deprivation (not for physical reasons), or a child may be abused physically because the boyfriend of the mother is angry.

TBB: All this can usually be picked up on in the Touchpoints assessments. These delays in motor development and the hypersensitivity or dysfunction in other areas could be brought to light if the parent has a good relationship with her provider.

We need more and better staffing for early intervention sites. 99-457[15] was a federal mandate (1978), that provided funding for delayed and impaired children. Early intervention for these children and their parents was seen as a *right* of such children. The Early Intervention Centers which are available in most cities and can be contacted through every Children's Hospital are available to any parents who suspect that their child is not progressing. The earlier such children are identified, the more progress they are likely to make. The United Cerebral Palsy Foundation has been a real supporter of these centers. It published a study that demonstrated the sensitivity of parents to their baby's progress. If parents referred their babies to intervention, they were referred as early as 4 months. If this was left for providers (such as pediatricians) they weren't referred until 16 months. Too often, a caring physician may say "Don't worry. He'll outgrow it." The early intervention programs have taught us so much about early development and the benefits of intervention to parents and children.

SIG: What's in place now in the way of services is a loose confederation. If, by chance, the abuse by the boyfriend gets identified, social services may get involved and there may be some assessment of whether foster care is needed or not. A community mental health center that has no experience with babies may be involved and not know what to do.

TBB: A baby who comes in for a three-week or six-month checkup is really at the mercy of whoever is the primary caregiver. In a good instance—say, here at Children's Hospital in Boston—the family would have access to all the different departments. Still we'd like to have more teamwork, people who know each other and know how to work with families and children. Within their relationship they could raise questions about development early, while there is plasticity and a better chance of recovery from insults at birth and during delivery.

SIG: Children's is one of the best hospitals in the country. What happens there if a six-month-old baby is brought in—and the doctor notices that he has low muscle tone and is delayed sitting up (but not enough to be called cerebral palsy)? The mother is quite depressed but manages to put on a good face for the visit. Father is an alcoholic. What's likely to happen at the best hospital in the country right now?

TBB: Nothing until the baby gets into more trouble than that. We don't always talk with them preventively nor do assessments. This is one of the things we're trying to do—to get people to come for our training and start watching for these signs at 2 months, and at 4 $1/2$ months. They learn about motor, cognitive, and affective systems and look at each one of those. [See Appendix for guidelines from Touchpoints program.]

SIG: The training is indeed critical. If you don't ask a mom about her husband, you won't find out that he's drinking. If you don't carefully observe the caregiver-baby interaction, you won't notice that a baby is not related or purposeful. Even when an adequate assessment is done, nothing is likely to happen because there's no backup team. The health insurance may not pay for services related to developmental challenges.

TBB: Some providers may simply call it genetic and leave it at that. One of our goals in our Touchpoints program is to train professionals to spot such conditions. We are now training nurse practitioners in many nursing schools, and in two medical schools we're training young doctors to evaluate newborns. Hopefully, this will increase referrals for early intervention rather than later, when deficits are fixed. Sharing observations with parents can alert them to their newborn's behavior and help them trust the provider.

SIG: But even if these trained individuals spot problems, right now children are likely to get referred to services where they wait in line. They won't get enough visits and most providers are not trained well enough to help. There has to be training both for those who assess children and for those who form an intervention team.

TBB: So what we need is not only assessments but services available that could get going right at that point and give people some hope. Even when there are early-intervention sites that are staffed with multidisciplines, pediatricians may not be aware of them.

SIG: Clinicians feel more empowered if when they first make the assessment they realize they have a good intervention team behind them. Then they'll be more likely to look for subtle things. What percentage of pediatric neurologists, behavioral pediatricians, or general pediatricians believe that we can do much about these problems? What percentage would say that even if we could assess this and have a great intervention team, we couldn't do much about it? Many will say, "Let's wait and see." In such a view a child is either heading toward developmental problems such as autism or he's going to outgrow it; his genes will determine what happens.

TBB: A large group of pediatricians won't even pick up subtle delays. Of those who do, 1 percent says we can do a lot about it and 99 percent say let's wait and see if it doesn't right itself. When it gets worse, we do know what to do about it.

SIG: That is a very important point. There's a real educational need here. We do know what to do for these children at an early stage.

TBB: But you know, all of this is still based on the pathological model, the medical school, pathological model. I'd like to turn that model completely around and say, "Look for people's strengths." What does this mother with this low-tone baby bring to you that you can build on as a strength? Is she really devoid of strengths? Is she so depressed that she can't help the child? Then you look at the baby and you see from its expression and responses that the baby has some motivation, even though his muscles don't express. You say, "OK, well, I can do something about that because the baby is motivated. Now I have to translate that motivation into action. Whom do I get to do that?" You're starting at it with a proactive point of view rather than just a label. If we change the model at medical school to a more positive model, a systems approach, then I think we would be much readier to act. Short of that, I think we just go on with the same old thing, waiting until the baby is clearly failing, before we can do anything.

SIG: By having a whole system in place that understands a child's developmental level and individual differences, and then having backups available if needed, you're working with creating mastery from the start. You're working with that low-tone baby and helping the mother interact with that baby and read the baby's signals before a serious developmental disorder is diagnosed.

TBB: The sites that have attempted to apply Touchpoints ideas to early-intervention outreach are finding that the opportunities in the first three years are magnified. When you have a mother who is grieving over the fact that she has a delayed or disordered baby, she's bound to be defensive. She'll listen to a professional who says, "He'll outgrow it," because she still has hope. But if a caregiver identifies the baby's strengths before attacking the mother with his failures, she can hear what is being said. Our Touchpoints program supports the mastery of the parent, recognizes that the parent is the expert on her child, that all parents have strengths, all parents want to do well by their child, and all parents can add something at each stage of development. We also stress that ambivalent feelings are *normal*. This approach fosters a relationship between a caregiver and a suffering parent, and parents are more likely to stay involved.

SIG: That's a very different way of thinking. We've got to have health insurance and HMOs cover this, and we've got to have the government involved in providing services for those who don't have health insurance or belong to HMOs.

TBB: There's another model in the Healthy Steps program that Margaret Mahoney at Commonwealth Fund has been backing.[16] You have child developmental specialists in HMO offices who can ascertain where babies are in their development and who do testing while they're in the waiting room. They're psychologists and are part of the HMO team. Parents learn to rely on them for advice about their child's development. Pediatricians in the HMO feel backed up and are willing to discuss developmental issues more often with parents. This is a very good model.

SIG: As you say, HMOs would have to be convinced that it would save them money in the long run to provide such services. But looking at this from the HMO's point of view, if the failure is largely psychological, social, and emotional, the HMO may not end up paying the cost. It may come out of the school system, jails, mental health services, and so on. Perhaps the government might say there are going to be bonuses for each HMO that produces healthy citizens. On the other hand, when HMOs are not attending to these things, there could be penalties, perhaps contributions to educational or special education programs. The problem is creating an incentive. Ideally, the different systems— health, education, social services—would work together, bearing responsibility together. I'm trying to think about how you change people's attitudes quickly. If you're a managed-care system and you're going to have to be concerned with how this child will do at school at age seven or eight and paying a penalty if the child can't learn, I think that would motivate some. If the managed-care people thought they were going to have to pay for the tutor down the road, it might be an incentive to work with the child now.

TBB: I don't think that managed care can think of the long haul. So far they're on a one- or two-year string, I think.

Individual Differences in the School System

SIG: Once the children get a little older, what should the responsibility of the educational system be, to augment the medical responsibilities?

TBB: I think we should have our most highly trained, expert assessors at work in the school systems (we learned it in Head Start). First grade ought to have plenty of trained people watching those children to see who's functioning well and who isn't. Then, we would need referral systems to pick up the pieces.

SIG: What sort of a team or person do we want in the schools to carry forth this philosophy?

TBB: Somebody who looks at the total child. This would be a child psychologist with developmental training. The person could tell the child's stage of development, temperament, and individual differences, and create some picture of the home for each child in the class.

SIG: Would that person work through the health system or through the educational system?

TBB: I think it ought to be done through both: first through maternal infant care in the health system, and then as soon as you get the children at school. If you get them in Head Start, then you begin back there. We've proved that, doing what we could, which wasn't very much. Head Start made a difference in children's outcome later on.

SIG: The Touchpoints model could continue all through adolescence, so the school person would be collaborating with the Touchpoints health person.

TBB: We haven't reached into the school system, but we've certainly tied into day care, and it's worked like a charm. The day care people say to a mother, "Is your one-year-old waking up at night?" and the mother says, "Yes, how did you know?" "Because she's working so hard on learning to walk all day long, she must be waking at night, and she must be hard to feed." The mother says, "Wow, she knows my baby!" and she becomes involved in day care in a way she wasn't before.

SIG: The public schools have to take a conceptual shift here. The public school system and, to some extent, the day care system really see themselves as purely educational. They have to change their scope, just as health care needs to broaden and consider relationships and interactions and emotional-social development as part of health care. Similarly, education can't have a narrow definition of intelligence. Once you broaden the definition of intelligence, you see the importance of early relationships. Interactive relationships are the basis of how you learn to think.

We're not talking about small numbers of children when we're talking about children who have especially challenging individual differences. Although it's been estimated that between 15 and 20 percent of children have clinically identifiable problems, the children who come to school trusting, capable of intimacy, capable of sharing, capable of empathy, and capable of using ideas in imaginative play and in reflective discussions (rather than acting needs out) are probably less than half of the children.

The purview of education must be broadened to consider all these individual differences we've been talking about. Schools can't close their eyes to them. They can't say, "This is asking education to do too much. Our job is to teach math and reading." For the child to understand the spatial relations involved in math, he has to be able to reason and think. To reason and think he has to be able to interact and communicate with others.

TBB: When I have had the chance to talk with people at the National Education Association (NEA), they say that right now they are bogged down with having to deal with social work problems, with learning-disability problems, and that they are over their heads and it uses all of their energy. If they were freed by specialists who can take over the work with children and families who need help, they would be ready to do any amount of diagnostic work. They certainly have the know-how.

SIG: What's preventing them from bringing in those specialists to help them right now? The prevention model that you are talking about would reduce the number of children in special-needs classes. By paying attention early to the children with motor, attentional, language, social and emotional, and family challenges, we would reduce the numbers who go on to need very extensive special classes.

If you follow this preventive model, you could redesign special education in this country at less cost and do much better. Right now, the model of special education is just what you criticize—a pathological model where the child's deficits are being assessed and labeled and the building blocks for mastery are not being laid. The kids are being "remediated" into deeper holes.

TBB: Now by the time children get help, they have been so battered that they're burned out and no longer have any hope.

Class Size and Individual Differences

SIG: One of the issues that comes up in school would be what class size we should have, if we really believe in individual differences and tailoring the approach to the child's nervous system.

TBB: I'm not experienced in schoolteaching, but in the first few years I think you'd start with what we said earlier for day care.

SIG: If you look at the size of classes in private schools, many have from 12 to 15 children. This makes a big, big difference. In a private schools, many of the classes tend to stay in that

12–15 range. Occasionally it will go up to 20 for a popular class. This is true from 1st grade right up to 12th grade.

My take on it is that there are two groups of children. There are children who can learn on their own. They can basically learn without school. Give them books and worksheets and they'll teach themselves. The children who really need to have a teacher to help them learn need to be in classes of less than 15 or 16 children. Otherwise, you'll begin to compromise what they're learning. People are talking about more technology in education, summer school for children, and longer school days, and yet they may not be looking at the most critical issue, which is that the class is too big, 25–30 children. You can't tailor the work to individual differences with that size class.

In preschool, for two-year-olds, I would say we could have 4 children per caregiver. For three-year-olds, we could go up to 5 children and in the next year up to 6 children per adult. We could have a class of 12 children with two adults. In the sixth year, kindergarten, we could have 7 children per adult or up to 14 children with two adults.

In the first grade, I would hold the class size at 15 or under and would do the same for the rest of the school years through high school—plus or minus a few. Some classes might be 18, some might be 13. Through the elementary grades, I'd prefer two adults per class. At this level, one of the adults could be an aide. This second person does not need to be a fully trained teacher. From the 6th grade to the 12th grade, you can go to one adult per 15 children. You might make that transition of one adult gradually in the 5th and 6th grades, too.

Most children need a lot more one-to-one work to be truly educated. If we're talking about helping minds develop and we're serious about education, we have to make changes. You can't farm out the human factor. Learning occurs through relationships and interactions. Trying to get technology or more hours of drilling to take the place of interactive problem-solving learning just doesn't work very well. The glue that makes minds grow is the glue of human interaction. If you try to substitute technology for the human factor, we'll come out dehumanizing our population. And they won't be well educated.

TBB: Some of these numbers may not be realistic. For two-year-olds, I think you could go up to 6 to 8, and for three-year-olds, 8 to 10. With four-year-olds, I think you could have 10 children per adult, and in kindergarten, 12–14. Then I'd keep to 12–6 in the rest of elementary school and not go above 16 until graduation. But we're asking for something that's rather expensive.

SIG: Basically, I think we're on the same wavelength. The idea is smaller class sizes throughout school. You are trying to be more realistic in terms of what's affordable, and I'm trying to be very idealistic. In the preschool years, for example, I'm trying to think of what's optimal in terms of these children not being emotionally hungry and getting enough adult contact. If there is one adult to four or five children, on the floor helping them play, moving in and out as needed, they would have a sense of security, just like kids playing at home. I'm trying to think of what makes an ideal experience for children. You have a few children from the neighborhood in to play and Mom is in and out. All 4 children have access to an adult. If you have 10 children, there's not quite that same access to the adult. They're dependent more on the child-to-child interaction, which is fine up to a point, but it leaves gaps.

TBB: Are you thinking more about children with special needs?

SIG: Perhaps in my practice I see more children with acute disabilities, but I see a lot with mild challenges and in normal range also. Our differences have more to do with the reality of what's fundable. I think if you were given a choice in setting up a day care center or preschool program and money was no object, and they wanted to know how many children would be optimal for each caregiver, I think you would say one to four rather than one to eight for two-year-olds.

TBB: Yes, I would say one to four.

SIG: The point is in order to tailor experiences to the child's nervous system and individual differences, an adult needs time for each child. After the physical safety and protection, and relationships with a lot of warmth and affect, our first two needs, children need this tailored attention.

TBB: One of the most tragic things that has happened in our educational system is that parents have become marginalized. They no longer feel necessary to their children's education. The parents' dedication to learning and their understanding of their child's needs are critical to a child's success in school. Asian families are a good example of this.

It's natural that teachers and parents get into competition over a child they care about. I call this *gatekeeping*. It occurs whenever two adults care deeply about the same child. It happens between parents and between parents and caregivers. It's bound to happen in schools. But today, especially, parents need to feel necessary and included in their child's education. They are often so torn by two full-time jobs that we need even more to include them in developmental processes like schooling. Maybe Parent-Teacher Associations aren't the answer any longer, but we should press for new, innovative ways of attracting parents.

Home Schooling and Individual Differences

TBB: In terms of individualized attention, many people speak of home schooling. I have been flooded with letters from people speaking of the advantages of home education, given what we have in the way of schools now. When I'm asked if I think home education is OK for children, I point out some drawbacks, including less chance to socialize. Children learn so much from each other that I would worry about isolating them to that extent socially. The letters I get speak of taking a child out of negative situations in the schools and what a difference this makes in terms of self-image. Many such parents go to a lot of trouble to keep peer groups going and athletics going and so forth among home-schooled children. Such parents stand up for their philosophy and work hard at it.

SIG: We've had some children with special needs whose parents have elected to do home education with my support, and some of these children have just done remarkably when their very thoughtful parents took control. Some hired one-to-one educational help for their child during the day (some were the educators themselves), they were in play groups in the afternoons, and they also were involved in activities, such as dance or music or athletics.

TBB: It can be done. Yet I think it can be a cop-out. I think we need to work on the schools, for not many parents have the means to do all this themselves. Some who try home schooling are likely to be disillusioned parents who feel shut out by our present system.

SIG: The ones I've known were parents who were forced into it because the school wasn't working and they weren't finding decent options. One was a little boy with severe cerebral palsy and language, cognitive, and social challenges. When I first saw this child, he was about four but had no language or motor planning capacities and very few cognitive islands. He was only making a little bit of progress. He had gotten a little more related and a little more purposeful, but he would still come in and the best he could do would be reach out for something or initiate with a motor gesture. There was physical and speech therapy and his parents were trying to do what I call "floor" time at home. But the school program he was in was not working for him. He was self-absorbed for hours in a row during the school day. His parents were justifiably concerned. They had not been able to get the school to tailor a program to his individual differences. They said, "Since this clearly isn't working, what if we try a home program that we can really tailor to him?" I agreed that it would be worth trying. They not only organized a home program but sued the educational system and got it to pay for the one-to-one helpers they needed at home. They put together a program in which the four or five hours that the child was losing at school were now being devoted to one-to-one learning interactions. These were on three levels. One involved following the child's lead and engaging him in back-and-forth communication. The second involved some structured problem-solving learning situations that would motivate new learning and mastery. The third involved motor, sensory, and visual-spatial activities. That child is now very related and purposeful, using words and constructing short sentences, and one can have a dialogue with him. Such children clearly can do better than we expect if we hang in there. But you have to get a program in place. If these children are left to be self-absorbed in big groups or programs that ignore individual differences, nothing will happen or their problems will get worse.

Recommendations

- **At Birth:** During the hospital stay, the newborn should be examined in the presence of the parents, with the Neonatal Behavioral Assessment Scale. Individual differences and developmental level should be explained and plans set in place if early intervention seems necessary.
- **Home Visit:** We recommend that every family be visited at home by a trained developmental nurse specialist, to watch for postpartum depression and parent-child relationships and ability of the parent to tailor care to the baby's individual differences. [See Touchpoints program in Appendixes.]

- **Well-Baby Care:** At the early checkups, attention should be paid to the formation of relationships, as well as assessment of any motor or neurological delays that require help.
- **Preventive Approach:** Early assessments, during which the child's strengths are pointed out to the parents, should be used to spot challenges or delays before they lead to patterns of failure. Recommendations for intervention should come *after* the caregiver has made a working relationship with the parent.
- **Support Services:** Each pediatrician or nurse practitioner caring for infants should be backed up by a team involving all the relevant disciplines concerned with early development. These services should be based on understanding individual differences in both the child and the family.
- **Insurance:** Screening, early assessment, and intervention should be mandated by HMOs and health insurance plans.
- **Education:** Education must build learning around new understanding of individual differences in the way children learn and interact with others and the world. This includes the ways they take in, comprehend, think with, and respond to information.

Class size in preschool, kindergarten, and elementary and high school should make it possible for children to learn at their individual levels and styles, and for teachers to recognize strengths and delays. This would mean no more than 4–6 children per adult in the third year (2-year-olds), 5–7 children per adult in the fourth year, 6–8 children per adult in the fifth year, and 10–12 children per adult in kindergarten. In the rest of elementary school, the class size should not exceed 12–15, and in high school classes should stay at 12–16 children.

Mastery-oriented approaches should replace failure-oriented approaches to the curriculum. Tests should be used to identify what children need to learn and to change the teaching methods for that child, not to blame a child. After-school programs, summer programs, and individual tutoring should be used to help children master the curriculum in a logical stepwise progression. A child should keep retaking a test until he is capable of doing a B or better work on that particular exercise, with the requirement that he or she be provided the help to master the test and move ahead. Some children move ahead more slowly, some more rapidly.

Separation should be made between the fundamentals of reading, writing, and math and subjects that require more discussion and are more content-based and on which children can work more in groups. The fundamentals have to be more individually tailored so that children don't wind up graduating from high school unable to read and do fundamental math. This approach will require small learning groups and lots of individual tutoring.

In addition, the fundamental building blocks of thinking and problem solving should be an explicit focus of education. The curriculum should therefore include work on auditory processing, visual-spatial processing, motor planning and sequencing, and sensory modulation. These building blocks can be worked with in the context of traditional academic subjects such as math, science, reading, English, and writing.

In addition, IQ or other structured tests should not be used as a primary way to categorize or label children. While such tests have a long tradition behind them, they may only measure selected cognitive capacities at a point in time. Furthermore, they don't measure all the critical processing capacities that relate to intellectual functioning and performance on them can be undermined by selective processing deficits such as severe motor planning and sequencing problems. For example, we have clinically observed children with severe motor planning and sequencing problems improve their performance on IQ tests by 30 to fifty percent over a five year period as their motor planning and sequencing improved. IQ-type tests are not nearly as helpful as observing a child learn over time through learning interactions tailored to his or her developmental profile of processing strengths and weaknesses. In fact, labeling a child and treating him as though he is similar to others in his category tends to decrease the likelihood of individualized learning interactions. In contrast, working with a child and constantly attempting to find better and better ways to understand his differences and create dynamic, individualized learning interactions often creates continuing opportunities for growth.

Education must employ dynamic interactive learning approaches that promote conceptual understanding rather than rote memorization. Parents and educators can work together to tailor learning experiences to each child's individual differences. This cooperation can extend to parents' involvement in school governance.

- **Special Education, Children with Special Needs:** A functional developmental, individual-differences approach (for example, the DIR Model) is needed throughout, one in which each child is worked with interactively in the context of his unique nervous system and developmental capacities. Sufficient one-on-one interaction mut be available, espcially for self-absorbed, aimless, or perseverative. These services should never wait until a child is failing. The backup services should be in place early, and the smaller class sizes should allow children to remain in regular classes. Home schooling for children with developmental delays should be an option for motivated parents.

Most recent studies support a functional developmental, individual approach.[17] Yet, many programs in schools and other settings for children with autism are based on an older behavioral model. This model pioneered intensive one-on-one work with an individual child, an important advance at the time. Behavioral approaches, however, attempt to modify surface behaviors without sufficient work on strengthing underlying individual processing differences or family relationships. New research and clinical observations enable us to go beyond this older model and construct intensive individualized approaches that strengthen underlying processing capacities.

Furthermore, the research on behavioral approaches is much more limited than commonly acknowledged by its proponents. The study often cited to support these approaches by Lovaas and collegues[18] was only on 19 children, was not done on a representative population of children with autism (the selection criteria excluded the moderate to severe end of the continuum), and did not measure outcomes most impaired in autism (e.g. the capacity for abstract thinking, such as making inference, using imagination, reading and responding to nonverbal gestures and emotional cues [social reciprocity], constructing novel solutions to problems, and understanding one's own and others' feelings.) It also did not compare its approach with other approaches of equal intensity or use a clinical trial methodology.[19] In selected circumstances, behavioral techniques can be one of a comprehensive approach, but based on current research and clinical practice observations, it should not be in the primary approach.

We are now, therefore, faced with a major national (and international) challenge. In order to provide appropriate care to children with developmental and learning disorders, including autism, we need to convert older, more limited programs to a functional, developmental, individual-difference approach which tailors the program to the child's unique developmental profile of underlying processing differences (rather than attempting to fit the child to a standard program). To help children and families at the earliest possible time, we also need routine screening for developmental, learning, and emotional problems as part of well-baby and child health care and early education. Meeting these challenges will require a major national training and program development effort.

- **Social Service and Legal Systems:** Approaches to problem behaviors, delinquency, and criminal behavior should combine both responsibility and punishment, with rehabilitation programs geared to individual differences. Rehabilitation programs should take into account the different processing capacities of the child and the characteristics of his environment. It should not assume a global inherited tendency toward antisocial delinquent behavior but rather look for such tendencies as involving inclinations such as sensory craving and impulsivity. Attempts should be made to improve family environments that have a hard time providing structure and guidance, empathy, and nurturing behavior.
- **Mental Health:** Therapy must also embrace an individual-difference approach.[20] The temptation to cluster individually different patterns quickly into larger syndromes should be avoided while awaiting more data. The individual profile should be the guide to an intervention program for the child which should include sufficient individual, family, and educational approaches, as well as a consideration of biological intervention. At present, there are often insufficient psychosocial interventions.
- **Educating Parents and Future Parents About Individual Differences and Early Development:** Through public education campaigns and through education in schools about the needs of children, parents should be

made familiar with the concept of individual differences. In this way, parents will be prepared for challenges such as the child who is sensitive to touch and sound or the child who is underreactive, along with many other variations. These expectations would go a long way toward preventing maladaptive patterns and helping each and every child master positive adaptive ways of interacting and learning.

4

The Need for Developmentally Appropriate Experiences

As children grow, they master different developmental stages. Each of these stages provides building blocks for intelligence, morality, emotional health, and academic skills. For example, during one stage children learn to relate to others with compassion and empathy, during another to read social cues, and in another to think imaginatively and logically.

At each stage certain experiences are necessary. To learn to relate to others with compassion requires caregivers who provide nurturing, empathetic interactions. Learning to read social cues requires that caregivers join in interactive play and negotiations. Creative and logical thinking requires that caregivers become partners in pretend play, opinion-oriented discussions, and debates.

As a child negotiates a new developmental stage, he continues to require the types of interactions associated with the prior stages. Because new types of interactions are added to the old ones, by the time a child reaches school age there is a variety of essential experiences he requires to sustain his development. Many parents intuitively sense what these essential experiences are. They also sense which ones their child has mastered and which ones require more emphasis or practice. Some children, for example, require more practice at learning to relate with warmth and trust. They may be more laid back and self-absorbed in the first year and only gradually become more intimate and related in the second year of life. Other children require a little more time to learn imaginative play.

Children master these developmental tasks at very different paces. Hurrying the child through any stage can actually slow him down. The cost is great. A shaky foundation is then built, just as hurrying up the foundation of a house may leave it vulnerable to the first hurricane.

Most early-childhood programs, as well as the recommendations of the National Association for the Education of Young Children, (See Organization list in Appendix) emphasize developmentally appropriate practices. The challenge of making this goal a reality, however, is figuring out the best way to characterize each child's developmental capacities. This is an important question because if we can tailor experiences to the child's most pressing developmental needs we can often help a child overcome challenges as well as promote healthy growth and development. Because motor, cognitive, language, emotional, and social skills can progress at a different rate, we must also look at the level children have reached in each of these areas. If there is a delay in certain skills we can then understand what it may be costing the child.

There are various ways in which the stages of a child's development has been described. One of us (S.I.G.) has outlined six primary stages, or six functional developmental capacities, plus three additional stages that characterize the school years.[1] In these basic capacities the child brings together all his different skills. These functions show the way his mental capacities work together as a team. Cognitive, motor, language, emotional, and social skills act together to help the child learn to deal with his world.

These stages can be described as follows.

Security and the Ability to Look, Listen, and Be Calm

One of the first abilities that all children, and certainly school-age children, need is to be calm and regulated and at the same time interested and engaged in their environment. That means being interested in and attentive to people, things, sights, sounds, smells, movements, and so on.

It's not easy for children to learn how to be calm and regulated and at the same time attentive to an exciting world. Normally, children start learning that task in the early months of life. By three or four months, infants should be focusing on what they touch, see, and hear without losing control. Some babies naturally smile and gurgle, taking in the sights and sounds, sleeping regularly, and eating easily. Other babies—and there are many—have more difficulty. If a child doesn't have this ability at any age, then we need to work with the child. You can't jump over this vital internal milestone.

Relating: The Ability to Feel Warm and Close to Others

The inner security that makes it possible for a child to pay attention also gives the child the capacity to be warm, trusting, and intimate, both with adults and with peers. Normally, we see this ability reaching an early crescendo between 4 and 6 months.[2] An infant studies her parents' faces, cooing and returning their smiles with a special glow of her own as they woo each other and learn about love together. We see it in a 7-year-old, working independently at his desk, who greets his teacher as she approaches him with a beaming grin and proudly shows her his work. We see it in a 12-year-old who strolls over to a group of friends at recess and begins to joke and talk with them, casually draping his arm around one friend's shoulders, playfully punching him in the ribs.

Children who aren't able to relate to people in this warm, trusting manner—children who are aloof, withdrawn, and suspicious, or who expect to be humiliated—become isolated and unable even to hear what someone is saying. They may decide that it's best to be a loner or to treat people as things, hurting others because they don't expect to get what they want. They may also decide that they can rely only on their own thoughts or experiences. Distrustful of others, they effectively march to their own drummer. Lost in their own sensations, feelings, and thoughts, they can become—to some degree—alienated from external reality and the world of logic and objectivity. Such children have a fundamental challenge to meet before they can go on to the next developmental level. The reason is that in the early years or life, most learning—insights, intuitions, and principles—comes from what we learn from relationships. All abstract, intellectual concepts that children will master at later ages are based on concepts they learn in their early relationships.

Intentional Two-Way Communication Without Words

The third basic ability builds on the first two (you must be able to focus on and relate to people before you can communicate with them). From an early age children learn to use and read signals that are expressed not through words, but through behavior, facial expressions, body posture, and the like. Children's ability to communicate unfolds in a sequence of stages starting between about 6 and 18 months of age. At first children communicate only nonverbally, but they can carry on a rich dialogue with smiles, frowns, pointing fingers, squirming, wiggling, gurgling, and crying. By 18 months children are often very good readers of nonverbal cues ("referencing").

Children who can use and understand nonverbal communication comprehend the fundamentals of human interaction and communication much better than children who can't. They tend to be more cooperative and attentive in school. They are able to pick up on unspoken cues and figure out situations that might baffle other children. Children who have a hard time with nonverbal communication are likely to have a hard time in school and with friends because they're still working on learning to read nonverbal cues and figuring out what the other person really means, rather than feeling comfortable enough to focus on their school lessons. The important point to remember here is that this ability to read and respond to nonverbal cues, which a child learns very early in life, plays a continuing part in a child's ability to socialize and to learn during the school years.

Solving Problems and Forming a Sense of Self

During this stage toddlers are learning how the world works. They are now able to recognize patterns and use these in problem solving. A recognition of which actions bring about a desired response in parents leads to a complex series of interactions. Now successful at getting what they want—juice, a toy, or a hug—children of 14–18 months begin to develop a sense of self. A number of cognitive abilities and the budding curiosity on which scientific investigations are built grow from these early emotional experiences of solving problems together with another person.

Emotional Ideas

Next children begin to learn to form mental pictures or images—to form ideas about their wants, their needs, and their emotions. A child who says, "I want that pencil," instead of just grabbing it, is using symbols. We see this capacity when children say, "Give me that" or "I am happy" or "I am sad." They begin to substitute a thought or an idea ("I'm angry!") for an action (kicking or hitting). They not only experience the emotion but are also able to experience the idea of the emotion, which they can then put into words or into make-believe play. They are using an idea, expressed in words, to communicate something about what they want, what they feel, or what they are going to do.

This ability opens a whole new world of challenges: Children can begin to exercise their minds, bodies, and emotions as one. It is crucial for children to have mastered this kind of communication by the time they get to the grade school years so that they can both understand words spoken to them and use words and ideas to express themselves.

Many children (and adults) continue to have difficulties with this ability. They equate feelings or thoughts with action. Children who can't identify their intentions and feelings and who have an action-only approach to life are more apt to use aggression as a way to cope with all challenging situations.

Children naturally learn these emotional labels in their families, through the day-to-day experience of connecting words with what's happening in their interactions and in their bodies. Children learn by hearing others use words to express their emotions in certain contexts, and then when they experience the same emotion or experience, they try the words out. If their efforts are greeted with empathy and are amplified, the connection of that word or concept to the feeling is consolidated.

Emotional Thinking

The next ability involves going beyond just labeling a feeling—children gain the ability to think with these images. Between the ages of 2 $^1/_2$ and 3 $^1/_2$, children take those emotional ideas that they have elevated from the level of behavior to the level of ideas and make connections between different categories of ideas and feelings: "I am angry today because you didn't come and play with me," or "I feel happy because Mommy was nice." If you think about it, this connection embodies a rather sophisticated viewpoint—it means connecting two feelings across time and recognizing that one is causing the other. This ability to build bridges between ideas on an emotional level underlies all future logical thought. More abstract logic and cause-and-effect thinking builds on this fundamental cause-and-effect thinking. In fact, emotional thinking is the foundation for all future thinking.

At this stage, children also link all those ideas that pertain to "me" and all those ideas that pertain to "not me." In this way, they begin to make the distinction between fantasy (things that are inside me) and reality (things that are outside me). They are also able to use this me–not-me distinction to control their impulses and to consider and plan for the future: "If I do something bad to someone else, I may hurt the other person, and I may get punished." In order to succeed in school, children need to be able to understand that actions have consequences—that is, to imagine how their actions today will affect them later—because much of school is geared to the future. Nightly homework assignments don't make much sense to children unless the children realize that the results will be increased knowledge, good grades, praise from their teachers and parents, and a good feeling inside themselves. They need to be able to tolerate frustration, persevere at a task, and anticipate accomplishment.

Triangular Thinking, The Age of Fantasy and Omnipotence

In the first stage of the grade school years, children further develop their abilities to relate, communicate, imagine, and think. In this stage, which tends to run from about 4 1/2 to about 7 years of age, all things are still possible. Selma Fraiberg first described the sense of grandeur and magic at this time.[3] Children have a curiosity about life, a bold expressiveness ("I am the best!"), and a deep sense of wonder about the world.

This stage is commonly called the Oedipal stage: Boys, it is suggested, have romantic fantasies about their mothers and girls about their fathers, and children develop strong rivalries toward the parent of the opposite sex that coexist with loving feelings. This phase ushers in a new type of relationship: the triangular relationship. Mother and father no longer easily substitute for each other, as they could when the child was younger, when the basic needs were security and trust.

Having three people in a system gives a child greater emotional flexibility. The child doesn't have to look at the relationship with each parent as an all-or-nothing situation. A triangle is an efficient system of emotional checks and balances, allowing children to work out complicated feelings without volatile outbursts. All sorts of rivalries and intrigues are played out.

At the same time, these years when "the world is my oyster" can be a time of great fearfulness. Children's sense of grandeur and rich fantasy life constitute a double-edged sword. They are easily frightened by their own power. They may fear witches under their bed and ghosts and crooks who are going to come in and kidnap them. They want to hop into Mommy and Daddy's bed to be protected.

If all has gone well, children emerge from this stage with certain capacities: Their grasp of reality begins to get firmer, though they still have an active fantasy life and a degree of grandiose omnipotence. They are able to grasp more complicated relationships and, in this way, become more emotionally stable. They begin to develop a capacity for more "adult" emotions, such as guilt or empathy (although empathy is easily lost when they are feeling jealous or competitive). They can experience a wider range of emotions and emotional dramas—revolving around dependency, rivalry, anger, and love, for example. All of these abilities equip children to move out from their families and into the wider world.

The Age of Peers and Politics

As children move through their seventh and eighth years, their horizons expand. Their world is other kids. They begin to move from the family-oriented stage of development and enter the multifaceted world of their peers, moving into the politics of the playground.

Children now define themselves more by how they fit in with their classmates. Their self-image begins to be defined, in part, by the pecking order that prevails on the playground. In everything from athletic ability to popularity, appearance, brains, and clothes, children rank themselves against others.

Children get big benefits from defining themselves as group members. For example, they gain an enormous ability for complex thinking. To negotiate the intricacies of multiple relationships within a group, they have to learn to reason on a very sophisticated level. They learn, "Nora might want to play with Emily, not because she hates me or because I'm a turkey, but because Emily is her best friend today, and I'm her second-best friend today, and Joey is her third-best friend. But that could change, especially if I invite Nora over to my house a few times and let her play with the new toys I got for my birthday."

This ability to diagnose group dynamics helps children to develop cognitive and social skills that will be very valuable in school—and beyond school, in the real world. They learn that most of life operates in shades of gray, not in all-or-nothing extremes.

Sizing up these subtle shades of gray requires understanding that feelings and relationships can exist in relative terms. A child begins to learn that "I can be a little mad one day, a lot mad the next day, and furious on still another day."

At this age, competition can be very intense. Games are taken very seriously ("You cheated, and I know it!"). Children may be intolerant of anyone (other than themselves) changing the rules, and they may take a loss personally. At this stage of life, humiliation, loss of respect, and disapproval may be a child's worst fears.

An Inner Sense of Self

From about the ages of 10–12 children begin to develop a more consistent sense of who they are. They are gradually more able to develop an inner picture of themselves based on their emerging goals and values, and on who they feel they are as people, rather than on how other people treat them from day to day. However, they may feel caught between their childhood longings for closeness and dependency and their desire to grow up and be teenagers and young adults. Sometimes they are defiant—"Who needs you?" or "I know better than you!" At other times, they are fearful of their independence—"I don't want to go to school. I just want to stay home!"

They can now hold onto two realities at once: their peer group reality and their emerging inner reality of values and attitudes (e.g., "I want to be a teacher someday").

These stages don't conclude the road map, of course. They take us only through the grade school years. During adolescence children continue this process of learning how to negotiate even more complex inner and outer worlds. But once children have mastered these basic abilities, they have the foundation for negotiating, with the help of family, teachers, and friends, many of the specific challenges and dramas that life presents.

We tend to focus on many isolated skills in the motor, language, or academic areas. Because these basic capacities, however, have the building blocks of the more integrated capacities for intelligence and emotional health, we believe they should be used by parents, pediatricians, and educators to follow and understand a child's growth. They can be used together with the Touchpoints model. For practical application they can be put in the form of a growth curve. (See Appendix.)

Paying attention to developmental levels and the experiences required for each level has far more than just academic value. It helps us understand where children are or what kind of experiences they require. It tells us how to balance a child's life and what kinds of experiences to make available to the child for healthy growth and development. (See Touchpoints guidelines and Developmental Growth Curve in Appendix.)

For example, do we have preschoolers doing imaginative play or sitting in front of the computer learning preacademic skills? One can argue that imaginative play is healthy for the emotional development, but that playing with the computer and learning spelling and reading will be better for academic and intellectual development. Understanding the experiences children need to master the different developmental levels, however, tells us that this argument is simply untrue. Imaginative play, coupled with long discussions, debates, and opinion-oriented conversations (where we ask children what they think and challenge them with "why" questions), is far more important than computer-based educational programs, which work more on rote memory skills or on very structured types of academic capacities. This is not to suggest that 20 or 30 minutes of academic-oriented computer games may not be helpful, but it does suggest that the bulk of the day should be spent in dynamic learning interactions.

Helping a child through these stages and fostering these core capacities requires a great deal of adult time and energy, lots of time down on the floor interacting with the child. This can't be done in 15 minutes a day or by a tired parent who simply wants to put his feet up and watch the evening news. This requires an energetic parent who can truly enjoy his toddler or preschooler and her emerging capacities.

Similarly, when the child moves through preschool into the school years, we need to engage in new types of interactions involving higher levels of creating and logically connecting and reflecting on ideas. There is so much at stake (i.e., feeling cared for and secure; developing the capacity for reflective, comparative, gray area thinking; applying these capacities to relationships with peers and academic work). A pattern of TV and homework simply won't work because although the child may temporarily do OK in school, he won't be mastering these fundamental skills. Each day needs to be balanced. There should be one-to-one play dates at least three to four times a week. There also need to be set times when parents follow the child's interests and they play together. When homework begins, a new opportunity opens for parent participation and discussion. Even negotiations over chores and doing housework together can involve lively interaction and problem solving.

To maintain this level of participation and involvement requires parental availability during most of the evening hours, for homework, mealtimes, and play, as well as discussions eliciting a child's emerging reflective skills (comparing friends, understanding materials and books that are being read). In short, the school years require a balance between peers, family time, activities, and schoolwork. When a child is spending inordinate amounts of time, for example, on homework just to keep up, it may not be in that child's best interest. Negotiations with the school may be needed. If the child needs to go at a slightly slower rate in order to keep a balance in his life and master fundamental thinking and peer skills, then academic progress may have to occur a little more slowly, with perhaps part of the summer being spent on some of the academic work.

This balancing of daily experience includes such basics as limiting computer and TV time which not only don't provide human interaction, but can overload a child's nervous system. Time with friends is a very important developmental experience for preschoolers and grade school children, as well as adolescents. Peer play helps a child's learning about relationships and involves advanced reflective skills to negotiate the complexities that come up in peer relationships. Developmentally appropriate experiences also involve family activities. These can be games in which children team up with Mommy and Daddy, or constructive family discussions about rules, or starting a vegetable garden, or planning a trip.

Siblings are more likely to play together when they each feel nurtured and secure and valued by their parents so that they don't have to compete for the needs of life. Then they can compete for the joy of competition itself, that is, to show mastery, rather than competing to be loved or valued. This playful kind of competition breeds a healthy sense of assertiveness that will play out in schoolwork, sports, or a career.

As we said, all the experiences we have discussed require significant parental time. One of us (T.B.B.) has often described the importance of the hour when the parents first return from work.[4] Parents need to save some energy for the return home. They need to be prepared for everyone to fall apart when they return. Children save up their protests and unhappy feelings until they are safe, while parents can gather the children to sit in a big rocking chair, "How was your day?" "Ugh." "Mine was, too. I missed you all day." Before starting dinner or any other task, parents and children need a lazy, relaxed time just reporting on the day and being together. Then, when everyone is close again, parents and children can work together in the kitchen. Children are often grateful to feel part of the solution.

For school-aged children, from about 6:00 P.M. on, both parents need to be fully available. In most families, there will be a seamless flow between homework, play activities, dinner, and even a little bit of TV and computer time. Parents can keep their eye on the general balance and make sure it's a healthy one.

This flow should occur in a rhythm that suits the needs of the family members. Children will generally orchestrate this rhythm if their parents are available (if Mom isn't hiding behind her Internet searches or Dad isn't too busy catching up on telephone calls). Being available (and kids sense parental availability) leads children to come and seek out their parents for play, advice, and help with homework.

In families, however, where one or both parents are getting home by 7:00, 7:30, 8:00, or later (rather than starting the family time at 6:00), a hurried, stressed atmosphere is created. If Mother comes home early and is then home alone with the kids, as happens in some families (in others, it's fathers who get home first), that parent feels stressed and overloaded by the needs of the children, who are invariably squabbling with each other and feeling overwhelmed. When both parents come home promptly together, a much different atmosphere is created. The two can make a wonderful team.

Many parents feel such a schedule is unrealistic. Some feel they can't afford to put food on the table or a roof over their children's heads if they are home by 6:00 or 6:30. In some cases this is true; in some it is a matter of priorities. Often, the late night or weekend time can be used so that parents can work the same number of hours without taking away from the vital 6:00 to 9:30 time required for family life.

For preschool- and school-aged children a parent or a very stable caregiver (a grandmother, aunt, or live-in nanny, for example) should be available to the children in the late afternoon. Being at school all day and then in extended school programs until 6:00 is not developmentally appropriate for most children this age. A two-hour after-school program from 2:00 to 4:00 or 3:00 to 5:00 where children can play with peers and be involved in organized clubs or other activities can work for school-aged children. Hawaii has a program (Five–0) in which the state subsidizes all after-school programs. By late afternoon, however, children need time with their parents in relaxed family life.

Discussion

SIG: What are typical, every-day experiences in the child's life? Are we substituting virtual experiences over real experiences or overscheduling kids with team sports rather than just going out in the backyard and throwing the ball together?

TBB: This is especially true for the wealthier children. Every hour may be programmed. There has to be a whole part of the child's life when the adult isn't trying to make him a better learner. He needs to relate to his peers.

SIG: When I was a kid we would go out to the playground across the street and we would choose up sides and make up our own games. Now you have coaches telling the kids what to do and everything is scheduled. It's a very different family who goes out in the backyard and makes up its own games and its own rules. At younger ages, it's much more creative and more fun than team sports. We need to raise questions about what children lose by not just hanging around with each other and getting their feet wet in the brook and making up their own games. So often, watching TV replaces playing cops and robbers out behind the house.

TBB: We need to look at how a child actually spends the day.

SIG: Say they are in school until 2: 30 or 3: 00. When they get home they have a snack and the parents insist that they hit the homework. They don't go out and play, they don't go out and build a tree house. At 4: 30 or 5: 00 they may have soccer practice or ballet class, often with a lot of driving in between, then dinner, a little more homework, and then go to sleep. That's their day. If there is time left over, it's usually TV. There is very little time in that for just hanging out with a friend around the block. What do we think about that? Given the nature of the nervous system . . .

TBB: There's a price to be paid. A child loses the spontaneity by not having a chance to try out his ideas in play. So much is learned from modeling on peers, from testing the limits, from finding out how to share.

SIG: With the families I see, I often say, "When Johnny and Susie come home from school, they need to go out and play for at least an hour." I insist that kids have four or more play dates a week. Susie comes home from school and finds some children in the neighborhood or has a friend over or goes to a friend's house to play for an hour or two. Start the homework at 5: 00. If there's soccer practice, let a child get together with another one before soccer practice for a half hour or 45 minutes just to hang around together. Most of the kids don't have a chance to learn about peer relating, as you said. Getting along with other children is a skill that has its own processes. In order to be able to deal with competition and rejection, both of which are a part of peer relating, children need many hours together. Without a chance to experience humiliation and teasing, a person is handicapped in adult relationships. If you don't log the hours, then you're not going to pick up these skills.

TBB: Children need a whole variety of experiences. They need time with peers, with computers, with family, and hours of just plain doing what they want to do. But I guess we have to program play into their lives since that seems to be our way of life.

Hanging Out Together

SIG: Kids and parents need unstructured time together, too, particularly in those formative years when the parents might be either at work or busy helping the children with their homework. But they need this unstructured time in the adolescent years and even after the adolescent years. Families need "hang-out times," not doing homework or structured activities.

TBB: We need to make room for an hour here and there when the kid doesn't have to do anything. I also recommend a date with each parent. Just one-to-one, time to be together. Each child needs this. Ellen Galinsky of the Families and Work Institute interviewed children of working parents. They all agreed that it was necessary for their parents to work. What they missed most (unless it was available) was "hanging out time" with a busy parent. Not "special time," just "hanging out" together.[5]

SIG: Yes, all kids in the elementary years need time to call a friend and chat, and also to hang out with Mom or Dad just shooting the breeze. These are times you remember as nice moments, because you are reaching each other.

TBB: I recommend that working parents come in the house and not do a single thing but sit down with the kids and say, "How was the day?" After a while, the kids will get all itchy and ready to move around, and you can taken them into the kitchen and let them help you as you get dinner. Children who help out in a busy family feel that they are contributing and needed.

Limits on TV and Computer Games

SIG: This takes us back to the earlier topic of protection and safety: There's a need to protect children from overuse of TV and computer games. These times together often never happen because the TV is on. When people worry about TV, the focus is on content, which is a problem, but the greater insult is the passivity. The great danger in terms of TV is the lack of two-way interaction. Children miss out on the give-and-take that mobilizes the central nervous system into integrated pathways and leads to growth. When this deprivation is combined with violence on TV, you've got a double whammy. You've got people in an almost hypnotic state being barraged by negative images. When you've got kids outside playing good guys and bad guys, that's OK because they're working it out and thinking about justice and injustice. They're working on the themes of life, which is very different from being passive and absorbing the images on TV.

TBB: We've studied what happens to three-year-olds when they sit in front of the TV and found how exhausted they are emotionally and autonomically. After 30 minutes of TV, they come away just zapped out. We did some heart rate and respiration tests on children and showed the effect on the cortex. The child was stimulated at first, then habituated. Once you stopped the habituation process, the child "exploded" and got into a discharge mode of motor and autonomic activity. Habituation is a way the brain protects the child from getting overloaded.

Do you remember Skinner boxes?[6] Parents would tell me that when their children were in them, they slept like logs and when they came out, they were climbing the walls. At the time, I saw that it was an effect of the homeostatic system. We saw the same thing with children in front of TV, testing their heart rates and respirations. They got into this hypnotic state and their EEGs [electroencephalograms] flattened out. When they came away from the TV, everything went crazy. To me, it was an example of the cost of these artificial situations.

SIG: If you didn't watch them post-TV but just measured their physiological functioning while they were watching, you might have thought they were in a resting, in-and-out state. It didn't look like an unstimulated state.

TBB: I always thought of it as an active, protective process. The heartbeat slowed down and got regular. There was no variability. The respiration slowed down and got regular, too, with no variability, in spite of the barrage of stuff coming in from the TV. Then the EEGs began to look like sleep.

SIG: That lack of variability was a sign of stress in the system. When I watch TV late at night, I find it hard to get back to work. I feel tired and don't have any energy left. Eventually, I get back to work, but it takes a lot of doing to get out of that passive mode. If I could avoid having to take the TV break, doing something else to relax, it would be much easier to come back. There seems to be something relaxing about not having to do anything, but it's a hard physiological state to break out of and reintegrate.

TBB: Do we want to put a limit on TV? I would say for school-aged children an hour a day during the week is plenty and two hours on the weekend. Let the child help you make the decision about which programs, but the parent is still in control. We should see TV as one of the biggest competitors for our children's hearts and minds. We should take it seriously.

SIG: An hour a day is realistic. But if we are talking about an ideal amount, I would try to reduce TV to a half hour a day during the school week and an hour a day or maybe two hours on the weekends. What often happens is that parents come home and put on the TV and watch the news and then the family watch TV together. It's very addictive.

TBB: There are other media with the same effect, like computer games.

SIG: Children, if they don't have something else to do, can sit there for four hours playing computer games. They are kind of mindless, repetitive games. Many kids will prefer more interactive play if given the opportunity. We videotaped kids playing computer games and old-fashioned games like cards. With computer games, there was very little emotional expression or interaction. With the card games, the kids came alive. They laughed and talked and problem-solved. So much more was happening.

TBB: But I've seen learning-disabled kids just come alive incredibly while playing these computer games.

SIG: Yes, we have programs we use with kids who have developmental problems, some speech and language programs or math programs. These involve computer games. They are OK, but even there if the kids spend hours a day doing them, the kids become perseverative and more self-absorbed. If the children do it for half an hour and then get a lot of interaction, it's fine and can be helpful.

TBB: Computer-assisted techniques are fabulous with some of these kids. But when you overdo them, then you've lost the benefit. So each of these things—TV, computer games—needs to be assessed for its effect.

Homework

SIG: While we are trying to make room for play and hanging out, we have to think about homework. Some kids sit down and spending four hours at it. Because the child can't stand sitting there for hours, he is getting up every 10 minutes, so two hours of homework becomes four hours of homework, and the whole afternoon or evening or Saturday is spent with the parent forcing the child to sit there and try to do his homework. He is not getting peer play, learning about nature, drawing, or building.

TBB: I don't really like directing kids what to do with their time. I want to get away from that. I like your idea of developing different areas of a child's life. Homework, I think, ought to be decided between parents and child. We have shoved parents away from being involved in our educational system and I think it is a big mistake. If there really is something the child ought to achieve at home rather than at school, then it really demands the whole family's participation.

SIG: I find that many families do that already.

TBB: Yes, but it certainly would helpful if the goal for homework were family participation. We might look at homework as an activity for the child and family to do together.

SIG: OK, let's say we take that as a basic principle, but for different ages and grades would you give some general guidelines? Should six year olds be spending a lot of time on homework? Shouldn't they be out with their friends? How much homework?

TBB: Not much, I would think. I don't know enough about levels of work in each class, but the fourth grade is when children begin to get more into symbolic thought and into reading well on their own. Certainly they can handle assignments independently then. Homework for learning could be instituted then. Before that, the goal might be involving the parent.

SIG: In first grade they are learning to read and do simple math—adding and subtracting. By second grade, they are beginning to do double-digit adding and subtracting and simple multiplication, and they are doing whole stories. A little extra practice might be appropriate.

TBB: Yes, it would be fun for children to participate with their families in things like this. It needn't be mandatory, but it's a chance for the parents to keep up with what the child is learning and where she is and for the child to show off to her parents. A little bit of practice, a half hour or so, would be good.

SIG: Most schools keep homework pretty light in the first and second grade and don't overdo it, but when you get to the third grade, there's a transition, and when you get into the fourth, it picks up and keeps growing into junior and senior high. For the fourth, fifth, and sixth grades—we are now talking about your 9-, 10-, and 11-year-olds—what's too much?

TBB: Anything over two hours. I think by high school that a child can get engrossed in what he or she is doing and then three hours would be OK.

SIG: So we might say two hours maximum from fourth through junior high and then two to three hours in high school. I think that third hour should be on a task the student is really interested in, as opposed to being forced to do something he may not care about. Two hours is plenty of time for required homework, especially after six hours in school.

TBB: The same amount of homework will not take the same amount of time for all children.

SIG: Yes, of course, the fast kid can get a lot more done in that two hours and another kid takes longer. But once you begin having any kid doing four or five hours of homework, the question is: What is it costing in the other areas of the child's development? You are teaching the class how to write an essay, but the slow child takes all afternoon and evening. He can't play with his peers, so he's not learning about relationships. He won't have the experiences he needs to eventually write a thoughtful essay or creative story.

TBB: So where does that leave us?

SIG: Well, the kids with special academic needs or learning disabilities may need extra work and extra practice in certain areas, but if that means a third or fourth hour every day, you may be asking them to pay a price that will rob them of too many other opportunities. What I suggest is that the kids who need extra help should have it in school as one-to-one help and then spend some extra time on weekends.

TBB: There's where the parents' coming in might take up the slack. Parents and the child working together for two hours in the afternoon or evening ought to be enough.

SIG: It would also help if instead of giving everyone 20 math problems, let's say for a fifth grader, the teacher gives 30 math problems, but 15 are optional. One kid does those 30 math problems in an hour and maybe the slower child does only 15 of the problems. I often suggest to parents, "Talk to your teacher and ask that Johnny be given credit for doing 15 problems, a few from each category so he gets the hang of it. If he needs more work to learn the stuff, not just to repeat himself, he can do it on the weekends." The teachers are often in agreement when parents go in and talk to them. I've seen cases where children are doing a painful third or fourth hour of work and have no time with friends and are hating it and becoming negative and resistant. This brings family conflict and the price is very high.

TBB: Maybe there needs to be a caveat that if the child needs more than two hours with parents' help, then it's time to ask for special dispensation or remedial help. Parents and teachers should see this as a sign, a touchpoint, in the sense that they need to look into what is happening for that child.

SIG: So many kids with motor planning problems are very good in terms of understanding the concepts, but they are very slow; it takes them five minutes to write a sentence out, as opposed to two minutes. Less, but well-designed, homework works for them. In school, for kids who are slow but bright and conceptually sophisticated, untimed tests can work very well. Instead of being robbed of a chance to show what they know, they are given time. After all, speed is not what we are testing;

we are testing knowledge. The teachers need to get away from the idea that they have to make it the same for everyone. There needs to be more flexibility and caring.

TBB: The same applies to parent participation. This can be very different at different ages. At some point it becomes intrusive or undermines initiative. Children need a chance to experiment, even to fail.

SIG: Regarding participation in high-school homework, some parents copyedit a little or a lot. Some may write the whole essay for the child, but I think that's rare. From my own experience with three children and all their buddies, I see a whole spectrum of help. Sometimes there is a minimum of help, like "Oh, you missed a comma here," or "My grammar is crummy. I need you to read it over." Some parents may say, "What do you mean here? I don't understand this paragraph." But I've seen times when it's midnight and the kid wants to go to sleep and says, "I still can't write this introduction. How would you write it, Mom?" Mom says, "Well, you could say it this way if you wanted to."

TBB: At that point, the child doesn't own the work. As I mentioned earlier, Asian parents have shown us what it means to be involved in a child's education. Much of what we blame on our school system is due to the fact that the parents are not motivated to be involved. If we are to give children varied experiences and freedom to explore, parents have to be involved in planning. It's a tricky balance, supporting kids without taking over for them.

Grades

TBB: In addition to recognizing and working with each child's developmental capacities and individual differences, here, too, we need a model built on strengths rather than failures. We've seen the Rosenthal effect.[7] You get what you expect when you label people so there's every reason to have a more optimistic, rather than a resigned approach, which passes on an expectation for failure to the people you are serving.

SIG: We have to begin with the assumption that every child can learn. There is no excuse for every child not being able to do the fundamentals. The key is the concept of developmentally appropriate experiences coupled with attention to individual differences. Developmentally appropriate means reaching the child where he is, not two steps ahead or behind. Each child has to build from his current level. Often, however, we are ahead of a child and he doesn't get the fundamentals. Taking it one step further, would you go so far as to say that the way we assess kids, in terms of testing at school, feeds into the failure model? In other words, kids get graded to figure out what they know and also what they don't know, and that is the grade that is fastened to them. Can we use testing in a different way? In other words, say you take the test once and you get an F. What if there is some accountability on the part of the teacher, and you don't stop there? If you get an F, you take it again and again and again, and so on, until you get a B or better grade, which means you know the work. If you get a C, you really don't know the work. If you get a B or better, you may have made a silly mistake, but you know the work. You keep working, but you work on it in a stepwise way, beginning where you are and working up the ladder one step at a time, not skipping steps to look good. There can be extra lessons after school and one-to-one time with a tutor or whatever. You won't fail, because you have the chance to build gradually with extra help and work.

TBB: What happens when it's April and Johnny is still taking Test One?

SIG: Then we aren't finding his level and building gradually. What's our goal? Is it to spread these kids out on a bell curve and judge them, or is our goal to get everyone to do B-level work? Shouldn't we change the whole way we grade kids?

TBB: It's true that grades, at present, are just labels, largely negative labels. If, on the other hand, we do what you've been doing with autistic children—look at the process rather than the grade—then I think we might break into the cycle of failure.

With young children, I would look at the process, the level they are at in each of the different compartments of their learning. In reading, for example, where are they? Are they at the point of just recognizing letters and sounds or are they really understanding what they are reading and can they analyze the work or look ahead or behind, and so on?

SIG: Let's say that on a 10-point scale you have a fifth-grader who is at Level 8 in reading, which means he can read and interpret and discuss concepts and other experiences, but he is not quite at Level 10, which means full comprehension and the ability to extrapolate. Another kid is at Level 5. Would you grade them accordingly, saying that one gets an 8 score and one gets a 5 score or just give each a verbal description of what he or she can do?

TBB: This is what a lot of private elementary schools do. A report says your son or daughter is at this level of comprehension and facility and so forth. But eventually you get grades or the child says, "I'm fifth in my class." It is interesting to ask a child, "Who is the smartest? Who is the next smartest?" They will tell you where they fit and even say, "Here I am right here."

SIG: Yes, the kids all know and they know better than the teachers, often.

TBB: So, by avoiding grades, you're not hiding anything?

SIG: But kids' ranking is different. What is interesting is that kids make their determinations of the pecking order based on abilities, not grades. Teachers do it on performance and the kids know better. The kids may see that someone who is smarter may not do well on a particular test. The kids always know who is really smart in different areas.

TBB: So grades really are not necessary.

SIG: But the schools will say, "Well, that's fine for grade school. We can just describe the kids and we don't have to give them letter grades. But in high school, these kids need records for college. What do we do when it gets serious like that? What system would you recommend?"

TBB: I would still be looking for an incentive system rather than a labeling system, and I'm not sure how that plays itself out. If there's enough motivation and the kids want to go to college and want to master all their subjects, maybe the labeling system works for them. I would look earlier into what we can do at the start. Earlier, I think a process approach gives children, as well as parents and teachers, insights into how the children might be learning. Requiring a breakdown of skills and strengths would demand that teachers really pay attention to their students. That would be the real value of the process approach. For instance, a teacher might say, "So-and-So learns by thinking things out at a quantitative level rather than a qualitative level. I would like to bring him around to more qualitative thinking, too, but at present he is so locked into measuring the world that I haven't been able to do that."

SIG: This is more child-directed than the current system, but not child-directed in the extreme sense. You are focusing your educational intervention and challenges on where children are in each area, on their level of understanding of the phenomenon you are trying to teach. So that means teaching that is developmental-level- and individual-difference-oriented, but not child-directed in the sense that the child gets to dart to the playground or the block corner when you want to work on reading skills. Teaching can be developmentally oriented because the child's interests are taken into account, without its being child-directed strictly in the sense of following the child's lead.

TBB: The second you begin to understand the child, the child knows it and begins to look at you to reflect the struggles he is aware of going through.

SIG: I think we need to learn more and spell out this process orientation, just as you are suggesting. An understanding of the building blocks of a particular skill needs to be part of the educators' training. Math skills progress in a certain sequence. Many educators understand the building blocks of where they are going in math and science skills. I think teaching is moving in that direction, so that if you are interested in history, you learn to think from a historical frame of reference. You can move backward from what you expect your 12th-grader to be able to do to understand history to what it really means to understand history. What are the steps, the building blocks, from a 1st-grade level to a 12-grade level? Once you have these steps defined, you can then say where a child is on this road. Same thing with math. What does it mean to be a mathematical thinker, to understand adding, subtracting, dividing, and multiplying? Where is the child in all this? Once educators do it that way, they understand a child better and understand what that child needs.

TBB: In looking at these building blocks, I'm out of my expertise. But I would look for two things: (1) an individuated approach, that is, looking at the effort that goes into mastering those building blocks and how much this is costing the child and (2) an attempt to work with the individual temperament of each child. If teachers would take these two things into account in their understanding of each child, they would have a much better chance to maintain positive expectations and not get bogged down in failure. Actually, I would be surprised if many teachers weren't eager for this approach.

The Mastery Model

SIG: The whole concept of process and building blocks is a positive model.

TBB: Yes, I think this approach applies very broadly. When kids hit a snag in some course—geometry, say—instead of just seeing it as a failure, you can look at it as a challenge to all the energies of the child. Using our Touchpoints model, when there is a regression or difficulty, it can be seen as a time to reorganize: "OK, this child is having trouble with geometry. What is this costing him in other cognitive areas? What is it costing him in peer relationship?" A teacher can use each of these vulnerable times as a chance to reevaluate the pressures on the child and a chance to reach the girl or boy as well as the parents and really connect. This can be an economical approach, too. You don't have to do this all year long because you do pick up on the times when a child seems in trouble. This doesn't necessarily mean remedial help or therapy or anything like that. When a child has difficulty with a course is a time to connect with the family. Given the kind of backup we spoke about earlier, a teacher might identify problems she probably wouldn't notice before and help the child before failure is locked in.

SIG: Exactly. A difficulty with geometry, to keep to that example, may reveal a difficulty in a basic skill, say, abstract or spatial thinking. So often it reveals not just difficulty with geometry, but something more significant. Perhaps practicing certain kinds of exercises can help. I've seen a lot of these kids with "math blocks" in second grade. They seem to lack a very basic feel for quantity. In working with them, we go back to the beginning and get them negotiating for cookies and coins or pieces of pizza. We say, "How much do you want?" and they can't show you. The basic sense of quantity is lacking. So we go back to just establishing quantity concepts visually, motorically, and spatially. We start by keeping the numbers small. We cut the pizza pie in six pieces: "OK, he gets two pieces of pizza and she gets three. How many are they going to eat altogether?" The kid has the pizza in front of him and he can see two plus three. He still has to count, because he can't do it. Then we have him close his eyes: "OK, now can you close your eyes and picture the pizza pie pieces? She gets two and he gets three. How many does that make altogether? Do it with your eyes closed and picture the pizza. Don't touch the pizza." When he can finally close his eyes and picture the pieces of pizza, then we know he has the concept. We work on adding and subtracting, multiplying and dividing, and fractions, all under six to keep the numbers small. We don't get them to memorize it but have them picture the quantities.

We use emotionally meaningful stimuli, like pizza or candy or coins. When they go back to math class, they feel more confident and often do very well with their math.

TBB: So that's the therapy for this!

SIG: The children weren't mastering math because they hadn't mastered a fundamental sense of quantity. By identifying that problem and working on it, you get a child back on track. Whether the child had missed this building block for central nervous system reasons or lack of experience or both, it was going to cause problems. This is a very different approach from just trying to teach each skill at a certain grade level and letting a child fail.

TBB: This is just what we do in our Touchpoints model of early intervention; we get back on the level of the child and the parents and work from there.

SIG: Yes, the approach works at every level. When a teacher tests a child to see if she knows 10 facts, that's a failure model. But if the teacher looks to see where the child is in her capacity to think historically, he is using a mastery model. This would be a profound difference. Education is going in this direction, but the only schools that are doing it now are private schools, usually for very bright kids. The irony is that all children need it, not just ones who are gifted in certain subjects. Many children figure out the challenges at each level, even if their school is not perfect. But other kids need this process orientation. The student with challenges especially needs it. The need and the reality in our system are reversed. Gifted children in small classes in private school or in an honors class often receive instruction tailored to their level of understanding, whereas children with challenges, including poverty, get more rote learning in very large classes. Much of the testing and labeling there is failure-oriented.

Recommendations

1. **Family.** Family experiences should provide the full range of developmentally appropriate experiences for a child of a certain age. This includes reaching the child at his level and working up the developmental ladder. For children of all ages, no more than a third of the child's waking hours (after-school, peer-play, and other scheduled activities) should be involved in independent activity, with two-thirds saved

for family involvement. These two-thirds should be divided up between facilitating the child's understanding and mastery of his world and direct interactive play and conversation. For infants and toddlers, at least four 20-minute (or more) sessions each day should be reserved for direct inter active play, activities, and conversations; for preschoolers, at least three; and for school-aged children, at least two. Children benefit from the involvement of each parent, each day, for this type of interaction. Some of the principles involved in making this developmental approach work include:

- Each child needs time with parents each day that is spent in activities that appeal to the child at his or her level. This could be pretend play with a younger child, or games and activities with an older child, or just a good talk with a teenager or older school-aged child. These warm, nurturing times, following the child's lead, provide a basis for the continuing security that all children require and also maintain the trust that will be needed at times when the going gets rough.

- From ages 3 $1/2$ to 4 on up through the grade school and adolescent years, all children require opportunities to talk with their parents about school, friends, and challenges, as well as to anticipate the challenges of tomorrow. Anticipatory problem solving involves discussions where parents and children together try to imagine or even visualize the challenges of tomorrow and imagine how they will feel in those situations, what one typically does in that challenging situation, and what alternatives might be considered.

- In discussions with children, it is important to empathize with the child's perspective, even when one disagrees. Whether in a play where the character is angry, or is in a vehement discussion about wanting to stay up later, or wanting to avoid a certain homework assignment—the parent should let the child know he's understood and find experiences of her own to show understanding before they problem-solve together toward a better solution.

- Whether they are mastering a math concept or learning to do chores around the house or learning to share toys, the challenges that adults negotiate with children need to be arranged in such a way that there are small steps, each one associated with mastery. Children will generally work hard where they feel a sense of satisfaction.

- All of the above means family time characterized by lots of parental availability. Parents need to be available to help with homework or hobbies, and to be involved in direct one-to-one conversations or play with children. For infants and young children, we have offered guidelines in Chapter 1. Preschool- and school-aged children need an adult at home when they return from school. All families of children through high school need regular time together from 6: 00 P.M. through the evening.

2. **Peer Play.** Children need time to play with friends outside school or formal activities four times a week or more to provide the complex processes of thinking and socializing that only such play can offer. Each child also needs unstructured time to explore and play with peers, siblings, or parents, as well as on their own without direction from adults.

3. **Homework.** Work brought home from school needs to be seen as just one of the experiences that promote intellectual and social growth. If homework begins to fill up all the time after school, it may compete with other experiences that are necessary for healthy growth and development. Conversations with parents and working out complicated relationships among peers are important sources of intellectual achievement, as is learning math facts or reading a book. The following guidelines for educators and parents are suggested.

- The involvement of parents in encouraging and facilitating homework should be welcomed.
- For children during the later preschool years through kindergarten, there should be no homework.
- For children in first and second grade, no more than an hour a day.
- For children in third and fourth grade, no more than 1 to 1 $^1/_2$ hours per day.
- For fifth and sixth grade, no more than 1 $^1/_2$ hours per day.

- For seventh and eighth grade, no more than 2 hours per day.
- For 9th through 12th grade, on average, no more than two hours per day except for special projects or papers, or before finals.

4. **Understanding and Following Children's Changing Developmental Needs.** Just as we follow children's physical growth (e.g., height and weight), parents, pediatricians, and educators should monitor the stages of intellectual and emotional growth to identify strengths, as well as needs for additional developmentally appropriate experiences. (See Appendix for the Touchpoints guidelines and the Functional Developmental Growth Chart.)

5. **School.** Making developmentally appropriate experiences available to children has profound implications for their education. Intelligence and cognitive skills develop from these experiences, which provide the building blocks of thinking and learning. Fact- and memory-based learning is not the same as learning how to think about and understand the world. Educational approaches that are truly developmentally appropriate are more likely under the following circumstances:

- **Small classes** (for recommended sizes see chapter 3.)
- A dynamic, interactive problem-solving curriculum focused on the child's **individual developmental profile**.
- **After-school programs and innovative programs in school** for children who require specific help, such as the need for a nurturing adult figure (e.g., mentoring programs for after school as well as being with the same teacher during the first six years of life), or tutorial help in subjects that are causing difficulty.
- **Extracurricular opportunities** for children who are interested in participating in sports, interscholastic debates and math competitions, drama, art, music, and so on. These should have various levels and be open to all children.
- **Grades** should be replaced, at least in elementary schools, and ideally through high school, with reports

that identify the child's level of understanding and grasp of basic skills in each subject.

- **Tracking** should be done only skill by skill, or subject by subject. Tracking and ability grouping on a classwide basis should be avoided.
- **Teacher training** should give more focus to breaking down the skills or type of thinking required in each subject rather than factual learning.
- There should be an **emphasis on mastery**. Failure to achieve a skill should not result in a permanent grade or label but instead should be used as a window to identify the level the child is at and the levels that need to be mastered as well as the difficulties (such as auditory or visual processing), which can be overcome with targeted help.

6. **TV and Computer Time.** Developmentally appropriate experiences also means limits on inappropriate experiences, such as excessive TV and computer programs. Parents must set limits on these activities. Therefore, computer time not being used for schoolwork and TV time should be limited to a total of one hour per day and two hours during the day on weekends. TV and computer time should come only if there is time *after* homework, peer play, and family time.

- Ages 1–3: No more than $1/_2$ hour per day
- Ages 3–5: No more than $1/_2$ hour per day
- Ages 6–9: No more than 1 hour per day
- Ages 10–16: No more than 2 hours per day

7. **Social Services and the Legal System.** The concept of developmentally appropriate experiences should guide rehabilitation efforts in terms of providing missing experiences, such as:
   - Stable, nurturing caregivers for children who are growing up in unstable families.
   - Appropriate limits and structure for children who are growing up without guidance.
   - Opportunities to master the different developmental stages outlined earlier for children who are involved in problematic behavior.

- Use by the legal system of a developmental model of children's functional capacities for accountability.
- Use by the legal system of a developmental model for rehabilitation. A profile of the child in terms of developmentally appropriate experiences mastered or not mastered can determine the types of experiences that would be helpful for the child.

8. **Mental Health.** Mental health approaches must also take into account the concept of developmentally appropriate experiences. It is not sufficient to treat symptoms or even underlying biological vulnerabilities. Treatment programs must include appropriate family and psychosocial supports so that developmentally appropriate experiences are provided for children with mental health problems.

This point is most important because most mental health problems are associated with a lack of developmentally appropriate experiences in one form or another. For example, children who have problems with relationships often have not mastered reading social cues and signals. Children who have extreme emotional reactions often have not mastered gray-area, relativistic thinking, particularly as it applies to feelings. Each set of problems, when looked at from the point of view of the developmental profile of the child, can lead to the identification of specific experiences that need an emphasis in that child's intervention program and life. In this way, mental health involves family and school, as well as other settings where the child is engaged in daily experiences.[8]

5

The Need for Limit Setting, Structure, and Expectations

Although there is general agreement about the need for limits, structure, and guidance in a child's life, there is a strong difference of opinion among many professionals about the best ways to meet these needs. Some believe in more educational approaches, explaining to children the "why" of it, and others favor very firm disciplinary standards even for toddlers and young preschoolers with an emphasis on discipline, structure, and respect. These debates hark back to the debates of the 1940s and 1950s, when there was a transition from the very strict and rigid approach to feeding and toilet training to the more individually- oriented approaches advocated by Dr. Benjamin Spock and others of his generation. It is interesting to watch the ebb and flow of the more structured and more flexible approaches throughout the generations. These basic themes are still being debated today, 50 to 60 years later.

To help clarify these issues it is important to understand how infants and young children learn. All learning, even of limits and structure, begins with nurturing care, from which children learn trust, warmth, intimacy, empathy, and attachment to those around them. Limits and structure begin with nurturance and caring because 90 percent of the task of teaching children to internalize limits is based on children's desire to please those around them. Children want to please for several different reasons: because they love their caregivers and want their approval and respect, or because they are afraid. Obviously, there is often a combination of fear and desire for approval. Children also learn by modeling themselves on those around them. Morality develops from trying to become like an admired adult.

The reasons children want to please by following rules and set limits are important because of the effect of different approaches on whether children broaden and generalize what they learn at home to other settings, such as school or with peers, or later when there are more temptations. Children who limit their aggression and "bad behavior" strictly out of fear are likely to behave themselves in situations where there is an authority figure present because that's who will dispense the punishment. Fear tends to be situation-specific. If the fear is excessive, it can lead to a child's being anxious and inhibited in most situations, even to the point of inhibiting healthy types of expression of assertiveness, also not a very good outcome. Many children don't generalize as well from fear. For example, a child who learns to be scared about hitting a sibling may not hit the sibling when the parent is present but may hit other children at school because she hasn't been punished explicitly for hitting other children at school. As children get older, those who have been disciplined through fear are more vulnerable to drinking, alcohol abuse, drugs, and delinquent behavior.

When discipline is seen as teaching and is conveyed with a great deal of empathy and nurturing care, children feel good when they comply. It is a warm, nourishing feeling to feel that you are the gleam in someone else's eye. When that child gets a disappointed look for hitting his sister, he feels a sense of loss because he misses the positive regard that he has received when he has behaved appropriately. If he never had those positive feelings, there would be no sense of loss or disappointment to motivate him *from the inside* to change his behavior.

Physical discipline, such as hitting or spanking a child is no longer an acceptable alternative to discipline. Discipline means teaching, *not* punishment. Physical punishment is not respectful and is bound to undermine the child's self-image. Anger may be stored up to be worked out later. In addition, we are living in a violent society today and using violence to settle an issue is saying to a child "This is the way we deal with things. Violence is the way to handle frustration or anger." We cannot afford such a message any longer.

Instead of punishment, parents need to take every opportunity to sit down with a child and say "Every time you do this, I must stop you, until you can stop yourself." Hence, upon the occasion of a need for discipline, the first step is to use any measure to break the cycle quickly (holding, isolation, time out). The next step is to sit down to explain it to them. Discipline is a long term not a short term affair. The goal is to teach a child to control his own impulses.

Do children still need help sometimes when the temptations are strong, when they are angry or in a hurry to go somewhere? Of course. Here, parents must combine nurturing, empathetic care with structure: "Sorry, buddy. We can't go until you pick up those toys. We are all going to be a few minutes late." There are, therefore, sanctions along with discussions and attempts to understand the nature of his behavior. Later on, children disciplined in this way want the respect of teachers because they, too, are adults who can be nourishing and caring and who offer admiration and approval. In this way, feelings of being cared for, empathized with, and loved build the foundation for feelings of being respected and admired, which in turn build the foundation for an inner sense of respect and admiration, internalized standards that can guide behavior.

Internalized standards have a number of levels. They begin with feeling nurtured and cared for by others. They then evolve into both feeling nurtured and cared for by others *and feeling respected*. Respect leads to a sense of inner goals and eventually inner values, and then meeting these inner goals and values can lead a child to feel nurtured and good inside, even in the absence of authority figures. Obviously, when such a system is in place and children or teenagers are guided by inner values and goals, they can be in a variety of situations and make wise judgments about the appropriateness of their behavior, because they are now pleasing not just their parents or their teachers or society norms, but they are pleasing their own inner sense of values and goals. In contrast to fear-based limits, which tend to be situation-specific and concrete, the internalized limits born lead to the much broader, finely discriminated, internalized set of guidelines so necessary for operating in our complex, multifaceted society.

How does a child develop this internalized set of guidelines? Through a number of steps at the different stages of the child's development.[1] Before the child can reason with words, limits are being set through nonverbal communication with gestures. We will frequently see 14-month-olds moving toward the area of the room that has the electrical outlet and Mommy shaking her head "no" and pointing "no" and baby looking up with a smirk on his face and stopping for a second and then moving toward his goal. This back-and-forth communication with gestures may occur five or six more times before Mommy has to physically block his access to the outlet or scoop him up in her arms and with a big grin say, "You can't do that. I have to stop you. You can't touch that."

Other gestural negotiations are not quite as serious, he comes to see, because when he is, for example, about to toddle into the living room even though Mom wants him in the playroom, she goes with him and shakes her head "no," but her voice has a playful quality to it, and only when he reaches for a vase does her voice become a little more serious. He is learning about different degrees of inhibition. He is also learning that sometimes he gets picked up and scooped away and sometimes he enters into a finely tuned negotiation that involves back-and-forth regulation of his behavior.

When this understanding is in place, it leads to a second level of limits. By 18–30 months, the child can usually form an idea, a symbol, or an image. Children can now say "no" or talk to themselves: "Don't do that." The child can now picture Daddy shaking his head and saying "no" and can say it to himself as an inner guiding idea.

As a child goes from 30 months to 48 months and is learning to connect ideas, he can now have an internal debate ("I shouldn't do that, but I want to") and also anticipate what may happen ("If I do it, I will lose TV or have a time-out" or "If I do the right thing, Mommy or Daddy will be proud of me"). The child isn't using all these words yet; by the time he is four, he will be able to. But he is now combining ideas to get a sense of consequences and reason out alternatives. At this point a parent can say to a child, "Whenever you do that, I am going to stop you, until you can stop yourself."

The foundation of each of these levels is children's desire to please, their desire for the respect of their caregivers, and eventually their ability to internalize this sense of respect and admiration into an inner set of goals and guidelines. Once this set is in place, children can constantly nourish themselves through striving toward these goals. Loving, nurturing care is therefore the foundation for any lasting sense of discipline and morality.[2]

At the heart of a teaching approach to discipline are *expectations*. Parents expect children to learn at school, to be members of a community, to care about other people, and to be empathetic. At the same time, we expect children to strive for goals that will be their own goals. We hope that they will feel fulfilled for reaching goals that are important to them rather than simply carrying out an agenda of their parents.

In our discussions we have found a few guiding principles. The key principle is that children learn from their relationships with us and they develop expectations from these relationships. They learn, though, not just from what we say but from how we relate to them and how we say it. Therefore, empathy, for example, is taught not by telling children to be nice to others or to try to understand others, but by parents' having the patience to listen to children and children's feeling understood. Once they understand what empathy feels like, they can create it in their relationships. Similarly, love can be described at length, but unless we've felt love, we may not have an emotional reference point to understand what it means. We have to experience these complicated feelings ourselves to understand them and to learn how to use them with others.

A second important feature of expectations is to provide the child with broad goals through the way we lead our lives and through what we encourage. Broad goals are better than narrow, concrete goals. Learning and discovering things about the world and the excitement of fulfilling one's curiosity is a great broad goal, for example, because it doesn't tell the child what to be interested in—biology or literature—but it does convey a sense of enthusiasm for the learning process so necessary in a complex society. Setting broad goals does not mean just a lecture on the importance of being smart. It means the child's feeling our excitement, modeling herself on our curiosity as we explore the woods or read a book to her or discuss politics or even play a game in an innovative way. A different example of expectations might be health—enjoying dance or sports or running or healthy diets. Children enjoy these activities together with parents, whether it is a game or a meal or a canoe trip.

The next step in creating healthy expectations is building children's sense of being respected for how they are unique. This enables children eventually to create their own particular stamp that makes them feel fulfilled in a personal way. The child's ability to select what he wants to do is grounded, however, in his sense that what is unique and special to him is valued. So here we get at something that we discussed earlier—the respect for individual differences. Children who feel unique and special are much more likely to develop a set of expectations for themselves regarding relationships and career and learning that will feel fulfilling and meaningful, rather than feeling as though he is carrying out someone else's agenda. This can lead to rebellion or a sense of compliance or just passivity.

There is one more piece, however, to developing expectations and goals that enable children to pursue meaningful inner-directed goals. Children need to feel a sense of pleasure in mastery in the areas of life that are important or will be important to them. This sense of mastery does not wait until a person is a professional athlete or a Nobel Prize–winning scientist; it starts with the small steps involved in the learning process itself.

When you are naturally gifted at something such as dancing you can try more complicated steps quickly and they will feel natural, satisfying, and rewarding. When you are not gifted at dancing, these complicated steps will feel awkward, clumsy, and not very rewarding. However, a first simple step may. A three-year-old who can't copy a circle or triangle may derive great satisfaction from simply making a scribble-scrabble. If the child and an adult each make a fist around the pencil and each makes a scribble-scrabble at the other, the child may take pride in his scribble-scrabble. If that scribble-scrabble evolves gradually over a few weeks into a line, then that line evolves into a circle, the child may gradually learn to take pleasure in making shapes. Another child can start with the circles and within three or four weeks be making different letters. Very different sequences are needed for each child, but if we respect the needs of children to develop skills in their own way, at their own pace, we build a sense of mastery and pleasure rather than of frustration.

Children who rebel against expectations often do not have the skills or capacities to meet those expectations. So it is incumbent on us as parents and educators to create opportunities for mastery, each small step associated with a sense of pleasure and mastery. This does not mean avoiding hard work. Quite the contrary. Children are willing to work much harder when they feel a sense of mastery and pleasure. No child elects to do things that are inherently difficult for him. A gifted reader or a gifted math student is not intrinsically more motivated or even more conscientious than a child who is avoiding those tasks. That child is simply one who finds reading or math somewhat effortless and therefore satisfying. On the other hand, the child who has trouble with them feels clumsy and awkward.

As we learn about the steps leading to different capacities, we are often able to tailor approaches to individual children so that more and more children can develop a sense of mastery.[3] By working on children's actual competencies and developmental steps, we are able to help the child associate expectations with an assertive, mastery-oriented attitude. From the early days of life, all through our life cycle, there are opportunities for assertive learning versus passive experiences. The newborn baby who is enticed to look around to examine where those interesting sounds are coming from as he follows Daddy's animated voice and face from left to right and up and down is asserting himself to discover his world. He is far different from the baby whose parents just sit in front of him and talk to him or simply rock him and soothe him. The caregiver of a 16-month-old who wants a favorite pop-up toy and simply brings it to him is encouraging passivity, whereas the parent who offers her hand and says let's find it together is offering opportunities for problem solving and assertive mastery. The parent who plops her toddler or preschooler in front of the TV is supporting passivity in comparison with the caregiver who gets on the floor in imaginative play and follows her child's lead. Imaginative play, opinion-oriented conversations where the child's thoughts are important, and active debates all foster an assertive attitude not just in behavior but in thinking as well. Using the Socratic method to brainstorm solutions or maybe the parent playing devil's advocate supports a much more assertive approach.

Such an approach also teaches children to tolerate frustration, and to deal with loss and disappointment. By giving children a chance to master the tools of learning in all the areas of life, we foster an assertive attitude and an ability to pursue and fulfill expectations. When we provide these types of incentives with appropriate structure and limits and couple these with nurturing warmth and a real of sense of admiration for the child's uniqueness, we are helping that child set his own inner goals and discipline.

Discussion

SIG: A lot of people think that when you respect individual differences and work at the developmental levels of children, you are catering so much to them that you spoil them. But actually, respect for developmental levels is a very important part of limit setting. Levels of development and differences must be taken into consideration. When families brainstorm together on what the consequences are going to be for not doing what you are supposed to do, then everyone becomes a participant in setting down the rules. An atmosphere where there are expectations, structure, and limits appropriate to a child's age and level is necessary for the basic security we've talked about earlier.

TBB: I'd say discipline is the second most important thing you can give a child. Love comes first, but very close on its heels comes discipline. The goal is teaching, not punishment. *Limits* may be too strong a word. The long-term goal is self-discipline. That means years of teaching; it doesn't happen overnight. What you do overnight isn't going to be that magical, ever. All the stuff about time-out for five minutes at such-and-such an age is not my idea of discipline. When a child misbehaves, you first break the cycle with whatever means works for you, time-out or whatever. Once you have the child's attention, you sit right down with the child and say, "Now, let's talk about this. This is something that you can't do. So every time you do it, I have to stop you. How should I stop you? Can you help me? You tell me what I should do, because this is your job, not mine. I would like you to take some responsibility in this." By four and five, the child can tell you what would help work for him and can already be involved in the process. This can have wonderful results. That's the way I would look at limits. Every misdemeanor becomes an opportunity for learning limits—a long-term goal.

Physical Punishment

SIG: What about physical punishment? I would agree with you and say no physical punishment. Unfortunately, there are too many families nowadays for whom it can lead to abuse.

TBB: But if I'm speaking to a mother who I know keeps whamming away at a child, I have to see it from her side. I might try to say, "You know it must be so hard to have a child that you care so much about and that you have to get so upset about. Can I help you? What would help to take a little of the pressure off for a while?" We need to find alternatives to landing on somebody who just landed on her child, who is out of control. Give her back a sense of control.

SIG: We need to get the child's attention with sanctions that are developmentally in keeping with the child's developmental level, for example, losing computer game privileges for a school-aged child, and other things. But the key is to get them motivated to listen and then talk it out and help them understand the where and why of it and how to approach things differently.

TBB: Discipline begins at 8 or 9 months when the child crawls up to the TV, looking around at you to be sure you are there. For the next few months (9–18), distraction or holding may be appropriate.

From 1 $1/_2$ to 3 $1/_2$ years, the need for firm, understanding limits is very powerful. When parents respond to provocative testing of firm limits you can see a look of relief from the child. Certain calm, respectful limits such as holding and time-out are a good way to begin. But immediately afterward the child needs an explanation: "Every time you do this, I have to stop you until you can stop yourself."

From 3 $1/_2$ to 6 years, the discussion can get more sophisticated: "Every time you do this, I get angry. I don't like to be angry with you. Can you suggest anything that might help me help you *before* we get in trouble?" Then, firm limits and discussion of why you need to be the monitor of limits until the child can set his own limits. Physical punishment doesn't bring this about.

Balancing Limits with Nurturance

SIG: Along with setting limits, I recommend that every day there is some relaxed time one-on-one with the parent and child. I call it *floor time*. Often, by following the child's lead for a time you can have problem-solving discussions where you work on the limits together. You also anticipate situations tomorrow. Also, you always empathize with the child's perspective, even if you disagree with it. You always try to encourage change in small steps. You make sure the child is experiencing success most of the time, rather than consistently failing. If you have to set lots of limits, you increase the warm, nurturing "hangout" time proportionately. If you find you are getting into a situation where you are setting more limits with your child, don't let your relationship deteriorate. What can happen is that you start getting angry with the child; the child is being aggressive, and you start pulling away and stop playing together because you are too mad most of the time. Life then becomes a power struggle all around. You are losing the nurturance and the warmth. So if you are increasing your limits, increase your nurturance and warmth. *By giving more you can expect more.*

TBB: It helps to comment each time the child uses his own internalized limits. Parents can also model controls for him. At certain times, verbalize them: "I got so angry at that woman cutting in front of me in line like that, I wanted to shove her, but I knew I shouldn't."

SIG: I like to see a child visualize ahead of time what's going to get him into hot water, whether it's hitting a brother or sister, how he feels, how the other person feels, and what led up to it. You can ask the child what she routinely does when her baby sister bites and what the alternatives are, what else she could do, so that she won't get into hot water. So the child is anticipating and participating and visualizing, especially the feeling part. Then you're the good cop. If she hits again, she gets a ticket and has to pay the "sanction" or whatever you have agreed on, but then you work with the child to picture what will happen tomorrow so she doesn't get herself into hot water again. Through this kind of experience, children are learning all these important lessons: They are learning how to cope with their own selfishness, anger, and entitlement. The most important thing for real maturity is how to cope with disappointment. That's a very important thing. By empathizing with children you help them express their frustration when they don't get their way or think something's unfair. Also, through the limits and through the talks, you are conveying aspirations, goals, and expectations for the child and this offers the child a sense of security.

Discipline and Working Parents

TBB: There's something else I've also seen: Working parents have a very tough time thinking about limits. Their ability to set limits has gone way down in this generation. Parents tell me, "I can't stand to be away all day and then come back and be the disciplinarian." They need a lot of reinforcement to realize that discipline is important to the child. One reason children act up, tease, disintegrate at the end of the day when the parent gets there is that they are asking for the security that comes with limits. We have to pay attention to how hard it is for people, for adults, to face disciplining these days. They don't want to be disciplinarians in the short time they have with their children.[4]

SIG: You raise a good question. If the parent hasn't seen the child all day and the child is acting up, the parent feels bad jumping in and setting limits right away because he feel guilty for having been away all day. The problem is two-sided: Parents are feeling guilty; they don't feel that they have earned the right to set limits, and the child who is acting up may be alerting the parent, just in the way you were saying before, that hey, there is something more complicated going on here. In order to successfully set limits, parents may have to allow time with the child, and then they can feel they've earned the right to discipline. If they are "in there," getting up at night with the baby, in the trenches with the child, they won't have too much guilt setting a limit. Then you feel pretty entitled as a parent to set that limit. But if you feel that you are not there enough for your children, you might not feel right asking that child to be quiet while you talk to Dad about something important.

TBB: As we discussed earlier, a welcoming routine at the end of the day can help the parent work back into the role of feeling entitled. I feel strongly about recommending to working parents that they set up a homecoming ritual in which everybody gets close all over again. Then they are ready to play a disciplinary role. But not until then.

SIG: And if the routine is slipping away, if both parents are starting to get home at 7: 30 at night (with two high-pressure careers), then they have to realize that a rushed evening is not enough.

TBB: Limits are too important for the child. They must come from parents first and other caregivers second. Parents have to be clear about that.

SIG: Along these lines, say a prototypical family, a new family with young kids, comes to us. They say, "OK. How much time do we have to spend with our kids when we get home? We want to do what's right. How much time is needed each day to stay close but also set limits?" What would you recommend?

TBB: I would put it in terms of "You're away all day. You owe your child a couple of hours of time when you get home." One hour should come first to cement your relationship and then if things are going well, you can use the next hour to organize limits, chores, and everything else. But at least one hour of warm, undivided attention is owed that child: reading, rocking, singing songs. All told, a minimum of two hours is absolutely necessary.

SIG: So you are saying for working parents, two hours with direct involvement with the child. One of those should be where it's really more child-directed around the kid, and the other can be sharing chores together. As we discussed in earlier chapters, approximately two-thirds of available time (e.g., after school and peer play) should involve different types of interaction with parents, and one parent needs to be home in the afternoon and both at home (in a two-parent family) by 6: 00 P.M. This

parental availability will make setting limits and providing
guidance a natural part of the day.

TBB: But that first hour is key. If parents can get close in that first
hour and the child then gets restless, they can go on and be
available to their children while cooking or cleaning up or
whatever.

SIG: I think all this is important because it bears on limits. The
needs for limits and ongoing relationships are closely connected.

TBB: This needn't mean that two-career families do a bad job
with discipline. I've seen the positive side of work for many
women in the last two generations. Some tell me that by
getting out of the family for at least part of the day, they
function better within the family. Parents who feel they are
pursuing their goals gain perspective on what issues matter in
the way of limits.

Setting Limits Together

SIG: One last aspect of this question of limits is that mother and
father have to work well together as a team. They're not going
to work well as a team unless they are nurturing each other,
giving each other some "chicken soup," which means sexual
intimacy, warmth and understanding, compassion, and making
time for all that. For some stressed parents, there is no time
alone. They are not going out on Saturday nights to dinner or
the movies or spending a few minutes shooting the breeze with
each other. That lost intimacy begins to make them more likely
to hit a child because they are frustrated. They aren't nurturing
the child because they aren't nurturing each other. Talking
about discipline means recognizing the needs of parents. This
doesn't necessarily mean you have to earmark time for this or
that. It should be natural, just the way a kid just goes out and
plays. But maybe in the toddler years there should be prescrip-
tions for parents to have time together. Spending a little time
in bed together after waking up in the morning is a prescrip-
tion in the Jewish religion. Rabbis discuss why it's necessary.
For workaholics who just want to get up and go to work, this
means paying attention to each other. Maybe in our society
such things need to be spelled out. Some time each evening
and getting out together on weekends seems essential. And single parents need to be aware of their own need for being nurtured and supported, which can easily get lost in the battle to
make a living and care for children.

Recommendations

Limit Setting in Families

- **Giving More and Expecting More.** This means coupling limits and expectations with nurturing care, we challenge our children as we nurture them. This vital combination is what works for our most productive members of society. It's when we lose this vital balance, when we expect without giving and give without expecting, that children become either angry and resistant or spoiled and passive.
- **Discipline as Teaching.** Discipline should be verbal and should include limits, problem solving, learning to anticipate difficult situations, and learning to deal with disappointment and feelings of loss and humiliation.
- **Corporal Punishment.** This is no longer acceptable in a world of continuing violence.
- **Never Humiliating.** Humiliation only breeds resentment, anger, and more rebelliousness rather than an internalization of societally important values and goals.
- **Embedding Expectations in Relationships.** Children must experience adults doing for them what we expect children eventually to do for themselves and others. It's not just the witnessing or the observing that teaches, it's being a part of a relationship where certain attitudes, values, ideals, and goals are part of supportive adult-child interactions.
- **Making Expectations Appropriate to a Child's Age.** Children can't be expected to internalize limits and enjoy learning unless they are provided with the tools to learn about and master and understand their world. This requires recognizing stages of development and using educational approaches that work for all children. (See Chapter 4.)
- **Self-Discipline.** The goal of parents in setting limits should be to turn this job gradually over to the child. Helping children choose their own sanctions and work out ways to deal with strong feelings encourages them to take responsibility.
- **Discipline At the End of a Working Day.** The first hour or so after parents get home should be spent focusing on the child's needs and getting close Then parents will feel more entitled to set the necessary limits.
- **Parents as a Team.** Discipline works best when parents have time with each other and can set limits and carry them

out as a team. Parents' modeling of self-discipline is an effective way for a child to learn self-discipline. Single parents need to recognize their need for nurturance and support.

Limit Setting in Institutions

- Vital institutions (education, legal, and social services) should foster developmentally appropriate experiences and respect for individual differences. This ethic of "give more and expect more" must characterize not just family life, but schools, educational institutions, the legal and social service systems, religious institutions, and other community organizations. Only children who are making progress can learn to internalize limits and develop constructive ideals. The ability to more fully form and internalize values and expectations often occurs between ages 9 and 12 in our ninth stage of development. This stage builds on the preceding eight years. It builds on nurturing, empathetic relationships, regulating environments, and the ability to communicate and think creatively and logically. It derives from negotiating the stages of triangular thinking, peer relationships, and relativistic thinking. It is a product of a long developmental pathway. We can't expect this attainment for our children unless we provide the ingredients for that pathway.

- In schools or in restrictive settings run by the juvenile justice system, children and adolescents must have a sense of protection and ongoing nurturing relationships as well as structure. In these settings, expectations born out of interactions with adults and the development of real skills are essential in providing opportunities for growth and development.

- In restrictive mental health settings (i.e., for children who must be in institutionalized settings for brief periods of time, or sometimes longer periods of time), regulating and nurturing relationships must be the essential feature. When coupled with firm but gentle limits and reasonable expectations geared to the children's gradually improving emotional and intellectual skills, children and adolescents learn to internalize limits and constructive expectations. Overly rigid, punitive approaches or overly permissive approaches don't embrace this combination of essential factors.

6

The Need for Stable, Supportive Communities and Cultural Continuity

Communities and cultures provide the context or framework for the other irreducible needs that we have discussed. It's easy to overlook this vital component. Efforts on behalf of children will only be as strong as the families, communities, and cultural supports within which the child develops. At the same time, there have been important debates on how to balance, for example, respect for cultural patterns while enabling families to adapt to a complex society, interact with other cultural groups, and meet the demands of school and eventually the workforce. These debates have flared around educational approaches for young children. For example, to what degree should the language of the family be the vehicle for learning in school and to what degree should the child be challenged to learn in English? How much should Western civilization be emphasized, and how much should be taught about other world civilizations, or the particular history of one ethnic group? As these questions get raised, it is possible to see that the issue of cultural continuity is not an easy one at the level of practice.

While everyone would agree on the importance of stable, self-sufficient communities that have a sense of identity and cohesiveness unto themselves, there are important debates occurring here, too. To what degree should federal or state grants be given over to individual communities so that they, through their citizens groups, churches, synagogues, or other organizations determine the priorities for these resources and their implementation and evaluation?

Or to what degree should these priorities be determined by federal or state or city agencies? Here issues of perspective and control are also important.

These issues of control get played out in schools, among other important places. To what degree do local families oversee and provide governance for public education? Or to what degree is public education controlled by state, city, and county agencies and boards of education that, although elected, seem far removed from the concerns of a family in a neighborhood that is using a local elementary school. Fervent debate surrounds charter schools and tax support for parochial or religious schools.

When a neighborhood creates a school or when a particular individual with the strong support of a group of families creates a school or when a school is governed by a religious organization with strong local roots and oversight, there is a much greater sense of intimacy and immediacy to the oversight and regulation of that school. Yet there is also strong support for state or national standards and free and equal public education for all. Although everyone agrees on the importance of families having some input, there are varying degrees to which that occurs, from the far-distant boards of education and state and city and county oversight to a neighborhood school governed by the families who all live within eyesight and earshot of one another.

How can we instill in our children a respect for their own cultural uniqueness and also help them master the tools of English, math, history, and the like that will be required to operate in the larger society? Here, the dilemma is more apparent than real. All children need to master certain forms of written language that characterize the society they operate in. The question is whether the language spoken at home is seen as a strength that helps them understand new concepts or is ignored and is seen as a competitor with new learning. If a particular language or dialect has unique terms to convey certain ideas or feelings, the question becomes whether there are comparable terms used by others so that there can be a shared vocabulary to convey these feelings and attitudes. Also, as one is struggling with new concepts, such as the concepts of justice, devotion, and responsibility, one should search for the language used in different cultural groups that are part of the discussion to help understand and often enhance these concepts. For example, Asian cultures may have a more developed set of concepts for understanding family responsibility and loyalty than American or European cultures.

Going back and forth between the subtlety of one's own language and the subtlety of a new language helps one master new concepts and terms. But the reference points for subtle emotional meanings are always stronger in one's basic language. For this reason, we encourage parents to interact with their own children in the first language of the parents for at least part of the day.[1] This should be the case whether one's own language is simply a variation on the common language due to neighborhood or cultural differences, or whether it is an entirely different language.

Similarly, teaching history does not require a choice between the history of particular cultural groups or the westernized form of history (e.g., the history of the European and American continents). The focus should not be on which history is studied and which content is studied, but rather on the processes of understanding history, the mechanisms by which the past can inform us. Asian history, African history, American history, and European history can all be studied with an emphasis on historical analysis rather than regional content. Becoming a "historian" is different from mastering the facts of the Civil War. Studying one war can be used as a window for understanding conflict and war in general. Approached in this way, neither history nor use of language need be conflictual. Different languages and different histories can be mutually enhancing if the goal is the process of learning, as opposed to the concrete memorization of specific facts.

As we look at the themes of cultural continuity, in terms of the way language, literacy, and history are taught, or as we look at the governing structure of schools, we see that the debate between assimilation and diversity is not one that can be resolved by broad global statements. Although certainly a general philosophy of respect for cultural and neighborhood differences is vital, these issues have to be debated and resolved in actual practice before a vital balance can be found.

This issue is even more complicated because many neighborhoods and most cities are quite diverse, made up of many different cultural groups with different backgrounds, adding to the complexity of how one can respect each and every aspect of diversity and at the same time bring families together for consolidated neighborhood functioning. Our efforts to foster stable, integrated communities that can embrace diversity while providing structure and support for families and children have a long way to go. Yet, if the irreducible needs of children described in this book are to be met, such communities must become the norm.

In order to understand how communities operate, one of us (S.I.G.) has explored the ways different levels of organization parallel the levels of development of individuals.[2]

The first level involves how well a community provides protection and physical safety and a sense of internal regulation. We know that many communities are characterized by fear and danger and are unable to provide safety. Other communities create a foundation of security.

At a second level, communities are characterized by their capacity to provide a sense of coherence and of connectedness among their different members. Is the community fragmented, composed of isolated families or small groups, or are there activities that bring many people together (e.g., religious organizations, civic associations, sports, zoning boards, parent-teacher associations, arts organizations)? Can the community come together in ways that are superordinate to individual cultural differences, such as on behalf of economic opportunity, health facilities, or improved education? Is the welfare of the children in the community an organizing principle?

At yet another level, communities are characterized by how well their members communicate with one another toward purposeful goals and to what degree they understand each other's expectations and cultural patterns. At a more advanced level, communities are characterized by the degree to which they share certain symbols, values, or ideals that are broader than individual beliefs and behaviors. An example would be support for values such as equality, the rights of the individual, justice, or environmental protection. In contrast, some communities come together around more polarized beliefs, sometimes creating "us" versus "them" mentalities leading to fear, suspicion, and aggression.

At the higher level, communities are characterized by the degree to which they are capable of self-reflection and active planning for the future. Mature communities can reflect on their own needs and take steps to plan and carry out actions that will lead to change and improvement based on changing circumstances.

Communities struggling with cohesion, safety and security, lack of communication among members, or polarized beliefs will generally not have the wherewithal or energy for reflective action. There are many examples of unsafe and chaotic communities that are fragmented into weary, isolated families or individuals or warring factions based on polarized beliefs. There are also many communities that have formed cohesive bonds that cross cultural divides and allow for reflective planned actions on behalf of education, health, open space, and other needs of children.

For all of us concerned with the well-being of children, the important question obviously becomes what types of steps foster cohesive, safe, reflective communities in comparison to unsafe, polarized, fragmented, and/or suspicious ones.

To begin with, groups that are supported, in terms of their unique cultural identity (and that therefore have a strong sense of personal identity), are, through that security, better able to embrace the differences of others. At the same time the sense of security, identity, and meaning that comes from support for one's own unique background needs to be balanced with the tools and knowledge of the larger community. These bring a sense of mastery of the environment within which one finds oneself. A cultural group in a larger society without the needed educational, political, and economic skills may well feel isolated and anxious and be less likely to participate in a reflective manner with the larger community around it.

What are some of the specific practical steps that can strengthen and integrate a community? We have already mentioned community oversight and appropriate levels of control of programs, including educational programs, by that community. Existing organizations, such as churches and synagogues or community organizations or neighborhood organizations, can be a beginning. Programs sited in these local organizations provide an opportunity for elements of the community to begin coming together and developing coherent structures.

In dealing with fragmented communities, it is often difficult to know where to begin. Communities that are organized and well functioning tend to get more support services because they are able to compete more effectively. Instead, certain services need to be directed at helping communities organize themselves in fundamental ways.

Communities often organize themselves successfully around schools. Schools provide a useful model for other community services because they already exist in every sizable community. In some schools there is already active participation of parents through the PTA, the local school board, and more informal arrangements (meetings with teachers and the like). In other schools, parents remain somewhat alienated and, although a few may attend meetings with teachers, are basically uninvolved in either the school's governance or its educational program. To serve the child and families in a neighborhood, schools must be under some degree of local control, with parents whose children are attending the school providing oversight (as in most private schools). Once such a governance structure is in place, parents and community representatives can enlarge the role of schools.

What type of after school-activities or evening activities can be a part of this important structure that stems from taxpayer funds? Could the school also answer some of the needs we have discussed in terms of afternoon activities, particularly for those at risk, or a place where health and social services can become more accessible to a community? In other words, schools have the possibility of being much more than they are.

It is also important for parents to have regular meetings with teachers and for the school to reach out to overly busy parents or parents who may be preoccupied with family problems and not involved in the educational life of their children.

Edward Zigler and James Comer of Yale have set up models to broaden the role and governance of schools. In their programs, parents and neighborhood members are involved in all facets of school activity, and school activity broadens into the community.[3] This goal of improved school governance is essential for the long-term goal of organizing and improving the entire community for families and children, as well as the immediate educational benefits.

In many communities there are enormous challenges, with children getting into difficulties after school due to lack of family supervision or lack of appropriate activities. "Hanging out" and troublemaking take the place of sports or music or dance or science or debate team or other activities that would be more constructive and have far more positive long-term value.

In high-risk neighborhoods and communities schools may need to become 24-hour-a-day institutions to support the development of children and families in that community. That means a much more ambitious after-school program with all different kinds of activities, from remedial educational work for those children who need it to enhanced learning opportunities in science, math, art, literature, and the arts and a variety of drama, music, and sports activities. Those children who have active family lives and supervision and want to just play with friends might not need these programs, but these other options would be available, not simply in a day care or holding environment, but with an ambitious after-school learning program.

At the high school level, we often see some children involved in many after-school activities, playing on one or two or three sports teams, in drama in a play, but although this activity looks good on paper, it is not really helpful to the large majority of children. Only 15 children make the varsity basketball team, for example, when perhaps 100 aspire to make the team. Is this emphasis on varsity sports really a fair use of taxpayer funds and community resources when being a member of the team provides not only healthy use of energies and athletic skills but also lessons in team membership, healthy behavior, and, when well run, positive values. Perhaps far better than just having one team with three coaches and all the resources would be to have at the school level a variety of different leagues. There might be three or four levels so that all the kids who wish to play competitive sports could be on a team and play against other schools in a competitive and joyful atmosphere. Although the school might have to hire some additional coaches or have community volunteers come in to help, nonetheless between the boys' and the girls' teams and the two or three levels of play, most children who are interested in a sport could be accommodated. Children who aspire to improve could move up from one level to another. This way no one gets left out and sports are for everyone.

Similarly, drama is highly competitive at most schools and only a handful of kids get a part and make the play. This, too, seems an unfortunate and unfair way to use taxpayer funds, where only the talented have a chance to fine-tune their craft and others wind up observing the few fortunate ones. There is no reason why the school can't be putting on two or three plays at a time, with community volunteers helping out. Each play may be less elaborate in production values, but more children would get a chance to participate. In other words, the principle is activities after school for all children. The way it turns out now is the most gifted students, athletically, musically, dramatically, or academically, find their way into afternoon activities, and other less gifted or timid students, who need the extra practice even more, wind up hanging out, getting into hot water, or simply becoming more passive and self-absorbed.

But after-school activities are just one element of the type of programs that schools could spearhead on behalf of creating cohesion, dialogue, and shared values and goals for a community. A community could have access to the schools for evening programs as well. These may involve education classes for parents, social service and health care for families, evening activities for older children and adolescents, and community members and leaders coming together for governance. In other words, the community should be able to use the tax-supported property (i.e., the school), for a variety of purposes in keeping with that community's priorities. The common interest in education and governance for education could then be the beginning of a process of collaboration that can extend into other community needs, including social service, health, education for adults, and preventively oriented afternoon programs for children and adolescents, which would include prevention of substance abuse, delinquent behavior, and poor health practices. Mentoring programs can also be a part of both school and after-school activities.

In most communities, however, there are also families who require more than simply supportive services organized through schools and other institutions. If an emergency room is not able to care for acutely ill patients, an entire hospital will become demoralized in its ability to carry out its main function of sustaining and improving health. Similarly, communities must have an ability to care for those most in need. There are multirisk or multiproblem families with depression or mental illness, substance abuse, severe marital difficulties, and, as a consequence, severe difficulties in rearing children.[4] Because of years of ingrained helplessness, passivity, suspiciousness, and avoidance, often occurring through many generations, many families with these characteristics are unable to use traditional health, social service, or mental health agencies for assistance. Instead of reaching out, they involve themselves in more self-destructive practices, such as substance abuse or social isolation. Many programs working with a range of such challenges have demonstrated effectiveness.[5] The key to such a program's being successfully launched in a community to reach and work with the families most in need is its comprehensiveness and its outreach capacities.

One way of creating such programs is through the formation of what has been described (S.I.G) as a Vertical Village. A sizable apartment building could serve as its physical frame. This Vertical Village would house a range of residents: some very dysfunctional households; some other families, both working and on welfare, who cope more competently with their lives; some older, perhaps retired, persons living either alone or with relatives; some adults without children.

Services aimed at both children and their parents would be available within the building itself. A well-equipped, well-staffed infant and child center, for example, would welcome youngsters essentially from birth. Both children and adults would come here daily, the youngsters spending their time in play and learning activities, the parents availing themselves of education and guidance suited to their needs. Knowledgeable staffers would work at forming lasting personal ties with each member, helping adults develop parenting skills while providing children with familiar, dependable care to backstop their often overstressed parents. For each high-risk family, one staffer would assume the role of surrogate "relative" along the lines of a sympathetic, capable aunt or grandmother. This trained caregiver would establish a permanent bond with the family, seeing that parents manage the personal problems that stand in the way of caring for their babies and that children get the nurturing they need at each developmental stage, regardless of their parents' ability to provide it.

The Touchpoints training (T.B.B.) is an example of support built around relationships. It is an outreach model designed to create working relationships between caregivers (health care providers), child care providers (day care), early interventionists, and parents. The theory is that if we can change the outreach model from a deficit or failure model to one which values the strengths of the parents, using the child's development as a language of communications, parents will become more involved in each of these programs. The staff around the provider is also trained to reach out for vulnerable parents. Each "touchpoint," or regression in the child's developmental progress becomes an opportunity for sharing and deepening the provider-parent relationship. Knowledge is shared not "taught," and parents become openly available. Compliance is miraculously increased when parents fill an intimate part of the child's progress. They feel supported and understood. The negative or illness-focused model has never worked to cement relationships. If we want to include parents we need to train supportive teams in each of these contact systems. Parents are available and needy. (See Touchpoints guidelines in Appendix.)

Working with the same trusted helper over a period of four or five years, the child could gain a center of stability that endured despite upheavals that might occur at home. A mother too depressed to respond to her baby appropriately would thus not totally deprive him of the support and interaction he needs to build relationships or master communication. Even addicted mothers can become available if their children's future is the focus of the outreach. A drug binge or episode of inpatient addiction treatment would not throw a child's world into turmoil and the child into the uncertainty of foster care. Staffed around the clock, the center would be a safe haven at any time and for as long as needed, cutting drastically the chaos in youngsters' lives.

Such a reliable, nearby resource would also bring order and responsibility to parents' lives, offering, in addition to instruction in parenting skills, opportunities for personal counseling, drug treatment, health and family planning education, courses toward high school equivalency completion, and work training or job search assistance.

A night staff would consist of familiar and trusted persons as well, removing from parents the pressure to care for children when they cannot. A parent in crisis would always have a place to turn for help, and in turn, center staff would demand that the parent meet a minimum level of maturity before family life could fully resume, thus enforcing standards of responsible care.

To make this system work, each troubled family would belong to a cohesive community, most of whose members functioned pretty well. The other families living in the building—some on welfare, some not—would also belong to the center, with children attending the nursery and adults taking part in classes, groups, and activities that suited their circumstances. Adults seeking job opportunities, for example, could be trained as child care workers in preparation for taking paid positions in the center. Other adults, especially older or retired persons with backgrounds in child care and education, could work in the center either as volunteers or paid staffers. A variety of financial incentives—low rents, reduced child care fees, educational opportunities—could attract residents to this diverse yet balanced "neighborhood."

Such an urban village would draw strength and support from the culture and institutions of the surrounding community. Churches, community centers, civic groups, and local charities, preferably associated with residents' cultural or ethnic heritage, could provide social, spiritual, recreational, and educational resources. Instead of being a ghetto for the most disadvantaged, like present-day public housing, the community would offer benefits not only to the very poor, but to households with other options.

Ideally, a parent and child at risk would be part of the village network from before birth. Rather than waiting to intervene until after a child has begun to have difficulties, staff would make help available early to maximize each baby's developmental chances.

Though highly cost-effective in the long run, a program like this is far from cheap. Lack of staff available 24 hours a day has sunk such efforts in the past. When families encounter crises, sufficient numbers of trained staff must be ready to step in and maintain children's development. Although difficult to implement, programs to help the families most in need reveal the essence of what a community is prepared to give.

Discussion

Gatekeeping

TBB: We are really talking here about a basic need of parents as well as children. Just as we were talking earlier about mothers needing to be mothered, parents need to be embraced within layers of community. Instead, we often have child care or social service that weakens the parent-child attachment. I see it as a kind of gatekeeping.

SIG: Gatekeeping meaning . . .

TBB: Well, everybody who cares about a small child is in competition for that child, and so they will unconsciously try to keep other people out of the relationship. They will blame the other person when something goes wrong with the child. This pertains not just to parents and child care people, but also to custody, all kinds of issues. Unless gatekeeping is brought to the surface, parents withdraw and feel resentful.

SIG: Yes, when parents don't have this support and help in being reflective about their needs, they can become hurt and angry. The situation then gets polarized. Parents and teachers or day care workers or social workers get locked into competition and petty rivalries. You see this in institutions all the time. When the funding and grants flow, everyone is happy. But when the resources get short, people regress down to the level where there is backbiting, people ganging up on people, and a lot of conflict. This is when what you call gatekeeping takes place. It's at a minimum when everyone is well nourished, when parents want to work together with teachers and caregivers as a team.

TBB: The attachment to a child that creates gatekeeping can be a strength, though. It can be turned into a good thing. It just needs to be brought to the surface. This is why I think it's critical that in day care parents and child care personnel talk all the time about how they feel, how they plan to handle this or that. They don't have to come to an agreement, but they have to be aware of each other's feelings: "When you do that, I feel very jealous" or "When I come to get her at the end of the day and she cries at seeing me, I feel rejected."

SIG: The day care worker who is not being nurtured herself will be more likely to be competitive with the parent and more judgmental. Caregiving isn't always easy to share. Parents should be concerned if the person taking care of their child is very unhappy and lacks support. Let's say day care staff aren't getting an adequate wage or the boss of the day care center is overly critical—caregivers in this situation are more likely to blame the mother for bringing in the child with a cold, for example: "If you took care of the kid, he wouldn't always have colds." That sort of thing. That adversarial relationship is more likely when caregivers come from a family situation where they themselves are stressed or the day care situation is not that supportive or paying them enough. If they have husbands who love them and the day care director is supportive and warm, they might be more apt to be sympathetic: "Is he feeling better? These colds are going around."

   None of this is particularly mysterious. In an institution or community with strong social support, we can see people are identifying their needs and working things out. In a deprived or chaotic setting, we see people acting out and becoming self-centered, with criticism and rivalries. So with both their parents and those who care for them in schools and day care, children's needs are directly dependent upon nourished, integrated families.

   But can we get families to nourish each other and society to nourish them? We often assume that this should be happening. But a lot of the time it's not, and how do we bring it about? Fortunately, there are a number of groups that have sprung into action around the country to reinforce families.

TBB: Family Support America in Chicago (See Organizations in Appendix) is an example of the potential for bringing parents together for mutual support. Organizations that link parents of special-needs children in mutual support groups are another instance of how vital these can be. The Child Care Action Campaign in New York City (See Organizations in Appendix) is another instance of a group that is trying to improve child care all over the country and to support parents who are having to work outside the home. Our Touchpoints programs (See Organizations in Appendix), in 30 sites around the country, are reinforcing child care, preventive health care, and early intervention for parents in their communities. These work, and they do give parents a feeling of being cared for.

Cultural Strengths

SIG: But there's another aspect to this, the cultural layer when you have programs like Touchpoints or intervention programs out in the communities. They succeed or fail to the degree to which they are sensitive to cultural needs and the degree to which the people who are a part of the culture shape them, as opposed to a federal program with all kinds of mandates that are passed down. With a patronizing program laid down from outside you get helplessness and dependency. On the other hand, if the participants are taking initiative themselves, there is the strength of feeling that you are doing it on your own and directing this effort to the real needs.

TBB: We've lost the extended family and the backing of cultures. We have downgraded ethnicity. We need to rethink all that. It always horrifies me, having worked with newborns of many ethnic and religious groups, and seeing what diversity brings to our culture via newborns, to see that we have turned ethnicity into something negative. I would like some day to have a chance to study, not only the roots that people come from and what they bring with them, but also what they are having to give up for our culture. I'd also like to look at the touchpoints or moments when these ethnic differences are called into question. Say a four-year-old comes home and says she's been teased for her curly hair or "My skin's too dark." If we knew more about these experiences, we could reinforce parents not to fall into a trap at that point, but to be ready for it. A parent might say, "Of course they tease you. They like you. Everybody teases people they like. They're trying to understand why you are different from them. Do you understand why you are different?" Then, get back from the child where she is with her understanding and talk about all kinds of differences: language, beliefs, skin color, and so on. If we were all ready for each of these turning points, we wouldn't just keep reinforcing the idea that diversity is a negative from one generation to another.

SIG: We can also look at different cultural groups, religions, and ethnic backgrounds and say, "In what ways can particular religious, cultural, or ethnic differences support families?" First, as you were saying, where are the strengths coming from? Certain religious beliefs may make it easier to meet a child's needs. For example, if a religion advocates very strong relationships and involvement with kids, it makes it easier to be available to your child, to spend more time with the child, to hang in there. You are following a religious teaching and feeling good about yourself because you are doing it. There is often more support than people realize embedded in the spirit or philosophy of the religion, but people may not be using it that way. Almost all of the religions advocate strong family involvement. You can harness that.

But there can be worrisome traditions, for example, if corporal punishment is advocated.

TBB: People use religion to advocate some pretty hard-line stuff. For the good of his soul, let your child cry, feed him only every four hours, don't spare the rod.

SIG: Let the child cry?

TBB: Yes. I've heard that from parents in certain communities.

SIG: But it's more helpful to focus on support and strengths. We can point to the involvement and responsibility a religion teaches.

TBB: You know, we all feel a sort of emptiness about value systems in this country. Many of the values that we have espoused as a nation aren't working. We are looking for better ones. When you begin to look, you realize there are some that we have left behind. Many of the cultures that blended into ours have had to leave their values behind. We would all do well to look back and say, "What have I lost and what have I gotten in exchange?" We've given up a lot of our religious values and our ethnic belief systems and we haven't gotten much back. We see that all around us, actually, people going back to their cultural, ethnic, and religious backgrounds.

Shared Values

SIG: When I work with groups of different cultures, I try to emphasize what in their culture strengthens them as parents.

For example, take a parent who has a hypersensitive child who is panicking because he is being handled roughly, but whose culture supports stern punishment. To help, I say, "Well, you know little Johnny has sensitive skin. A little spank to you may seem like nothing, but to him it's like a huge blow. It's really scary stuff to him. I don't think you really meant to scare him. There is nothing in your beliefs that says to scare children, but it does say to discipline him. There are ways to discipline him and let him be respectful without scaring him." The larger goals of the religion or culture are usually very constructive. It is very interesting to look at religious beliefs in the context of our psychological concepts of what makes a mature, healthy human being.

All religions and cultures help survival in some ways or they wouldn't have lasted. But it's important to individuals to figure what in their culture may offer help for a particular issue they are confronting with their child. Our goal here, to support the development of a healthy, creative, thoughtful, respectful person, is likely to be shared by most religions and cultures. In most instances, a culture has its own unique way of meeting the basic needs that we've advocated here. Most cultures advocate strong family ties, committed relationships, limit setting, and individuals who balance autonomy and compassion.

TBB: Many of the minority cultures, though, have given up positive values in order to fit into our dominant society. I think we need to make parents more aware of that and to give them permission to look for support in their own traditions. But this means openness and understanding on everyone's part. For example, in traditional old Greek culture, babies are not given a name as a newborn. The mother doesn't even want an outsider to admire her baby for fear he will be taken away from her. If a neonatologist or nurse in one of our obstetrical hospitals ran into these practices and wasn't aware of the reasons, the medical person might feel, "They aren't bonding."

Latin American parents often must give up the close family traditions that they bring with them as they enter our society. As a result, they do not feel supported. They have left behind many of the close family ties that might have strengthened them as they face the enormous job of integrating into our society.

Recommendations

Stable family neighborhoods and community organizations are necessary foundations for meeting the irreducible needs of children. Supports for families and cultural strengths can come from several directions.

Cohesive Neighborhoods

- Community support at the neighborhood level includes familiarity with other neighbors, block watches (monitoring of each other and each other's property), and social exchanges, such as block parties. Families derive a personal identity from a neighborhood and relationships that are supportive.
- Churches, schools, civic associations, parent groups, and service agencies knit the fabric of a community. In turn, they are strengthened by collaboration for community good—cleaning up the streets, creating a park, and having after-school care, community activity centers, and so on. The community's environment is also enhanced by organizations funded beyond the neighborhood level: police protection, fire protection, public health nurses, libraries, co-ops. Much of this social infrastructure, which can support families, is missing or eroding in many communities (e.g., visiting-nurse programs, churches, libraries).

Federal and State Programs

- These must be designed, as many increasingly are, to work together with local efforts as fully as possible. Attempts to control local schools and organizations and practices (e.g., nonproductive paperwork and accountability) often demoralize local efforts. Such programs could take more advantage of existing community and cultural networks. New programs could be evaluated by a litmus test: "Do they support or undermine family functioning and community-based social infrastructure" (education initiatives do little to support family functioning). Such a test would help us avoid the often wishful thinking that isolated program initiatives can make up for missing or vulnerable basic foundations. New research efforts are adding to our ability to evaluate programs.[6]

Multiproblem Families

- Programs for multiproblem families must provide 24-hour availability to infants and children, parental, and family support and guidance; outreach and crisis services; diagnostic and early-intervention capabilities; and educational and vocational training opportunities, all integrated into what we (S.I.G.) have called a Vertical Village. Such a Vertical Village must be characterized by unfailing respect for multirisk and multiproblem families and the capacity to persist with warmth and compassion in spite of enormous challenges. Such relationships are part of the Touchpoints program (see Appendix).

Day Care and Schools

- In order to create family involvement and make schools more responsive to the communities they serve, parental and community governance is therefore essential as a first step. Parents and community members working closely with teachers would set up a structure for each public school (similar to that of a private school) with a local board of advisers and working committees in all the important areas (including curriculum, special activities, drama, dance, music, and after-school activities).
- Both families and neighborhoods would be strengthened if schools evolved into having a broader role in the community than simply academics. This would be particularly true in high-risk neighborhoods and communities. This role means a much more ambitious after-school program, which includes different kinds of activities, from remedial educational work for those children who need it to enhanced learning opportunities in science, math, art, literature, and the arts for those children who are interested as well as drama, music, and sports activities. All children have to be given equal opportunity to participate in high-demand activities such as sports and drama by having different teams and leagues and many performance opportunities. Health services could be made more accessible through schools.

Evening meetings for the community could use school buildings.[7]

- For multirisk or multiproblem families, schools might be set up as 24-hour institutions.

- Those who work with young children—in day care, health care, schools, or social service agencies—should do all they can to work with parents as a team, rather than set up competition (gatekeeping). Becoming aware of competition and discussing it together can be a major step toward cooperation.

- Without adequate wages and respect for the importance of their work, day care personnel or teachers cannot be expected to back up anxious or stressed parents. Elevating the status and wages of teachers and child care workers must be a national priority. Giving them the necessary education and supervision afterward would go a long way toward preventing burnout.

- Those who work with families need to search constantly for the traditions and teachings that support a parent's role. The values and long-term goals shared by diverse religions and cultures outweigh conflicts over means and styles of parenting. Churches that address these basic needs are already contributing much to easing the stresses of modern parents.

7

Protecting the Future

No discussion of the fundamental needs of children would be complete without questioning the commitment of rich developed nations to the children in troubled or less developed parts of the world.

Those of us in developed nations decry the conditions in countries that permit or cause massive starvation, illness, and family dissolution to persist. We make attempts through various relief organizations and international groups to improve some of these conditions. Nevertheless, worldwide we have not made the type of commitment on behalf of the world's children that we have to other political and economic goals. We have not elevated children's starvation and illness to the top of international priorities. Although we rationalize that there are political obstacles (and at times cultural ones) to protecting the world's children, we all know that we could do much better were this goal number one on our international agenda.

As we look at our overall policies toward children, we need to remember, too, that emotional deprivation can wreak just as much havoc as physical and nutritional deprivation. In some respects, the stunting from emotional deprivation is even more devastating because of the emotional pain and disorganization it causes. Such deprivation saps the human spirit and the ability to parent future generations. Caring for children doesn't permit separating physical needs from emotional needs. In fact, part of our motivation for this work on the irreducible needs of infants and children is to unite all the basic needs of children into one framework, where physical, social, emotional, and intellectual fulfillment are all seen as equally essential for the continuation of human life the way we know it, and certainly for the continuation of worldwide social, political, and economic progress. This framework would make possible "report cards" for each nation based on how well they fulfill these basic needs. The irreducible needs report card would enable us to go beyond such indicators of children's well-being as infant mortality, morbidity and poverty and consider key "indicators" for each need based on the recommendations made earlier in this book. For instance, one could consider parental work leave policies, child labor laws, the quality of nurturing care for abandoned babies, and family support programs in regard to the irreducible need for ongoing nurturing care.

When we consider the future of children, whether in the developed or developing nations, nuclear, biological, and ecological threats immediately come to mind. The ability to limit the proliferation of nuclear weapons appears to involve only a slowdown rather than a true limit. Ecological challenges such as global warming and toxic substances from industrial waste spoiling the water supply or plant life or life in the sea are increasingly serious concerns. New diseases such as AIDS that can rapidly cross national boundaries constitute yet another broad threat to our future, as do biological weapons of mass destruction, which are now also growing in their availability along with nuclear weapons.

These are the visible threats to our future. They elicit two reactions. One is fear and helplessness, often coupled with denial and avoidance. The second reaction is to increase international collaborations to slow down or combat the threats. Fear, denial, and avoidance, however, slow down needed international collaborations.

All this would seem far removed from the irreducible needs of children, were it not that all other needs pale before the need to survive and give birth to new generations. Any one generation can now undermine life on earth to the extent of endangering the habitat for and survival of future generations. The ultimate irreducible legacy for our children is a safe planet that will maintain and support human growth. No doubt it should be the first rather than the last of the essential needs, but because of its frightening nature (and the tendency we have to deny it as a major concern) it's best considered as an overarching need with an obvious close relationship to all the others.

In order to protect the future, all nations on earth will need to work cooperatively with a far greater efficacy than has heretofore been the case. The unprecedented international cooperation required, however, reveals a deeper level of this seventh irreducible need.

We are now confronting a new type of interdependency, a new type of psychological challenge that humanity has never before confronted. A number of factors have shifted us from relatively small groups with boundaries into one large world group. No longer can the United States hide behind its boundaries, Canada behind its, India behind its, and so forth. The ties, in terms of national values, ideals, political systems, or cultural characteristics that help relatively defined groups form cohesive relationships and maintain communities and societies, are being broken down by more global concerns and influences.

First of all, the threats already mentioned—nuclear weapons, ecological disaster, and biological challenges—bring us into an interdependency of fear. Burning oil in the Middle East can create clouds that block the sun in other parts of the world. Viruses created in laboratories in one part of the world can affect citizens elsewhere. Despite attempts to create an umbrella to protect a country from nuclear attack, no such umbrella has been devised. Biological, ecological, and nuclear interdependency therefore create fears that connect us all. Only common solutions can reduce this fear.

Second, we are increasingly tied together economically. Markets that drop in Indonesia or South America can affect markets in the United States and in Europe. These events have become all too obvious in recent years, when there has been a flurry of activity by Western countries to bolster the economies in Asia and in South America. Related to the economic interdependency is the way in which large companies and corporations are creating new organizations that cross international boundaries. Some worry because these large companies can operate like governments without rules or regulations. The world trade agreements under which they operate preempt the health and environmental regulations of individual countries. Whatever the risks, they create yet another line of interdependency.

A third factor is the interdependency due to communication. Television is everywhere, bringing all parts of the world community together. Soon the Internet will tie every individual in every far corner of the world to every other person. Interestingly, the commonality of interests and cultural patterns, be they in music, clothing, or movies, is tying people of the world together more quickly than their governments can come together. We are also seeing younger leaders sharing values with other emerging younger leaders in many countries of the world. These shared values emerge from either common educational experiences or the interdependency of communication.

We are therefore all tied together, whether through fear, communication, or economics. How do we operate as a true global village or family?

In the past, we dealt with international conflicts through either cooperation or intimidation. If cooperation didn't work, there was always intimidation. Countries with greater military power could succeed by using a survival-of-the-fittest, might-makes-right mentality. We are seeing, however, that such strategies, as evidenced by the experience of the United States in Vietnam and of the Soviet Union in Afghanistan, often don't work even with superior military force. In any case, smaller, less powerful countries will soon have sufficient biological and nuclear weapons to create unacceptable damage either in their own backyard or elsewhere. In other words, when most nations can destroy the planet, the risks of the use of intimidation are too high.

Typically, when groups become very large, it's hard for individuals to organize themselves. They resort to the primitive psychological mechanisms that we often see governing international relations, such as polarized "we-versus-them" thinking, nonrecognition or withdrawal, suspiciousness, and attempts at manipulation and intimidation. These primitive tactics, whether used by individuals or among nations, however, were only partially successful in keeping groups organized in the world of the past. In the world of the future, because of the greater interdependency, these primitive mechanisms will not be able to build the cooperation necessary to protect the future for subsequent generations.

Therefore, the future can only be protected by the development of a new psychology that can deal with the fact of our interdependency. The worldwide family needs methods and patterns of communication that won't break down into distortions, polarizations, or patterns of withdrawal, avoidance, and suspiciousness.

How can such a new psychology of cooperation be developed? How can we mobilize our unprecedented interdependency to embrace diversity, broaden a shared sense of humanity, and work cooperatively together?

In attempting to facilitate large-group behavior that can work cooperatively in the future, we need to look at the factors that tend to increase polarized, suspicious thinking and withdrawal or aggression.

Here we come full circle: The factors that lead to a broadening of our sense of shared humanity are the basics we have been discussing. We need these basics in greater depth and continuity than at any time in our history. We therefore need to change course, interrupt the movement toward impersonality and fragmentation, and embrace a few basic principles of human growth that can foster collaboration among peoples in the future.

- **The Security of Having Physical Needs Met.** Groups concerned with survival are going to band together around very concrete needs and do not have the luxury of reflecting on long-term worldwide goals. Making sure the world's population has ample food, housing, and medical care is an essential foundation, just as it is for individual children. Here, economic gain can no longer be simply a personal matter, it must be a broad international concern. Strategies that foster each and every country's ability to grow economically will help ensure a secure and safe environment for all.

- **An Ethic and Worldwide Philosophy That Fosters Ongoing Human Relationships That Preserve and Support Families and Communities.** Only secure, well-nurtured individuals are capable of joining together and embracing a broader ethic of shared humanity. Deprived individuals, like stressed and hungry ones, take a concrete and narrow view based on their own anxiety and fear. Lack of basic nurturance sharply reduces their ability to extend caring to other members of the human race. We have focused on the "survival of the fittest," the competitive theme in evaluation, but have denied the importance of nurturing care that enables human beings to form and maintain relationships and families, cooperate in groups and communities, and work together toward political, economic, and military goals. In a complex society, nurturing care is the foundation for the collaboration necessary for survival. With an interdependent world demanding that we all embrace a wider range of "others" than ever before and project ourselves into the future way beyond our own and our children's lifetimes to protect the planet, we can no longer underestimate the importance of nurturance in human evolution. Ongoing, nurturing care in stable families, therefore, is a prerequisite for producing children who will be able to feel broader responsibility and stewardship.

• **Families, Educational Settings, and Communities That Help Children Become Communicative, Reflective Members of Society.** As we discussed in earlier chapters, it is necessary to build on this nurturing base developmentally appropriate interactions tailored to individual differences. We therefore need individuals around the globe who have an opportunity for an advanced, problem-solving education. We also need to foster stable communities to support families and the educational system and other institutions that will enable citizens to develop the reflective skills necessary for solving the world's shared difficulties.

Providing for the irreducible needs of infants and young children and their families is the first step in producing citizens of the world who can broaden their sense of humanity sufficiently to cope with the new interdependency of the world. Our seventh irreducible need, therefore, requires meeting the other six for its solution. This means creating citizens of the world who have a sufficiently broad sense of their humanity to embrace all others so that they can move toward truly reflective collaborative efforts. Our sense of justice must extend as well to intergenerational equity, to concern for the kind of world our grandchildren will face. Without such a perspective, we cannot begin the unprecedented effort to start long-range, 50-year planning sequences to reduce the risk of biological, ecological, and nuclear catastrophe.

To meet this goal, we must elevate the irreducible needs of children to the highest international priority, alongside human rights, as a "right" for all. The seven irreducible needs can serve as a framework (a report card) for nations and regions within nations and the international community as a whole to monitor current status and provide incentives for progress.

Throughout the world future generations of children and families will be much more interrelated. In order to protect the future for one child, we must protect it for all.

The Touchpoints Model

T. Berry Brazelton, M.D.

Acknowledgements: The author would like to thank Maureen O'Brien, Kristie Brandt, and other Touchpoints' colleagues for their contributions to this work. This article is based on a paper originally published in *Infants and Young Children*, 10, 74–84, 1997.

All parents benefit from information about child development and the importance of providing their children with a nurturing environment. Our goal as caring professionals should be to join them as allies in the system of care for their children. Our present systems are too often crisis-driven, deficit-oriented, and unwelcoming to parents. Many families, particularly those who have a child with special needs, are often left feeling isolated and unsupported (Bowman et al., 1994; Turnbull, Turnbull, & Blue-Banning, 1994). Our focus instead should be on developing a system where providers are thinking preventively and where parents' ethnic, religious, and lifestyle attributes are valued. Rather than treating a pregnant teenager as a failure, which will turn her away and mitigate our opportunity for successful interaction with her, we could accept her pregnancy, point to the potential future opportunity for her baby, and offer her our support. If we, as supportive providers, can offer the necessary information and modeling for the parents to understand their young child's development and to enhance it, we can play a crucial role toward the success of the family system.

For the past several years, I have been working on the Touchpoints model (Brazelton, 1992). Touchpoints are periods during the first three years of life during which children's spurts in development result in pronounced disruption in the family system. Touchpoints are like a map of child development that can be identified and anticipated by both parents and providers. See Figure 1. Thirteen touchpoints have been noted in the first three years, beginning in pregnancy. They are centered around caregiving themes that truly matter to parents (e.g., feeding, discipline), rather than traditional milestones. The child's negotiation of the points can be seen as a source of success for the family system. Awareness of these touchpoints and strategies of dealing with them can help reduce negative patterns that might otherwise result in problems in the areas of sleep, feeding, toilet training, etc. The timing of touchpoints may be somewhat delayed for a premature or fragile infant, but they will be even more important as opportunities for supporting their anxious parents. The guiding principles of the Touchpoints model can be found in the box below.

Professionals can use these touchpoints as a framework for each encounter with families during the first three years of a child's life. Several guiding assumptions about parents form the core of Touchpoints' practice with families. Together, professionals and the parents can discover themes that recur and strategies to negotiate upcoming challenges. For example, for four-month-olds, one can predict that there will soon be a burst in cognitive awareness of the environment. The

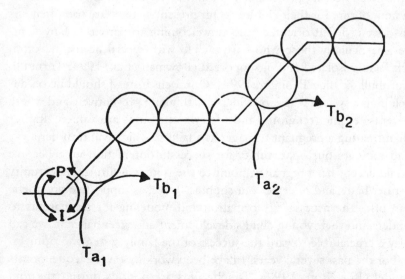

FIGURE 1   Touchpoints for Intervention

Touchpoints Guiding Principles

1. Value and understand the relationship between you and the parent.
2. Use the behavior of the child as your language.
3. Recognize what you bring to the interaction.
4. Be willing to discuss matters that go beyond your traditional role.
5. Look for opportunities to support parental mastery.
6. Focus on the parent-child relationship.
7. Value passion wherever you find it.
8. Value disorganization and vulnerability as an opportunity.

---

baby will be difficult to feed. He will stop eating to look around and to listen to every stimulus in the environment. To parents' dismay, he will begin to awaken again at night. Yet, when parents understand this period as a natural precursor to the rapid and exciting development that follows, they will not need to feel as if it represents failure. From the Touchpoints framework, the guidance or "scaffolding" professionals can give parents is supportive rather than prescriptive. Anticipatory guidance is not just delivery of "expert advice," but having a dialogue, a shared discussion around how the parents feel and would react in the face of new challenges. This is, in part, based on how they have dealt with related issues in the past.

Parents find it reassuring that bursts and regressions in development are to be expected. The concept of overlap in different lines of development is often a shift in thinking for parents, who without this concept would often question their own caregiving efficacy. In the face of their children's behavioral regressions, they wonder what they are doing wrong. Sharing these touchpoints helps parents feel more confident in themselves and in their child.

The Touchpoints model was originally developed for the primary health-care setting. However, our model is now being utilized by professionals from various disciplines who work in a variety of settings. We value practitioners' own expertise and encourage them to adapt the model to their own population and settings. The assumptions about professionals using this model can be found in Table 3. The essence of Touchpoints' training is in preventive anticipatory guidance, its approach is multidisciplinary, and its focus is on the common interest in the child that parents and providers share. Touchpoints focuses on building relationships as an integral *goal* of parent and practitioner interactions in diverse settings: childbirth education classes, during office and home visits, in encounters at child care centers, etc. Continuity of care for families in the face of fragmented services is also a focus of our work. How can individual practitioners work as a team to maintain a sense of connection with families that is meaningful for children's health and development? From a systems perspective, we believe that building community around practitioners is essential to best practice with families.

Our goal is both changing individual practice and causing a shift in the larger system of care around families. Accomplishing this shift at a community level requires an expansion of the definition of "practitioner" to include the full range of providers serving families from the prenatal period through early childhood, and the inclusion of practitioners from diverse practice settings (e.g., pediatric offices, hospitals, private/non-profit and public agencies, child care facilities, etc.). This community-based multi-disciplinary model is being pilot-tested in 13 communities and initial results are encouraging.

As a conceptual model, we see the Touchpoints' framework as a foundation for helping individuals and their systems to enhance care for families. With a dual focus on development and relationships, the model has implications for multidisciplinary providers and diverse families. As practice settings move toward greater collaboration, orientation to a community of practitioners must include an explicitly articulated conceptual framework. When espoused by the organization and shared by colleagues, this framework can form the basis for professional development within the work-setting and the community. Only then will we be able to move beyond the current state of fragmentation of services to more effectively join families as allies within a more caring, seamless system.

References

Bowman, P., Grady, M., Kendrick, M., Ladew-Duncan, J., Mentzer, S., Newman, R., Pease, R., Son, K., & Spandinger, L. (1994). *From the heart: Stories by mothers of children with special needs*. Portland, ME: University of Southern Maine.

Brazelton, T. B. (1992). *Touchpoints: Emotional and behavioral development*. Reading, MA: Addison-Wesley.

Turnbull, A. P., Turnbull, H. R., & Blue-Banning, M. (1994). Enhancing inclusion of infants and toddlers with disabilities and their families: A theoretical and programmatic analysis. *Infants and Young Children*, 7, 1–14.

Major Themes at Each Touchpoint

The Prenatal Touchpoint

Preparation—Parents are preparing for parenthood both physically and mentally. Anticipation and anxiety about the birth process is foremost in their minds as the delivery date approaches.

Imagined babies—Imaginary babies—idealized, damaged, and real—are active elements of the parent(s) inner lives. They are evidence of their emotional commitment to the baby, changes in their view of themselves, and anxiety about the demands of the future.

Relationships—A realignment of relationships accompanies preparing for a child. Mothers' relationships with their own mothers often become more intense. Friendships with peers who don't have children may lose importance. As a practitioner you play a role in the constellation of support around a new mother.

Imagined parent—Parents-to-be may feel both pride and self-doubt as they picture themselves as parents. The imagined parent is associated with the imagined baby.

The Newborn Touchpoint

Health Is my baby okay? Parents need to be reassured that their baby is healthy. And if she is not, they require honesty and support in addressing the issue of her health.

Parental emotions—Parents experience intense and often polar and confusing emotions upon the birth of a baby. Exhilaration, relief, anxiety, love, anger, loneliness, joy, and doubt can all arise. The baby is a powerful elicitor of the range of parent's own emotional strengths and vulnerabilities.

The real baby—The baby's unique characteristics—gender, size, color, temperament—are discovered and are given meaning by the parents as they begin replacing the idealized children of their imaginations with the real one they have received.

Attachment—The relationship with the baby will grow and develop as the first year progresses, but the initial emotional ties between parent and child are given impetus by the events of the first minutes and hours of life together.

The 3 Week Touchpoint

Parental exhaustion—Parental emotional well-being is particularly vulnerable at this point. Mothers are still recovering from the birth and may be experiencing postpartum depression. The demands of the baby are great, but her capacity to interact is not yet clearly defined.

Feeding—The caregiving demands of the baby center around feeding and sleeping. Feeding is the strongest representation of a parent's ability to nurture a baby. Issues of weight gain, feeding schedule, and elimination are often at the forefront of parents' minds at this early visit.

Individuality—The baby's behavioral organization and temperament are beginning to become more apparent. She is gradually showing her parents how she reacts to their efforts at caregiving.

Relationships—The changes in parents' lives are now more salient. The relationship between the parents themselves is changing. And relationships with extended family, friends and society in general are now recognizably different than before the arrival of the baby.

The 6–8 Week Touchpoint

Sociability—The baby is beginning to become more social. Her increased capacities to engage with the world—longer periods of alertness, visual attention, social smiles—offer parents the opportunity for interaction with their child beyond the demands of caregiving.

Parental self-confidence—The exhaustion and emotional depletion that parents experienced at three weeks has typically been replaced with a more settled outlook toward parenting. New mothers and fathers are no longer simply surviving; they are parenting. As routines of feeding and sleeping are becoming more stable and predictable parents tend to become more self-confident. For example, they can discriminate between the baby's cries and manage their own sleep schedules better than at three weeks.

Relationships—Parents are reentering the outer world. The exhilaration and exhaustion of the delivery and initial adjustment to the child have passed, and issues of reestablishing relationships and returning to work become more salient. At this point they are often concerned that their relationship with each other is altered forever.

The 4 Month Touchpoint

Attachment—Strong emotional ties between the baby and her parents are forming through more definite and predictable patterns of interaction.

Interest in the world—The baby is beginning to direct attention outward. She begins to become engaged and interested in the outside world.

Patterns of care—Caregiving routines are established—often with the effect of more parental self-confidence. Feeding and sleeping routines are becoming more predictable.

Baby's demands—Increased and more effective demands for attention from the baby can satisfy parents' desire for relationship or frustrate parents who can't meet this demand.

Father engagement—As the baby becomes more interested in the world, fathers may see more opportunities for engagement with thebaby. Mothers may feel this external orientation as a loss of intimacy.

The 7 Month Touchpoint

Motor abilities—The baby's motor abilities along with a greater cognitive awareness bring her more control over her environment. Increased trunk control allows her to explore with her hands more freely, and the emergence of a pincer grasp allows her to use her hands more effectively. She explores with more purpose.

Feeding—Her new cognitive and motor abilities affect her feeding in that she is no longer satisfied with simply being fed. The distractibility of the last few months is replaced by the need to be actively involved in the feeding process and everything else that is going on as well.

Sleeping—The excitement of exploring the world extends to nighttime. Getting the baby to go down to sleep and attending to her when she wakes at night return parents to challenges they may have thought they left behind.

Object Permanence—The baby is beginning to understand that objects have an existence separate from her own sensory perceptions. She shows an interest in manipulating objects and discovering their physical properties.

The 9 Month Touchpoint

Mobility—Motor skills are at the forefront of the baby's activity. At this point she can typically stand but not yet balance well enough to walk. At the same time she can effectively crawl or creep around and get into a thousand places she couldn't reach before.

Social referencing—The baby is now becoming more aware of parental reactions to her activity. She may crawl to a forbidden place and look for a reaction. This opens up a whole new world of shared understanding and misunderstanding for parent and child.

Person permanence—The cognitive advance of understanding that objects have an existence of their own separate from the immediate sensory perception of the child is now freely applied to people. As people come and go the baby wants to keep them or push them away.

Control—Both sleeping and feeding are affected by the baby's newfound abilities to move and think. The new awareness of each other's intentions brings issues of who is in charge to the fore.

The 12 Month Touchpoint

Independence—The balance between independence and dependence is based upon a secure attachment between a child and her caregiver. His ability to explore his world is supported by the security of her relationships. The paradox of greater dependence leading to more independence is often hard for parents to accept at a time when dependence is so strongly expressed.

Motor skills—The ability to move on two feet is an achievement that is filled with significance for the parents and excitement for the child. Anticipating the ability but not yet having the skill can be frustrating for babies. Parents expectations for the first steps and their surpass at the baby's negativity may make the achievement of this milestone more difficult than it needs to be.

Learning—The months after the first year of life are full of discovery. Now that she has a sense of object permanence she begins to explore the properties of objects and the larger world with interest and purpose experimenting with objects and looking for others' reactions to what she discovers.

Irritability—With advances in her ability to move and communicate on her own the baby may begin to demand to use her new skills. Her communications may now take on a negative tone as he learns that her directives have the effect of mobilizing her caregivers.

The 15 Month Touchpoint

Autonomy—The physical and intellectual burst in development that marks the entry into toddlerhood demands that the child exercise his new capacities. The challenge to the parent is to encourage these new skills while at the same time keeping the child safe and teaching him what his limitations are.

Play—The child is now a true explorer. His transactions with the physical world are characterized by experimentation and discovery. Taking a bath is an examination of water and the properties of objects that sink and float. Every nook and cranny in the house is another region to be explored. In addition to his interest in exploration he is now interested in the effect he has on objects and people.

Motor skills—There is large variation in the age at which children begin to walk. Most, but not all, typically developing children are on their feet by this age. If they aren't their parents are likely to be worried. Fine motor skills are now more refined. The child can reach for, grasp, and let go of small objects with greater ease than at 12 months. And he can run away with a giggle, combining his emergent autonomy with his newfound motor skills.

Dependence—The flip side of autonomy is the extreme dependence that is often experienced at this age. As the child exercises his newfound abilities he often discovers that he is out there on his own and needs to assure himself that his parents are there when he needs them. This is when stranger and separation anxiety are at their peak.

Language—Language learning is beginning to take more of the child's energy. A few words may be used, but more importantly an understanding of their impact is more apparent. The frustration of wanting to say something, knowing that it can be said, making the attempt, but not being understood can be large. Understanding well outpaces expression at this age.

The 18 Month Touchpoint

Cognition—This is a time when the child's ability to think moves from the here and now to the symbolic. This is best seen in a dramatic increase in the use of language not only to get what she needs but also to describe and organize what she experiences. It is also seen in more sophisticated pretend play.

Sense of self—This period is marked by a large shift in the child's self-awareness. The frustration that she expresses when she fails to successfully imitate an adult, her increased awareness of good and bad behavior, and her expressions of pride at her successes and empathy for others all mark the development of a clearer sense of selfhood.

Battles for control—New skills are inevitably accompanied by the desire to exercise them. Remarkable growth in personal and intellectual capacities leads to conflicts between the child and caregivers. Every limit is a challenge to the child's autonomy. Parents are often caught off guard by the intensity that their previously easy to manage children bring to these conflicts.

Language—At this age a child typically has a set of a few words that she can use repeatedly and effectively, but her understanding of language continues to outpace her ability to express herself. Adults can use language to explain things and to manage her behavior more effectively than in the past. But she is still tied to the physical and sensory. Expectations for language understanding must be tempered with the knowledge that she continues to need direct contact with people and things.

The 2 Year Touchpoint

Pretend play—The child is now entering a whole new world of imagination. He can begin to act out the routines of his life in his play and imitate the roles of the adults around him. He uses the objects which he manipulates—his blocks, dolls, and trucks—to make sense out of a complex world.

Language—His capacity to assign meaning in his play parallels the ability to do so with language. He now uses verbs in short sentences and begins to use language as a means of interpreting his own actions. The dramatic increase in ability to understand and use language allows him entrance into the community of speakers.

Autonomy—The famous willfulness of the two year old has two sides. It is the culmination of newfound physical, cognitive, and social abilities that need expression. And it is the overgeneralization of those perceived abilities to everything imaginable. Parents who have been lulled into caring for a baby are now confronted with a personality who believes himself as having a more important agenda than his parents.

Motor skills—At two years the child has far better motor control than only a few months ago. His large motor skills have developed to the point that he can climb over almost anything. His fine motor skills allow him to handle a cup with one hand and manipulate small objects. He now moves with greater confidence and mastery, a reflection not only of motor proficiency but also of a stronger sense of self.

The 3 Year Touchpoint

Imagination—With her ability to use symbols the child now develops a vivid and active imagination. She represents aspects of the world and her relationships with others in her mind. And, since she now has the capacity to generate new ideas separate from her experience, she begins to use fantasy in ways that help her make sense of a complex world. An imaginary friend or a transitional object like a teddy bear may become particularly important at this age.

Fears and phobias—Along with the ability to use imagination to help her sort out her experiences and feelings come fears and phobias when that capacity to imagine focuses on particularly bothersome aspects of experience. The line between fantasy and reality, particularly as she is emerging from sleep, is not clear. The feelings are real and must be responded to with assurance and respect.

Language—Language is exploding. It is becoming the primary means through which the child relates to others. And, it is also beginning to be used by her to organize her world. This is when many children seem to ask questions constantly, when they often talk to themselves while at play, and when they are asked to "use words" when they need something. How parents and other adults use language is incorporated into how she uses it and has major implications for her later school experience. Reading can begin to become a more cooperative process as she begins to expand her ability to represent ideas with words.

Peer relations—The three year old is typically a very social person. She is much more able to tolerate separations from caregivers than a year ago and be strongly attracted to truly interactive play with peers. She doesn't yet have the social skills to share and cooperate on play agendas, but she is capable of actively working at such interaction.

Social understanding—He is now better able to read others' cues, understand the impact of his behavior, and act accordingly. More mature behavior is expected by parents, and misbehavior takes on more meaning. The three year old is much more capable of manipulation by pitting parents against each other and not revealing his own intentions.

Functional Developmental Growth Chart and Questionnaire

STANLEY I. GREENSPAN, MD

To assess if your child has achieved a new functional milestone, the answer must be "yes" to all the questions under that milestone. If you've answered "no" to even one question, the child has not yet mastered the stage. Remember, this chart is simply a visual tool to draw your attention to those developmental areas where your child is progressing as expected and those where he or she may be facing some challenges.

Three Months
(Stage 1: Regulation and Attention)

- Does your infant usually show an interest in things around him/her by looking at sights and turning towards sounds?

Five Months
(Stage 2: Engaging in Relationships)

(Ask the questions from the prior category plus the new one from this category.)

195

- Does your baby seem happy or pleased when he/she sees his/her favorite people: looking and smiling, making sounds, or some other gesture, like moving arms, that indicates pleasure or delight?

Nine Months
(Stage 3: Interacts in a Purposeful Manner)

(Ask the questions from all prior categories plus the new ones from this category.)

- Is your baby able to show what he/she wants by reaching for or pointing at something, reaching out to be picked up, or making purposeful special noises?
- Does your baby respond to people talking or playing with him/her by making sounds, faces, initiating gestures (reaching), etc.?

By 14 to 18 Months (Stage 4: Organizes Chains of Interaction; Problem Solving)

(Ask the questions from all prior categories plus the new ones for this category.)

- Is your toddler (by 14 months) able to show what he/she wants or needs by using actions, such as leading you by the hand to open a door or pointing to find a toy?
- Is your toddler (by 18 months) able to orchestrate more complex chains of interaction as he/she solves problems and shows you what he/she wants, including such things as getting food, for example (does he/she take your hand, lead you to the refrigerator, tug on the handle, and point to a particular food or bottle of juice or milk?)
- Is your toddler (by 18 months) able to use imitation, such as copying your sounds, words, or motor gestures, as part of a playful, ongoing interaction?

By 24 to 30 Months (Stage 5: Uses Ideas—Words or Symbols—to Convey Intentions or Feelings):

(Ask the questions from all prior categories plus the new ones for this category.)

- Does your toddler (by 24 months) ever respond to people talking with or playing with him/her by using words or sequences of sounds that are clearly an attempt to convey a word?
- Is he/she (by 24 months) able to imitate familiar pretend-like actions, such as feeding or hugging a doll?
- Is he/she (by 24 months) able to meet some basic needs with one or a few words (may require parent saying the word first), such as "juice," "open," or "kiss"?
- Is he/she (by 24 months) able to follow simple one-step directions from caregiver to meet some basic needs, for example, "The toy is there" or "Come give Mommy a kiss"?
- Is he/she (by 30 months) able to engage in interactive pretend play with an adult or another child (feeding dollies, tea parties, etc.)?
- Is he/she (by 30 months) able to use ideas—words or symbols—to share his/her delight or interest? ("See truck!", for example.)
- Is he/she able to use symbols (words, pictures, organized games) while enjoying and interacting with one or more peers?

By 36 to 48 Months (Stage 6: Creates Logical Bridges Between Ideas)

(Ask the questions from all prior categories plus the new ones for this category.)

- Is your toddler (by 36 months) able to use words or other symbols (for example, pictures) to show what he/she likes or dislikes, such as "want that" or "no want that"?
- Is your toddler (by 36 months) able to engage in pretend play with another person in which the story or drama makes sense? (For example, does he/she have the bears go visit grandmother and then have a big lunch?)
- Is your toddler (by 36 months) able to begin to explain wishes or needs ("Mommy, go out." "What are you going to do outside?" "Play")? May need multiple choice help from you ("What will you do, play or sleep?")
- Can your preschooler (by 48 months) explain reasons why he/she wants something or wants to do something ("Why do you want the juice?"…"Because I'm thirsty").

- Is your preschooler (by 48 months) able occasionally to use feelings to explain reasons for a wish or behavior (because I'm happy/excited/sad)?
- Is your preschooler (by 48 months) able to engage in interactive pretend dramas with both peers as well as adults in which there are a number of elements that logically fit together (The children go to school, do work, have lunch, and meet an elephant on the way home)?
- Is your preschooler (by 48 months) able to make a logical conversation with four or more give-and-take sequences about a variety of topics, ranging from negotiating foods and bedtimes to talking about friends or school?

Between Ages 4 – 7 Years

- Is your child developing friendships with peers, including play dates outside of school?
- Is your child warm and close with his parents?
- Is your child able to negotiate with two or more people at the same time (e.g., go back and forth between mom and dad to try to get a later bed time or an extra cookie or try to convince two peers to play the game his way)?
- Is your child able to compare two ideas such as explain why he likes one friend better than another friend or one food better than another food?
- Is your child able to discuss how and why he feels a certain way?
- Is your child able to regulate his impulses and his fears and anxieties (control his behavior and calm down with a little bit of support)?
- Is he beginning to master academic challenges, such as learning to read, count, add and subtract, and write?

By Age 9

- Is your child fully involved in peer friendships?
- Is your child warm and close with his parents?
- Is your child able to deal with disappointment and/or frustration in peer relationships and/or family patterns without major tantrums?
- Is your child able to engage in gray area (relativistic) thinking (e.g., discuss how he likes one child more than another child or is a little bit sad, a lot sad, or very very sad)?

- Is your child mastering age-appropriate academic skills, such as reading paragraphs, adding, subtracting confidently and moving into multiplication and division and writing down a number of ideas in a row in organized sentences?
- Is your child able to regulate impulses, fears, and anxieties and feel good about himself most of the time?

By Age 12

- Is your child warm and close with his parents?
- Is your child able to be fully engaged in peer friendships and at the same time able to have his own opinions about himself and others?
- Is your child beginning to form his own inner ideas about what's right and wrong, what he likes and doesn't like, and what he wants to do in the near future?
- Is your child able to do gray-area thinking and weigh a number of factors in coming to a conclusion (whether it's discussing a story or his own feelings or friendships or the reasons for or against an action and taking into account the present as well as the short-term past and future)?
- Is your child able to reason at least a little about his own moods and feelings and regulate his impulses, anxieties and fears, and moods enough not to be swept away by them?

THE FUNCTION

Developmental Stages

$\Downarrow$

9. Constructs inner world of emerging standards along with world of family/peers

8. Moves more into peer friendships and relativistic thinking

7. Expands family & peer relationships & complexity of thinking

6b. Creates logical bridges between 3 or more emotional ideas

6a. Creates logical bridges between ideas

Chil

5b. Uses ideas beyond expression of basic needs and for pretend play

5a. Uses ideas (words/symbols) to convey intentions or feelings

4b. Organizes chains of interaction (complex problem-solving)

4a, Organizes chains of interaction (simple problem-solving)

3. Interacts in purposeful manner

2. Engages in relationships

1. Focuses and attends to sights and sounds

Developmental probl the chil

Age in Months/ Years $\longrightarrow$

| 0 | 3 mo | 5 mo | 9 mo | 13 mo |

AL DEVELOPMENTAL GROWTH CHART

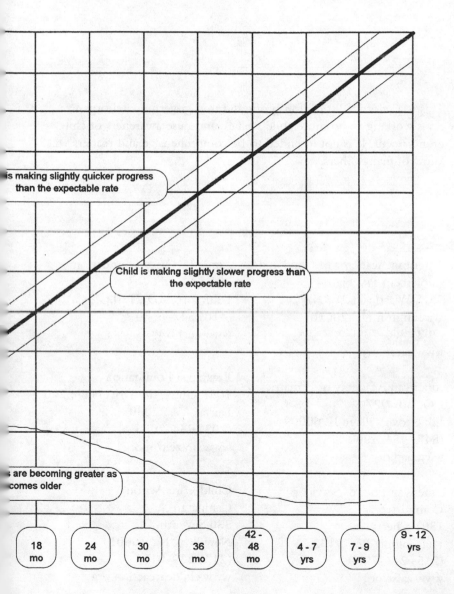

is making slightly quicker progress
than the expectable rate

Child is making slightly slower progress than
the expectable rate

s are becoming greater as
comes older

| 18 mo | 24 mo | 30 mo | 36 mo | 42 - 48 mo | 4 - 7 yrs | 7 - 9 yrs | 9 - 12 yrs |

Organizations

This is a selective list of non-profit and non-governmental organizations working to promote child welfare and raise awareness of children's needs. It is not intended to be comprehensive and readers will know of many others.

American Academy of Child and
Adolescent Psychiatry
3615 Wisconsin Ave NW
Washington DC 20016
(202) 966–7300
www.aacap.org

American Academy of Pediatrics
P.O. Box 927
Elk Grove Village IL 60009
(847) 434–4000
www.aap.org

American Friends Service
Committee
1501 Cherry St.
Philadelphia PA 19102
(215) 241–7000
www.aafsc.org

Annie E. Casey Foundation
701 St. Paul St.
Baltimore MD 21202
(410) 547–6600
www.aecf.org

Brazelton Foundation
4031 University Drive Suite 200
Fairfax VA 22030
(703) 934–2036
www.brazelton.org

Child Care Action
Campaign
330 Seventh Ave
New York NY 10001
(212) 239–0138
www.childcareaction.org

Children's Defense Fund
25 E Street NW
Washington DC 20001
202–628–8787
www.childrensdefense.org

Children's Health Envi-
ronmental Coalition Network
P.O. Box 1540
Princeton NJ 08542
(609) 252–1915
www.checnet.org

Child Welfare League of
America
440 First St. NW 3rd Floor
Washington DC 20001
(202) 638–2952
www.cwla.org

Early Head Start
National Head Start Association
1651 Prince St.
Alexandria VA 22314
www.nhsa.org

Educating Children for
Parenting
211 13th St # 701
Philadelphia PA
(215) 496–9780
www.ecparenting.org

Erikson Institute
420 N. Wabash Ave.
Chicago IL 60611
(312) 755–2250
www.erikson.edu

Families and Work Institute
330 Seventh Ave.
New York NY 10001
(212) 465–2044
www.familiesandwork.org

Family Support America
20 N Wacker Ave.
Chicago IL 60606
(312) 338–0900
www.fsca.org

Healthy Families America
Freddie Mac Foundation
8250 Jones Branch Drive
Mailstop A–40
McLean VA 22102
(703) 918–8888
www.freddiemacfoundation.org

Healthy Steps Program
C/o Commonwealth Fund
1 E. 75th St.
New York NY 10021
www.healthysteps.org

I Am Your Child
Foundation
335 N. Maple St.
Beverly Hills CA 90210
www.iamyourchild.org

Interdisciplinary Council on
Developmental and Learning
Disorders
4938 Hampden Lane
Suite 800
Bethesda MD 20814
www.icdl.com

International Childbirth
Education Association
P.O. Box 20048
Minneapolis MN 55420
(612) 854–8660
www.icea.org

March of Dimes Birth Defects
Foundation
1275 Mamaroneck Ave.
White Plains NY 10605
(888) 663–4637
www.modimes.org

National Association for the
Education of Young Children
1509 16th St. NW
Washington DC 20036
(202) 232–8777
www.naeyc.org

National Association of
Pediatric Nurse Associates and
Practitioners
1101 Kings Highway N
Suite 206
Cherry Hill NJ 08034
(609) 667–1773
www.napnap.org

National Black Child
Development Institute
1023 15th St. Suite 600
Washington DC 20005
(800) 556–2234
www.nbcdi.org

National Center for Education
in Maternal and Child Health
2000 15th St N Suite 701
Arlington VA 22201
(703) 524–7802
www.ncemch.org

NetAid.org Foundation
136 East 45th St. 2nd Floor
New York NY 10017
www.netaid.org

Planned Parenthood Federation
of America
810 Seventh Ave.
New York NY 10010
(212) 541–7800
www.plannedparenthood.org

PLANet
www.familyplanet.org
A public awareness campaign
funded by the David and Lucile
Packard Foundation and the
William and Flora Hewlett
Foundation, and involving Save
the Children, CARE, National
Audubon Society, Planned
Parenthood, and Population
Action.

Physicians for Social
Responsibility
1101 14th Street NW Suite 700
Washington DC 20005
202–898–0150
www.psr.org

Pew Environmental Health
Coalition
111 Market Ave. Suite 850
Baltimore MD 21202
www.pewenvirohealthjhsph.edu

Rheedlen Center for Children
and Families
2770 Broadway
New York NY 10025
(212) 866–0700
www.reeusda.gov

Robin Hood Foundation
111 Broadway 19th Floor

New York NY 10806
(212) 227–6601
www.robinhood.org

Save the Children
Att. Donor Services
54 Wilton Road
Westport CT 06880
www.savethechildren.org

The School of the 21st Century
Yale University Bush Center in
Child Development and Social
Policy
310 Prospect St.
New Haven CT 06511
(203) 432–9944
www.yale.edu.bushcenter

Society for Research in Child
Development
505 E. Huron Suite 301
Ann Arbor MI 48100
(734) 998–6578
www.srcd.org

Touchpoints Project
Children's Hospital – Boston
1295 Boylston St. Suite 320
Boston MA 02215
(617) 355–6947
www.touchpoints.org

UNICEF
UNICEF House
3 United Nations Plaza
New York NY 10017
www.unicef.org
UNICEF International Child
Development Center

UNICEF Innocenti Research
Center
Piazza SS Annunziata 12
50122 Florence
Italy
www.unicef-icdc.org

Unicorn Children's Foundation
1501 Maple #501
Evanston IL 60201

World Association for Infant
Mental Health
WAIMH ICYF
Kellog Center Suite 27
Michigan State University
East Lansing MI 48824
www.msu.edu/user/waimh

Zero to Three: National Center
for Infants, Toddlers and
Families
734 15th St. NW Suite 1000
Washington DC 20007
(202) 638–1144
www.zerotothree.org

Notes

Introduction

1. *Beyond Rhetoric: The New American Agenda for Children and Families.* Report of the National Commission for Children, Department of Documents, Washington, DC 20402 (1991).

2. Children's Defense Fund. *Child Care Challenge:* Washington, D.C., 1998

3. Helburn, S.W., et al. (1995). "Cost, Quality, and Child Outcomes in Child Care Centers," Public Report. Denver. Department of Economics, Center for Research in Economic and Social Policy. University of Colorado-Denver.

4. Galinsky, E., Howes, C., Kontos, S., Shinn, M. (1994). "The Study of Children in Family Child Care and Relative Care: Highlights of Findings." Boston, MA: Families and Work Institute.

5. Young, K.T., Marsland, K.W., Zigler E., (1997) "The Regulatory Status of Center-Based Infant and Toddler Child Care," *The American Journal for Orthopsychiatry* 67(4):535-44.

6. Fuller, B., & Kagan, S.L. (2000). *Remember the Children: Mothers Balance Work and Child Care Under Welfare Reform.* Growing Up in Poverty Project 2000. Wave 1 Report. Berkely, CA: University of California Berkeley.

7. National Institute of Child Health and Human Development. *NICHD Study of Early Child Care, Executive Summary.* NIH Pub. No. 98-4318 Washington, D.C.: National Institute of Health 1998

8. Kaiser Foundation Kids and the Media in the New Millennium, Publication No. 1536, Menlo Park, CA, 2000.

9. Greenspan, S. I. *The Growth of the Mind.* Cambridge, MA: Perseus Books, 1997.

10. Zito, J.M., Safer, D., dosReis, S., Gardner, J.F., Boles, M. & Lynch, F. (2000). "Trends in the prescribing of psychotropic medications to preschoolers." *Journal of the American Medical Association, 283(8),* 1025-1030.

Chapter 1

1. Experience can stimulate hormonal changes; for example, soothing touch appears to release growth hormones, and hormones such as oxytocin appear to foster critical emotional processes such as affiliation and closeness. Furthermore, emotional stress is associated with changes in brain physiology. S.M. Schanberg and T.M. Field, "Sensory Deprivation Stress and Supplemental Stimulation in the Rat Pup and Preterm Human Neonate," *Child Development* 58 (1987): 1431–47.

2. See T.N. Wiesel and D.H. Hubel "Single-Cell Responses in Striate Cortex of Kittens Deprived of Vision in One Eye," *Journal of Neurophysiology* 26 (1963): 1003-17; W. Singer, "Neoronal Activity as a Shaping Factor in Portnatal Development of Visual Cortex," *Developmental Neuropsychobiology*, ed. W.T. Greenough and J.M. Juraska (Orlando: Academic Press, 1986): 271-93, A. Hein and R.M. Diamond, "Contribution of Eye Movement to the Representation of Space," *Spatially Oriented Behavior*, ed A. Hein and M. Jeannerod (New York: Springer, 1983): 119–34.

3. See, for example, B.D. Perry, "Incubated in Terror: Neurodevelopmental Factors in the 'Cycle of Violence,'" *Children, Youth and Violence: Searching for Solutions*, ed. J. Osofsky (New York: Guilford, 1995).

4. See, for example, M.A. Hofer, "On the Nature and Function of Prenatal Behavior," *Behavior of the Fetus*, ed. W. Smotherman and S. Robinson (Caldwell, NJ: Telford, 1988); idem, "Hidden Regulators: Implications for a New Understanding of Attachment, Separation, and Loss," *Attachment Theory: Social, Developmental, and Clinical Perspectives*, ed. S. Goldberg, R. Muir, and J. Kerr (Hillsdale, NJ: Analytic Press, 1995): 203–30; P. Rakic, J. Bourgeois, and P. Goldman–Rakic, "Synaptic Development of the Cerebral Cortex: Implications for Learning, Memory, and Mental Illness," *The Self–Organizing Brain: From Growth Cones to Functional Networks*, ed. J. van Pelt, M.A. Corner, H.B.M. Uylings, and F.H. Lopes da Silva (New York: Elsevier Science, 1994): 227–43.

5. Brazelton, T. B. "Behavioral Competence of the Newborn Infant." In *Neonatology*. Ed. E. B. Avery et al. Philadelphia: Lippincott, Williams and Wilkins, 1999.

6. Brazelton, T. B. and B. Cramer, *The Earliest Relationship: Parents, Infants and the Drama of Early Attachment* (Cambridge, Mass.: Perseus Publishing, 1990); T. B. Brazelton, *Touchpoints: Your Child's Emotional and Behavioral Development* (Cambridge, Mass.: Perseus Publishing, 1992).

7. For a more detailed discussion of the relationship between emotional interactions and intelligence and emotional growth see S. I. Greenspan, *The Growth of the Mind* (Cambridge, MA: Perseus Publishing, 1997), and S. I. Greenspan, *Building Healthy Minds* (Cambridge, MA: Perseus Publishing, 1999).

8. Greenspan, S. I. and Wieder, S. *The Child With Special* Needs. Cambridge, MA: Perseus Publishing, 1998. S. G. Greenspan with Jacqueline Salmon. *The Challenging Child*. Cambridge, MA, Perseus Publishing, 1995.

9. [T. B. B.]: The neonatal assessment (Neonatal Behavioral Assessment Scale, or —NBAS) was developed in 1973 to assess the complex behaviors of the newborn baby. Not only can newborns see and hear, but they can maintain attention and register excitement and interest in faces, voices, a red ball, a soft rattle. They can shut out repeated intrusive auditory or tactile stimuli. It is the way newborn babies respond to these stimuli, and to the reflex check on their neurological systems that gives an observer an indication of the kind of person this baby may be. Her reaction to soothing techniques when she is active or crying can let the new parents become aware of their future job in caretaking. Not only is the NBAS diagnostic of any compromise or intrauterine effects, but sharing the newborn's behavior with new, hungry parents is the most valuable use of the assessment. We have 48 studies demonstrating the power of the newborn's behavior in capturing the new parents for attachment to the baby, but it also can be demonstrated that the parents become more attached to and compliant with the medical system available to them and the baby. Being aware of the newborn baby's marvelous use of states of consciousness (asleep, awake and alert, crying) was the key to the parents' budding attachment. For further information, see T. B. Brazelton, and J. K. Nugent, *Neonatal Behavioral Assessment Scale*, 3rd ed. (New York: Cambridge University Press, 1996).

10. Greenough, W. T. and J. E. Black, "Induction of Brain Structure by Experience: Substrates for Cognitive Development," *Developmental Behavioral Neuroscience* 24 [1992]: 155–299; I. J. Weiler, N. Hawrylak, and W. T. Greenough, "Morphogenesis in Memory Formation: Synaptic and Cellular Mechanisms," *Behavioural Brain Research* 66 [1995]: 1–6). R. L. Holloway, "Dendritic Branching: Some Preliminary Results of Training and Complexity in Rat Visual Cortex," *Brain Research* 2 (1966): 393–96; A. M. Turner and W. T. Greenough, "Synapses per Neuron and Synaptic Dimensions in Occipital Cortex of Rats Reared in Complex, Social, or Isolation Housing," *Acta Stereologica* 2, suppl. 1 (1983): 239–44; idem, "Differential Rearing Effects on Rat Visual Cortex Synapses, I: Synaptic and Neuronal Density and Synapses per Neuron," *Brain Research* 329 (1985): 195–203; C. Thinus–Blanc, "Volume Discrimination Learning in Golden Hamsters: Effects of the Structure of Complex Rearing Cages," *Developmental Psychobiology* 14 (1981): 397–403. T. N. Wiesel and D. H. Hubel, "Single–Cell Responses in Striate Cortex of Kittens Deprived of Vision in One Eye," *Journal of Neurophysiology* 26 (1963): 1003–17; W. Singer, "Neuronal Activity as a Shaping Factor in Postnatal Development of Visual Cortex," in *Developmental Neuropsychobiology*, ed. W. T. Greenough and J. M. Juraska (Orlando: Academic Press, 1986): 271–93; A. Hein and R. M. Diamond, "Contribution of Eye Movement to the Representation of Space," in *Spatially Oriented Behavior*, ed. A. Hein and M. Jeannerod (New York: Springer, 1983), pp. 119–34. B. D. Perry, "Incubated in Terror: Neurodevelopmental Factors in the 'Cycle of Violence,' " in *Children, Youth and Violence: Searching for Solutions*, ed. J. Osofsky (New York: Guilford, 1995).

11. Brazelton, T. B. and H. Als, "Four Early Stages in the Development of Mother–Infant Interaction." In A. Solnit et al. (eds.), *The Psychoanalytic Study of the Child*, Vol. 34 (Madison, CT: International Universities Press, 1979).

12. Brazelton, T. B. *Infants and Mothers: Difference in Development* (New York: Delacorte Press, 1969, 1983).

13. Winnicott, D. W. (1896–1971) influential British pediatrician and psychoanalyst.

14. Norton, D., "Diversity, Early Socialization and Temporal Development," *Social Work* 38: 82–90.

15. Field. T., "Affective and Interactive Disturbance in Infants." In J. D. Osofsky (ed.). *Handbook of Infant Development*, pp. 972–1005. New York: Wiley, 1987.

16. Tronick, E., H. Als, L. Adamson, S. Wise, and T. B. Brazelton. "The Infant's Response to Entrapment Between Contradictory Messages in Face-to-Face Interaction." *Journal of the Academy of Child Psychiatry* 17, 1–13, 1978.

17. The Touchpoints project at Boston Children's Hospital trains professionals from various disciplines in early intervention with parents and infants. The goal is to improve preventive health care and child care with parents involved. For a further description of this project, see Appendix.

18. Association of Family and Visitation Courts. 329 West Wilson St. Madison, WI 53703. 608-251-4001.

19. Governor's Blue Ribbon Commission on Foster Care, March 1992.

20. Brazelton, T. B. and J. K. Nugent. *Neonatal Behavioral Assessment Scale*. 3rd Edition. New York: Cambridge University Press, 1996, pp. 1–4.

21. Skeels, H. M. and H. Skodak. "A Study of the Effects of Environmental Stimulation." In *University of Iowa Studies in Child Welfare*. Vols. 15 and 16. University Park, IA, 1939.

22. Lvoff, N. M., U. Lvoff, and M. H. Klaus. "Effect of the Baby–Friendly Initiative on Infant Abandonment in a Russian Hospital." *Archives of Pediatric and Adolescent Medicine*, Vol. 154, May 2000, pp. 474–477.

23. See *Building Healthy Minds* 1999 and *Playground Politics* 1993 by S. Greenspan both Cambridge M.A: Perseus Publishing for detailed discussion.

24. Hopper P. and E. G. Zigler, "The Medical and social science basis for a national infant care leave policy." *American Journal of Orthopsychiatry* 58: 324–338.

25. Halcomb, B. *et al* "Childcare: How does your state rate?" *Working Mother*, July/August 1998.

26. These guidelines were kindly supplied by Dr. Carol Grey, a forensic psychologist in Seattle, Washington.

Chapter 2

1. California Department of Developmental Services. (1999). *A Report to the Legislature: Changes in the Population of Persons with Autism and Pervasive*

Developmental Disorders in California's Developmental Services System : 1987 through 1998. Department of Developmental Services, California Health and Human Services Agency, Sacramento, CA: March 1, 1999, section IV, *Rates of Occurrence,* p.5.

2. Ibid.

3. See Environmental Protection Agency. (1988). *The Inside Story: A Guide to Indoor Air Quality.* Washington, D.C. and www.CHECnet.org for further information.

4. For more information see the following Center for Health, Environment and Justice. (November, 1999). *America's Choice: Children's Health of Corporate Profit, the American People's Dioxin Report.* Falls Church, VA; Myers, J.P. (2000). "Hormone Disruption and the Precautionary Principle." Paper presented at the Delegate Science Briefing at the UN POPs Negotiations, INC 4, March 22, 2000; Herman–Giddens, M.E., Slora, E.J., Wasserman, R.C., Bourdony, C.J., Bhapkur, M.V., Koch, G.G., & Hasemeier, C.M. (1997). "Secondary Sexual Characteristics and Menses in Young Girls Seen in Office Practice: A Study from the Pediatric Research in Office Settings Network," *Pediatrics,* 99(4): 505–512; Paulozzi, L.J., Erikson, J.D., & Jackson, R.J. (1997). "Hypospadias Trends in Two US Surveillance Systems," *Pediatrics,* 100(5): 831–34; Rothman, N., Cantor, K.P., Blair, A., Bush, D., Brock, L.W., Helzisouer, K., Zaum, S.H., Needham, L.L., Person, G.R., Hoover, R.N., Comstock, G.W., and Stricklan, P.T. (1997) "A Nested Case–Control Study of Non–Hodgkins Lymphoma and Serum Organochlorine Residues," *Lancet,* 350 (9073): 240–44.

5. Kaiser Foundation Kids and the Media in the New Millennium, Publication No. 1536, Menlo Park, CA, 2000.

6. Zigler, E. E. and N. W. Hall, *Child Development and Social Policy: Theory and Applications.* New York: McGraw Hill 2000.

7. Klaus, M. H., J. H. Kennell, and P. H. Klaus, *Mothering the Mother.* Cambridge, MA: Perseus Publishing, 1993.

8. B. F Greenspan, S. I. *Infants in Multi–Risk Families* (New York) International Universities Press, 1987.

9. Brazelton, T. B. *Touchpoints: Your Child's Emotional and Behavioral Development.* Cambridge, MA: Perseus Publishing, 1992.

10. Greenspan, S. I., with N.B. Lewis, *Building Healthy Minds: The Six Experiences That Create Intelligence and Emotional Growth in Babies and Young Children* (Cambridge, Mass.: Perseus Publishing, 1999).

11. Lecanuet, J. P., C. Granier–Deferre, and M. C. Bushel. "Human Fetal Auditory Perception" *Fetal Development: A Psychological Approach* (Mahwah, NJ: Lawrence Erlbaum, 1995).

12. Scanlon, J. W., "Dangers to the human fetus from certain heavy metals in the environment." *Review of Environmental Health* 1995 2(1) 39–64.

13. Colburn, T., J. Meyers, and D. Dumanowski, *Our Stolen Future.* New York: Dutton, 1997.

14. Nathanielsz, P. *Life Before Birth: The Challenges of Fetal Development.* New York: W. H. Freeman, 1998.

15. Fein, G. G, P. M. Schwartz, S. W. Jacobsen, and J. L. Jacobson, "Environmental toxins and behavioral development." *American Psychologist* 38, 1198–1205.

16. Tronick, E. E., "The NBAS as a Biomarker of Environmental Agents on the Newborn," in G. Lucius (ed.), *Environmental Health Perspectives,* Proceedings of the National Research Council, 1987. 74: 185–89.

17. Sparrow J. D., *Psychiatric Research and Prenatal Diagnoses,* American Psychiatric Association, Federation Française de Psychiatrie, Paris, France, June 1998.

18. Klaus, M. H., J. H. Kennell, and P. H. Klaus, *Mothering the Mother* (Cambridge, MA: Perseus Publishing, 1993).

19. Educating Children for Parenting. 211 N 13th St. #701, Philadelphia, PA 19107, www.ecparenting.org

20. Brazelton T. B., et al. "The Behavior of Nutritionally Deprived Guatemalan Infants" *Developmental Medicine and Child Neurology* Vol 19. No. 3 364–367, 1977.

21. Bok, S., *Common Values* (Columbia: University of Missouri Press. 1995).

Chapter 3

1. Chess, S.and A. Thomas, *Know Your Child* (New York: Basic Books, 1987).

2. Brazelton, T. B., *Infants and Mothers: Differences in Development* (New York: Delacorte Press, 1969, 1982). T. B. Brazelton, and J. K. Nugent, *The Neonatal Behavioral Assessment Scale.* 3rd Edition. New York: Cambridge University Press, 1996.

3. Greenspan, S. I., and J. Salmon, *The Challenging Child: Understanding, Raising, and Enjoying the Five "Difficult" Types of Children* (Cambridge, MA: Perseus Publishing, 1995); S. I. Greenspan, *Infancy and Early Childhood: The Practice of Clinical Assessment and Intervention with Emotional and Developmental Challenges* (Madison, Conn.: International Universities Press, 1992); S. I. Greenspan, *The Development of the Ego: Implications for Personality Theory, Psychopathology, and the Psychotherapeutic Process* (Madison, Conn.: International Universities Press, 1989); S. I. Greenspan and N. T. Greenspan, *First Feelings: Milestones in the Emotional Development of Your Infant and Child from Birth to Age 4* (New York: Viking Press, 1985).

4. *Infants and Mothers. Ibid.*

5. Greenspan, S. I.and S. Wieder, "Developmental Patterns and Outcomes in Infants and Children with Disorders in Relating and Communicating: A Chart Review of 200 Cases of Children with Autistic Spectrum Diagnoses." *Journal of Developmental and Learning Disorders,* 1:87–141, 1997;

Greenspan, *Infancy and Early Childhood;* Greenspan and Wieder, *The Child with Special Needs.*

6. Bowlby, J., "Forty–Four Juvenile Thieves: Their Characters and Home Life." *International Journal of Psycho–Analysis* 25:19–52, 107–127, 1944.

7. Greenspan, S. I. and Salmon. *The Challenging Child.* Ibid.

8. Greenspan, S. I. and S. Wieder. "Developmental Patterns and Outcomes"; Greenspan, *Infancy and Early Childhood;* Greenspan and Wieder, *The Child with Special Needs.* Ibid.

9. Calfee, R., Lindamood, P. & Lindamood, C.(1973). "Acoustic–Phonetic Skills and Reading—Kindergarten Through Twelfth Grade," *Journal of Educational Psychology* 64: 293–98.

10. See Greenspan, *Infancy and Early Childhood;* S. I. Greenspan, with Lewis, N.B., *Building Healthy Minds* (Cambridge, MA: Perseus Publishing, 1999); and Greenspan and Wieder, *The Child with Special Needs, Ibid.*

11. See ICDL website (www.icdl.com) for information about the *Clinical Practice Guidelines* and the Council's activities.

12. Shore, M. F. and J. L. Massimo, "Contributions of an Innovative Psychoanalytic Therapeutic Program with Adolescent Delinquents to Developmental Psychology." In S. I. Greenspan and G. H. Pollock (eds.), *The Course of Life,* 2nd ed., Vol. 4: *Adolescence* (Madison, Con.: International Universities Press, 1990).

13. Family Resource Coalition (now Family Support America. www.fsca.org. 20 N. Wacker St. Chicago, IL 60606. (312) 338–0900.

14. Klaus, M. H., J. H. Kennell, and P. H. Klaus. *Bonding: Building the Foundation of Secure Attachment and Independence* (Cambridge, MA: Perseus Publishing, 1995).

15. Healthy Steps Program, c/o Commonwealth Fund. www.healthysteps.org. 1 E 75th St. New York, NY 10021.

16. Greenspan and Wieder, *The Child with Special Needs.* Ibid.

17. ICDL *Clinical Practice Guidelines,* Chapter 4, "Intervention Research," on the ICDL website www.icdl.com, or from ICDL 4938 Hampden Lane, Suite 800, Bethesda, MD 20814.

18. Lovaas, O.I. (1987). "Behavioral Treatment and Normal Educational and Intellectual Functioning in Young Autistic Children," *Journal of Consulting and Clinical Psychology* 55:3–9; McEachin, J.J., Smith, T., & Lovaas, O.I. (1993)"Long–Term Outcome for Children With Autism Who Received Early Intensive Behavioral Interventions," *American Journal of Mental Retardation* 97: 359–72.

19. ICDL *Clinical Practice Guidelines,* Chapter 4, "Intervention Research."

20. Nugent, J. K. and T. B. Brazelton, "Preventive Infant Mental Health: Use of the Brazelton Scale." In H. E. Fitzgerald and J. D. Osofsky (eds.), *Handbook of Infant Mental Health* (New York: Wiley, 1999).

Chapter 4

1. See Greenspan, S. I., with N. B. Lewis, *Building Healthy Minds* (Cambridge, MA: Perseus Publishing, 1999); S. I. Greenspan, with J. Salmon, *Playground Politics* (Cambridge, MA: Perseus Publishing, 1993). S. I. Greenspan, with B. L. Benderly. *The Growth of the Mind and the Endangered Origins of Intelligence.* Cambridge, MA: Perseus Publishing, 1997.

2. Brazelton, T. B. and B. G. Cramer, *The Earliest Relationship: Parents, Infants, and the Drama of Early Attachment* (Cambridge, MA: Perseus Publishing, 1990).

3. Fraiberg, S., *The Magic Years.* New York: Scribners, 1959.

4. Brazelton, T. B., *Touchpoints: Your Child's Emotional and Behavioral Development* (Cambridge, MA: Perseus Publishing, 1992). T. B. Brazelton, *Working and Caring.* (Cambridge, MA: Perseus Publishing, 1985).

5. Galinsky, E., *Ask the Children: What America's Children Really Think About Working Parents.* (New York: Morrow, 1999)

6. Skinner, B. F., a professor of psychology at Harvard University, developed transparent enclosed cribs for observing small babies' behaviors. The cribs had motors for air conditioning that made a hum. The infants habituated to the hum in deep sleep.

7. Robert Rosenthal, a professor of psychology at Harvard University, demonstrated the effect of a teacher's preconceptions on a child's performance.

8. See Greenspan, S. I. *The Growth of the Mind,* Perseus Publishing, Cambridge, MA and Greenspan, S. I. *Developmentally Based Psychology,* International University Press, Madison, Conn.

Chapter 5

1. Brazelton, T. B., D. M. Snyder, and M. W. Yogman, "A Developmental Approach to Behavior Problems." In R. A. Hockelman et al. (eds.), *Principles of Pediatrics* (New York: McGraw-Hill, 1994).

2. Brazelton, T. B., *Touchpoints: Your Child's Emotional and Behavioral Development* (Cambridge, MA: Perseus Publishing, 1992); S. I. Greenspan, with J. Salmon, *The Challenging Child: Understanding, Raising and Enjoying the Five "Difficult" Types of Children* (Cambridge, MA: Perseus Publishing, 1992).

3. See S. I. Greenspan and S. Wieder, *The Child with Special Needs* (Cambridge, MA: Perseus Publishing, 1998). ; S. I. Greenspan, *Infancy and Early Childhood* (Madison, CT: International Universities Press, 1992).; Greenspan, *The Challenging Child.*

4. Brazelton, T. B., *Working and Caring* (Cambridge, MA: Perseus Publishing, 1985).

Chapter 6

1. Wharton, R.H., Levine, K., Miller, E., Breslau, J. & Greenspan, S.I. (2000). "Children With Special Needs in Bilingual Families: A Developmental Approach to Language Recommendations," *The ICDL Clinical Practice Guidelines,* ed. S.I. Greenspan. In press. Bethesda, MD: ICDL.

2. See S. I. Greenspan, with B.L. Benderly, *The Growth of the Mind and the Endangered Origins of Intelligence* (Cambridge, MA: Perseus Publishing, 1997), Chapter 14.

3. Zigler, E. "Addressing the Nation's Child Care Crisis: The School of the 21st Century." *American Journal of Orthopsychiatry,* 59:484–491, 1989; for information on Comer Schools, see E. Zigler, *Child Development and Social Policy: Theory and Applications* (New York: McGraw–Hill, 2000), pp. 245–246.

4. See S. I. Greenspan, S. Wieder, A. Lieberman, R. Nover, R. Lourie, and M. Robinson, *Infants in Multi–Risk Families* (New York: International Universities Press, 1987); S. I. Greenspan, *Infancy and Early Childhood: The Practice of Clinical Assessment and Intervention with Emotional and Developmental Challenges.* (Madison, Conn.: International Universities Press, 1992).

5. Greenspan et al., *Infants in Multi–Risk Families;* Stanley I. Greenspan, *The Growth of the Mind* (Cambridge, MA: Perseus Publishing, 1997), Chapter 13.

6. Karr–Morse, R. and M. Wiley, *Ghosts from the Nursery.* New York: Atlantic Monthly Press, 1997. S. Provence and A. Naylor, *Working with Disadvantaged Parents and Their Children: Scientific and Practical Issues* (New Haven: Yale University Press, 1983); A. S. Honig and J. R. Lally, *Infant Caregiving: A Design for Training* (Syracuse, N.Y.: Syracuse University Press, 1981); J. R. Berrueta–Clement, L. J. Schweinhart, W. S. Barnett, A. S. Epstein, and D. P. Weikart, *Changed Lives: The Effects of the Perry Preschool Program on Youths Through Age Nineteen* (Ypsilanti, Mich.: High/Scope, 1984); C. T. Ramey and F. A. Campbell, "Preventive Education for High–Risk Children: Cognitive Consequences of the Carolina Abecedarian Project," *American Journal of Mental Deficiency* 88 (1984): 515–23; Greenspan et al., *Infants in Multirisk Families.*

Index

About the Authors

T. Berry Brazelton, MD, founder of the Child Development Unit at Children's Hospital Boston, is Clinical Professor of Pediatrics Emeritus at Harvard Medical School. Currently Professor of Pediatrics and Human Development at Brown University, he is also past president of the Society for Research in Child Development and Zero to Three: The National Center for Infants, Toddlers, and Families. A practicing pediatrician for over forty-five years, he introduced the concept of "anticipatory guidance" for parents into pediatric training. The author of over 200 scholarly papers, Dr. Brazelton has written twenty-eight books for both a professional and a lay audience, including *Touchpoints* (translated into eighteen languages), *To Listen to a Child,* and the now-classic trilogy *Infants and Mothers, Toddlers and Parents,* and *On Becoming a Family.* He is also the co-author, (with Bertrand Cramer, MD) of *The Earliest Relationship.*

One of Dr. Brazelton's foremost achievements is the Neonatal Behavior Assessment Scale (NBAS). Known as the "Brazelton" it is used worldwide, clinically and in research, to assess not only the physical and neurological responses of newborns but also their emotional well being and individual differences. Increasingly, the NBAS is being used to help parents understand and relate to their new babies and research is underway to study how it can be used to enhance early discharge after childbirth. To continue his important research and implement its findings, Dr. Brazelton founded, and co-directs two programs at Children's Hospital: the Brazelton Institute (furthering work with the NBAS) and the Brazelton Touchpoints Center (training professionals across the country in the Touchpoints preventive outreach approach).

Dr. Brazelton is the recipient, among his very numerous awards, of the C. Anderson Aldrich Award for Distinguished Contributions to the Field of Child Development, given by the American Academy of

Pediatrics, the Woodrow Wilson Award for Outstanding Public Service from Princeton University, and ten honorary doctorates. He has served on the National Commission for Children appointed by the U.S. Congress and recently became a Living Legend at the Library of Congress in Washington, DC.

Stanley I. Greenspan, MD is Clinical Professor of Psychiatry and Pediatrics at George Washington University Medical School and Chairman of the Interdisciplinary Council on Developmental and Learning Disorders. He is also a practicing child psychiatrist, founding president of Zero to Three: The National Center for Infants, Toddlers and Families, and a supervising child psychoanalyst at the Washington Psychoanalytic Institute. A nationally known advocate for children, he has been director of the Mental Health Study Center and the Clinical Infant Development Program at the National Institute of Mental Health.

Dr. Greenspan is the author or editor of over 30 books and 100 articles. His many influential works include *The Growth of the Mind and the Endangered Origins of Intelligence* (with Beryl Lieff Benderly); *The Challenging Child* (with Jacqueline Salmon); *Infancy and Early Childhood; First Feelings* (with Nancy Thorndike Greenspan); *Playground Politics; The Child With Special Needs* (with Serena Wieder and Robin Simons); *Intelligence and Adaptation: An Integration of Psychoanalytic and Piagetian Developmental Psychology; The Development of the Ego and Developmentally-Based Psychotherapy.*

Among Dr. Greenspan's many national honors and awards are the American Psychiatric Association's Ittleson Prize for Outstanding Contributions to Child Psychiatry Research, the American Orthopsychiatry's Ittleson Prize for pioneering contributions to American Mental Health (the only individual to receive both Ittleson prizes) and the Edward A. Strecker Award for Outstanding Contributions to American Psychiatry.